STUDIES IN MODERN BRITISH RELIGIOUS HISTORY

Volume 3

Bishops and Reform in
the English Church, 1520–1559

The English bishops played a crucial role in the process of Reformation in the sixteenth century, from the first arrival of continental Reformed thought to the virtual extinction of the office in 1559. This work has at its core the bishops' own understanding of the episcopate, from their surviving writings and other contemporary discussions; it supplies a key to understanding what became of the English Church of the middle ages and what it was to become under Elizabeth, and fills a gap in the existing literature on the period.

A thematic approach is adopted, looking at the interplay between bishop and king, the episcopate in the context of other orders, and the social context of the office. This is complemented by a study of episcopal activity in key areas such as preaching, ordaining, and opposing heresy, which were defining features of the role of the bishop in the Church. The influence of the models which the bishops themselves set up as ideals, most notably Christ himself as the ideal bishop, further colour the picture. The backgrounds of the bishops themselves are set out in the appendix.

STUDIES IN MODERN BRITISH RELIGIOUS HISTORY

ISSN 1464–6625

General editors
Stephen Taylor
Arthur Burns
Kenneth Fincham

This series aims to differentiate 'religious history' from the narrow confines of church history, investigating not only the social and cultural history of religion, but also theological, political and institutional themes, while remaining sensitive to the wider historical context; it thus advances an understanding of the importance of religion for the history of modern Britain, covering all periods of British history since the Reformation.

I
Friends of Religious Equality
Non-conformiat Politics in mid-Victorian England
Timothy Larsen

II
Confirmity and Orthodoxy in the English Church,
*c.*1560–1660
edited by Peter Lake and Michael Questier

Bishops and Reform in the English Church, 1520–1559

KENNETH CARLETON

THE BOYDELL PRESS

First published 2001
The Boydell Press, Woodbridge

ISBN 0 85115 816 1

The Boydell Press is an imprint of Boydell & Brewer Ltd
PO Box 9, Woodbridge, Suffolk IP12 3DF, UK
and of Boydell & Brewer Inc.
PO Box 41026, Rochester, NY 14604–4126, USA
website: http://www.boydell.co.uk

A catalogue record for this book is available
from the British Library

Library of Congress Cataloging-in-Publication Data
Carleton, Kenneth, 1958–
   Bishops and reform in the English church, 1520–1559 / Kenneth Carleton.
      p. cm. – (Studies in modern British religious history, ISSN 1464–6625; v.3)
   Includes bibliographical references and index.
   ISBN 0–85115–816–1 (alk. paper)
      1. Reformation – England.   2. Episcopacy – History of doctrines – 16th century.
   3. England – Church history – 16th century.   I. Title.   II. Series.
   BR377.C37 20001
   262′.12342′09031–dc21   00–052918

This publication is printed on acid-free paper

Typeset by Joshua Associates Ltd, Oxford
Printed in Great Britain by
St Edmundsbury Press Ltd, Bury St Edmunds, Suffolk

Contents

List of Illustrations   vi

List of Abbreviations   viii

Acknowledgements   ix

Introduction   1

1. Theologies of Episcopacy in mid-Tudor England   7

2. Models of Episcopal Office   43

3. Bishops of the English Church, 1520–1559   61

4. The Bishop and Preaching   81

5. Bishops and the Provision of Education   99

6. Prayer and Sacrifice: the Life of the Bishop   117

7. Episcopal Activity I: the Eradication of Heresy   132

8. Episcopal Activity II: the Propagation of the Ministry   156

9. Conclusion: the Old Episcopate in a New Order   179

Appendix I. Prosopography of the bishops in office, 1520–1559   188

Appendix II. The dioceses   202

Appendix III. The education of the bishops   205

Table 1. Membership of Oxford and Cambridge colleges   205

Table 2. English and Welsh bishops at foreign universities   206

Appendix IV. The bishops of Sodor and Man   207

Bibliography   209

Index of Scriptural References   219

General Index   220

ILLUSTRATIONS

Plate I	The arms of Reginald Cardinal Pole, Archbishop of Canterbury	111
Plate II	The modern arms of the See of Canterbury	111
Plate III	Henry VIII delivers the Great Bible to his bishops and ministers	112
Plate IV	Edward VI delivers the Bible to his bishops (Cranmer, *Cathechismus*)	113
Plate V	John Fisher preaching (title page, J. Fisher, *Hereafter foloweth a mornynge remembraunce*)	114
Plate VI	The burning of Nicholas Ridley and Hugh Latimer (from J. Foxe, *Acts and Monuments*)	115
Plate VII	The burning of Thomas Cranmer (from J. Foxe, *Acts and Monuments*)	115
Plate VIII	Henry VIII on the marriage of bishops (marginal note on fol. 94v of Bullinger's *De episcoporum . . . institutione et functione*)	116

To Ruth Chavasse

ABBREVIATIONS

BL   The British Library Department of Manuscripts

DNB   *The Dictionary of National Biography*, ed. L. Stephen and S. Lee (Oxford 1917–).

LP   *Letters and Papers, Foreign and Domestic, Henry VIII*, ed. Brewer, J.S., and *et al.* (London, 1862–1920)

ACKNOWLEDGEMENTS

This book is a revised version of my PhD thesis 'Episcopal Office in the English Church 1520–1559', written and researched at King's College, London. A grant towards its publication, from the late Miss Isobel Thornley's bequest to the University of London, is gratefully acknowledged. I wish to thank the many people who have read and commented upon this work, or parts of it, in the various phases of its life, especially Judith Champ, who encouraged me at an early stage to consider publication, and Susan Hardman Moore and Eamon Duffy, who examined the thesis and whose positive and helpful suggestions have been taken into account in its revision. The many useful and positive ideas of Kenneth Fincham, who has read the work more than once in its later stages, are most gratefully acknowledged. Full responsibility for this book's shortcomings, however, remains entirely my own. Many friends and colleagues have been a source of encouragement; in particular, the support of two former colleagues, Ian Robinson and Paul Tyler, has been very much valued, and this work would have been much more difficult without them. My wife and I have discussed and argued over many of the ideas in this book. She has also shared me with a hundred or so dead bishops for the whole of our married life. Without her encouragement this work would probably never have been completed.

Since I first arrived at King's College, one person has been a constant source of inspiration to me and to my work. The immense debt of gratitude I owe to Ruth Chavasse, as teacher, supervisor and mentor, cannot be expressed and can never be repaid. It is to her that this book is dedicated.

The verye office of a bushop is *predicare, orare, &*
sacrificare sive offerre.
To preache, to praye, to do sacrifyce and to offer.

JOHN LONGLAND, *A Sermonde made before the Kynge*, 1538

INTRODUCTION

The office of bishop was central to the Church from its earliest days. By the second century, the fundamental structural principle of the local ecclesial community was that of a single bishop, surrounded by a college of clergy, who together governed and served the people of the local Church or diocese. Together the bishops ruled and governed the whole Church, binding it together in unity (Cyprian called the bishops its 'glue'). Though splits and schisms appeared over the next fourteen hundred years, the greatest and most enduring being the Great Schism between east and west in the eleventh century, the fundamental principle of the single bishop at the head of the local Church remained the touchstone of the authentic Christian community. The late medieval bishop stood at the centre of a complex web of relationships. He was at one time both the king's man and the pope's, owing allegiance to both and deriving from each some of his authority and power. Dependent upon him to a greater or less degree were the clergy of his diocese, his lay officials and stewards, and the whole panoply of secular estate which had grown over the centuries around the office of a lord and pastor. The bishop sat in the Upper House of Parliament amongst his peers, Lords temporal as well as other Lords spiritual, by virtue of the temporal baronetcy which was attached to his see and which was conferred upon him around the time of his appointment. Alongside his responsibilities to the state as a whole, each bishop had charge of a specific area within which he exercised a true power of governance. Pastor as well as prelate, his role was one of shepherd guarding and tending his flock, through well-established means both sacramental and administrative. While the growth in importance of the parish in the Middle Ages had devolved much of the day-to-day sacramental and pastoral activity away to a local level, the bishop was still responsible for maintaining a body of clergy within his diocese through the ordination of suitable men to the ministry. Where his diocese was large, or relatively inaccessible, it was common for him to seek the appointment of an assistant bishop (sometimes more than one) who could carry out on his behalf the various sacramental tasks which were reserved to the episcopate alone. These included ordination to minor and major orders, the consecration of churches and churchyards, and (occasionally) the confirmation of children, though this was more often carried out by the bishop during a visitation of his diocese.

In the sixteenth century, the fundamental principle of the single, monarchical bishop as the essence of the Church was called into question with the result that in many places the episcopate ceased to exist in any recognizable form. Other models of the Church gained currency, the result of the development of the thought of the many promoters of Reformation. Insights into the nature of salvation, and the means by which the individual is put in a right relationship with God, led to an increasing emphasis away from the need of an earthly mediator in the form of the Church. Where the new reforms held sway, the monarchical episcopate was swept away, and new structures of governance for the local Church were set in place which no longer mediated God's grace but instead fed his people with his Word while the justifying power of God carried out its saving work in the individual soul. In counterpoint with these developments, the process of Catholic Reformation maintained and strengthened traditional teaching and structures in order to combat what its proponents saw as the dangerous heresies which were perilous to the soul, and which both starved it of the grace which Christ had promised to his people through the Church and its sacraments, and belittled the good works most necessary to its salvation. It is true to say that eucharistic theology was one of the fundamental areas of disagreement in the middle years of the sixteenth century. In Catholic thinking, while it was the priest (presbyter) who had the power to confect the eucharist, it was the bishop who was able to endow others with that power. The sevenfold hierarchy of minor and major orders, the priesthood at the top being possessed in its fullness by the bishops and in a more limited way by the presbyters, was supplanted in Reformed thought by a simple threefold structure of office holders, whose ministry lasted as long as their office was held. Only those who held such office were authorized to minister the word and sacraments to the congregation. The lowest of the three, in the Anglican scheme of orders, the deacon, was seen as one whose ministry was transitory, almost probationary, on the way to the ordinary ministry of priest. The senior ministers, the bishops, were those who had the mission of governing the Church and of appointing (or ordaining) other suitable men to the ministry. The same scheme is behind the complex Catholic hierarchy; offices largely of transition (though some remained in minor orders permanently), through subdiaconate and diaconate, leading to the permanent ministry of priest. Above the seven sacramental grades, as they came to be called, was the bishop, with the ordinary power of governing the Church (so far as the pope allowed) and of conferring the ministry on other suitable men. When reduced to the essence, the two at first very different understandings of the Church's ministry are seen to be at heart very similar. All agreed that the Church was served by a variety of ministries, and that it pertained to the office of bishop to set apart ministers for the Church in all normal circumstances. How the bishops responded to this need provides an insight into their perception of the changes to which their office was being subjected.

The daily practicalities of being a bishop in the English Church at this time were governed by precedent and custom. As the office was subjected to scrutiny, so the holders of that office responded in a variety of ways. The breaking of the mould often signified the practical carrying out of a new insight into the office held. Bishops differed in their responses, and yet often drew inspiration from common models. This study takes different aspects of the office of bishop in turn, and looks both at the theological context for that area of study and seeks to establish the understanding of the bishops in relation to it, highlighting points of consensus and of discord. It looks also at the bishops themselves, attempting to draw from their diverse backgrounds those influences which led them to develop this historic office in a period of rapid change and uncertainty for the English Church and its polity.

In England the process of Reformation, despite Lollardy's long history, was allowed to flourish first as the result of a political necessity, rather than a religious conversion. Christopher Haigh has postulated not one, but a number of English Reformations, some sequential and others overlapping, and his arguments are so convincing that it seems inappropriate any longer to refer to a single 'English Reformation'.[1] More controversial, perhaps, has been the revisionist thesis that, far from being a logical and necessary consequence of the decay and deterioration, Reformation was imposed upon an unwilling people who were content in a flourishing and thriving Catholic Church. Such has been the debate stirred up by this thesis (debate which led to a revised edition of Geoffrey Dickens' *The English Reformation*) that there is a danger of returning to the more confessional approach to ecclesiastical history where each side, Catholic and Protestant, saw Reformation as a victory or defeat, a Good Thing or a Bad Thing, dependent entirely upon the ecclesial allegiance of the writer. It is certainly the case that the outsider might form the impression that the opposing views of Eamon Duffy and Patrick Collinson, at least as far as their value judgements of the English Church as it emerged in the Elizabethan period are concerned, grew (however unconsciously) from their love and devotion to the particular traditions from which each of them is drawn.

There have been many studies of key figures from the episcopate in this period. Principal characters such as Cranmer have naturally attracted most attention, with the recent major study by Diarmaid MacCulloch set

---

[1] Haigh, C., *English Reformations: Religion, Politics, and Society under the Tudors* (Oxford, 1993).

to take centre stage for the foreseeable future.[2] Other important figures such as Stephen Gardiner and Thomas Wolsey have had recent, thorough biographical treatments.[3] John Fisher, bishop of Rochester and Catholic martyr, has recently been the subject of both a collection of essays edited by Brendan Bradshaw and Eamon Duffy, and a detailed exposition of his theology by Richard Rex, the latter succeeding in avoiding the confessional or apologetic tendencies to which some recent works have unfortunately been subject.[4]

Studies of individual aspects of the life and work of the bishop during the Tudor years have tended to focus on the Elizabethan episcopate (the works of Patrick Collinson being central to this corpus), while the early Stuart episcopate has been thoroughly examined by Kenneth Fincham in his *Prelate as Pastor: The Episcopate of James I* (Oxford, 1990); its thematic treatment of the office of bishop has provided a model for the present work. Much important work has been done by Felicity Heal on the social, administrative and financial aspects of the episcopate (both alone and with Rosemary O'Day), while her ground-breaking work on the practice of hospitality has greatly informed the debate on that fundamental and important duty of every churchman of the time.[5] While studies of the lives of the bishops, and aspects of their activity, exist for the period under scrutiny, no recent work has attempted to understand the office of bishop itself, at least for the episcopate of the years before the accession of Elizabeth I in 1558. This book attempts to fill part of that gap in a number of ways. First, it seeks to take a theological view, seeking to discover from the bishops' own writings, and relevant contemporary and official documents, how the office of bishop was understood by its holders in the years from about 1520 to 1559. The latter *terminus ad quem* was an obvious choice; by December of that year, thirteen months after the death of Queen Mary and the accession of her half-sister, the entire episcopate (save for one lonely and isolated exception) had been entirely removed. The study concludes on the eve of the consecration of Matthew Parker as Archbishop of Canterbury, a point in the life of the English Church where, for the first time perhaps since the arrival of Augustine, almost every diocese was without a bishop

[2] MacCulloch, D., *Thomas Cranmer: A life* (New Haven, CT, and London, 1996).
[3] Gwyn, P., *The King's Cardinal: The Rise and Fall of Thomas Wolsey* (London, 1990); Redworth, G., *In defence of the Church Catholic: The life of Stephen Gardiner* (Oxford, 1990).
[4] Bradshaw, B., and Duffy, E., eds., *Humanism, Reform and the Reformation* (Cambridge, 1989); Rex, R., *The Theology of John Fisher* (Cambridge, 1991).
[5] Heal, F., *Hospitality in Early Modern England* (Oxford, 1990); *Of Prelates and Princes* (Cambridge, 1980); Heal, F., and O'Day, R., eds., *Church and Society in England: Henry VIII to James I* (London, 1977); O'Day, R., and Heal, F. eds., *Continuity and Change: Personnel and Administration of the Church in England, 1500–1642* (Leicester, 1976).

and the very continuity of the episcopate was in serious doubt.[6] The study commences around 1520, as the writings and ideas of Continental Protestantism were beginning to enter England in a significant and substantial fashion, and when episcopal responses to the new heresies began to gather pace.[7] A second purpose of the present work is to contribute to the development of the history of ideas. The activity of the bishops has been used to illuminate their understanding of the office itself, in conjunction with both current teaching on the nature and purpose of the episcopate, and the surviving writings of the bishops themselves. A variety of interpretations were held amongst the hundred or so bishops whose office is the subject of this work. Moreover, the influence of doctrinal change led a number of the bishops to modify their idea of the office they held; in many cases, this also affected the way in which they carried out the requirements of their office, though it must be admitted that in some individuals, theory and practice failed to interact in any noticeable or meaningful way. Certain broad shifts of emphasis may also be perceived over the forty years covered by the study. The clearest of these was a tendency towards undertaking more pastoral and liturgical functions in the Church, alongside the beginnings of a reduction of the role of the bishop in matters of state and the civil government. The bishops began to drift back to their dioceses, and with pressure from both Catholic and Protestant Reform movements to take the practice more seriously, many bishops undertook a substantially increased role in the preaching of the Word of God, sometimes personally, occasionally through the publication of homilies, and not infrequently through the appointment and promotion of qualified preachers who could carry out this vital task either with, or instead of, the bishop himself. There was also a tendency, in some quarters at least, to modify the place of the bishop in society. While the provision of hospitality, enjoined by canon law and required by current social norms, continued to flourish, where an individual bishop took to himself a wife and started a family (in some cases before the freedom to do this was granted by law in the reign of Edward VI), there was an inevitable effect both upon the dynamics of society and on the manner in which the traditional requirement of hospitality was carried out.

The absence of a detailed recent study of the idea of episcopacy in the years leading up to the Elizabethan settlement of religion has meant that the theological debate on the nature of the Anglican Church, and especially the standing of its ordained ministers, has been lacking in an

---

[6] For a discussion of the Marian bishops who had survived past that date, see Carleton, K.W.T., 'English Catholic Bishops in the early Elizabethan Era', *Recusant History* 23 (1996), pp. 1–15.

[7] See Chapter 7.

area fundamental to that Church's self-understanding. Furthermore, the debate over the validity of Anglican orders, which rumbled for three centuries then exploded with their condemnation at the end of the nineteenth century, has been missing some of its context. The episcopate is key to the Anglican claim to catholicity, to continuity with the past, and to its place as an authentic part of the Church founded by Christ. It is important to study not only the early years of the Church which knew itself to be separate, though still a part of the Church of Christ, self-sufficient and needing no external validation, but also the years which led up to its definitive separation, covering the first break from the rest of Catholic Christendom and the temporary reversal of that situation which immediately preceded the final break. This work seeks to fill that gap, and to contribute to a better understanding of what actually became of the English Church of the end of the Middle Ages.

Abbreviations in quoted texts have been expanded, and dates cited take the commencement of the new year to be 1 January. Quotations in foreign languages have been translated, while the original spelling has been retained in texts in English. The names of individual bishops have been spelt throughout following the *Handbook of British Chronology*, ed. F.M. Powicke and E.B. Fryde (Royal Historical Society, London, 1961).

Chapter One

THEOLOGIES OF EPISCOPACY IN MID-TUDOR ENGLAND

Throughout the later Middle Ages the appointment of bishops to English sees took place as a result of mutual co-operation between the king and the pope. The fourteenth-century Statute of Provisors had rejected papal claims to appoint directly to bishoprics. The bishop was too important a figure in government to be left entirely to the nomination of the pope. The free election of bishops had been conceded to cathedral chapters by Henry I in the twelfth century, but with the king's effective veto of an unsuitable candidate the choice passed in practice largely into the hands of the Crown. The usual procedure was for the king to indicate his choice to the chapter by means of a *congé d'elire*, who would proceed with the election; the bishop-elect would then be recommended to the pope. In most cases, the pope accepted the royal candidate, and where the pope showed opposition to the choice, a compromise was reached; the pope then issued a bull of provision to the vacant see. A mutual understanding had been arrived at by the end of the fourteenth century that if the pope did not oppose the royal nominee, the king would not take exception to the bull of provision, except that the bishop, on doing homage to the king for grant of the temporalities of his see, was required to renounce those clauses in the bull which were seen to be prejudicial to the authority of the Crown. This procedure was invariably followed for the appoint-ment of bishops for the English Church up to and including that of Thomas Cranmer as Archbishop of Canterbury. The situation was of mutual benefit; the pope retained his appointing power over the Church's bishops in theory, while the king was able in practice to appoint those men who could be most useful to him and to the government of the realm. When Henry VIII claimed for the English Crown the right to appoint bishops directly and without reference to any foreign power, he was abrogating to himself a jurisdiction which for many years had *de facto* been exercised by the Crown; the claim was for the *de iure* right to exercise that appointing power.

The bishops of the late Middle Ages were at once both the king's men and the pope's men. To the king, they owed their choice for the episcopal office (or at least his active agreement to it), and the temporal estates attached to their sees, which they held on the same basis as lay lords. To the pope, they owed obedience (by virtue of their oath on appointment), and, according to most contemporary theologians, depended upon him for their episcopal authority. The pope was the universal ordinary, claiming direct jurisdiction over all local churches, in the same way that St Peter, having received authority from Christ to govern the Church, had delegated that authority to the other apostles. The bull of provision was an essential step in the appointment of a bishop, who was required to take an oath of personal obedience to the pope which unambiguously affirmed his direct dependence on the pope. Furthermore, the title of *legatus natus* held by the archbishops of Canterbury and York clearly implied that their status as metropolitans directly depended upon the pope, a view supported by the fact that the bestowal of legatine authority *a latere* on another person could override their authority and jurisdiction.

William Warham had been appointed Archbishop of Canterbury in the reign of Henry VII. His training and ecclesiastical career were typical of many late medieval bishops, and as a servant as much of the state as of the Church, was Chancellor of England from 1504 to 1515. In 1532, shortly before his death, he was threatened with a charge of Praemunire for consecrating the bishop of St Asaph in 1518 before the King had confirmed the grant of his temporalities. Warham's reply, which survives in the form of a draft speech which he apparently intended to deliver in the House of Lords, makes a number of points which clarify the understanding of the relationship of the episcopal office to the Crown which existed before the Henrician reforms. He argued firstly that archbishops have never before been accustomed to examine bishops coming to them for consecration whether or not they have exhibited the appropriate bulls to the king for restoration of temporalities. To oblige archbishops to undertake this would be a serious burden upon them. Many bishops in the past 200 years had been consecrated without first suing for their temporalities; if archbishops had been bound to ascertain whether bulls had been presented, there would be certificates on record to show this, and neglect of this duty would have been punished by wise princes. Then, significantly, he argued

> If the archbishop cannot give the spiritualities to one who is pronounced a bishop at Rome till the King has granted him his temporalities, the spiritual power of the archbishops will depend on the temporal power of the prince, and thus would be of little or no effect, – which is against God's law.

He also argued that an archbishop had no right to keep the spiritualities after an elect had been pronounced a bishop, particularly as many kings

8

had kept the temporalities for many years. To wait for the king to grant them would have the effect of depriving the elect of both. In any case, once the bishop-elect had exhibited his bulls and done homage to the king, the temporalities could still be held, as had been the case for many archbishops and bishops including Warham's own thirteenth-century predecessor John Pecham. With this possibility, Warham argued, the king suffered no injury should consecration precede exhibition of bulls. Warham's training as a civil lawyer led him to lay considerable emphasis on the jurisdictional nature of episcopal office; his understanding of the point at which a man becomes a bishop is significant:

> A man is not made bishop by consecration, but is pronounced so at Rome in Consistory; and he has no jurisdiction given him by consecration, but only the rights of his order, viz., consecrating of children, &c. If the king by detaining temporalities could cause consecrations to be deferred, the Church might have no bishops at all, and consequently no priests, and sacraments would cease.

The same logic could be applied to the situation whereby the pope should therefore not be crowned until he had sued the temporalities of the Holy See from the Emperor 'which Constantine gave to the see of Rome', so that there would be no Pope except by the Emperor's pleasure. Warham's argument then turned from legal arguments; the spiritual man should first seek the things necessary for spiritual functions, not temporal things, and should give his oath of obedience to the pope before his temporal prince. In consecrating the bishop of St Asaph, he claimed that he was acting as but the pope's commissary; the act he performed was in fact the pope's act.[1] For Warham, the ultimate source of episcopal authority was the papacy; he was quite clear that the spiritual power of the episcopal office did not depend in any sense upon the will of the king.

It is hard to say when Henry VIII first began to consider that the spiritual authority of the pope might subsist also in the English Crown. Popes at least since Pius II in the mid-fifteenth century had claimed the union of both temporal and spiritual power, as 'two souls' in the one papacy. This was reflected in England by the example of Wolsey who was at one time both papal legate and chancellor of the kingdom, uniting the two powers to a high degree, foreshadowing Henry's claim to unite both powers supremely in his own person. Certainly, by the end of 1530 the King was aware of the arguments in favour of the vesting of supreme authority and jurisdiction over matters temporal and spiritual in the secular prince. William Tyndale's *The Obedience of a Christian Man*, which was known to Henry, taught the supremacy in matters both secular and spiritual of the king in his realm:

---

[1] *LP*, V, 1247.

God hath made the king in every realm judge over all, and over him there is no judge . . . he that resisteth the king resisteth God.

The clergy and even the pope himself are subject to 'the temporal kings and princes'.[2] In addition, the writings of Marsilius of Padua were known to many at court, and the notions derived from his *Defensor pacis* written in 1324 lent considerable weight to the assertion of the royal supremacy. Marsilian teaching supported conciliar authority over papal, and vested all coercive jurisdiction in the secular arm alone. On the one hand he taught that the sacramental power belonging to the bishops was theirs alone. The power to effect the transubstantiation of bread and wine into the body and blood of Christ and the authority to bind and loose from sin, which he referred to as the 'power of the keys' were bestowed by Christ on the apostles and their successors alone. Particularly important and relevant was his teaching that only they possessed the power of appointing other men in their place with the same authority.[3] On the other hand, he taught very clearly that the ecclesiastical power has no authority either in secular matters pertaining to ecclesiastics or over the civil power.[4] An English version of the *Defensor pacis* appeared in 1535, translated by William Marshall, sponsored by Thomas Cromwell and edited to reflect a particular picture of monarchy; around one-fifth of the original text was omitted.

A collection of over 200 citations from Scriptural, patristic and medieval sources made around 1530 and supportive of the royal supremacy has been preserved in a manuscript in the British Library commonly known as the *collectanea satis copiosa*.[5] The principal collector and editor of the documents was Edward Fox, provost of King's College, Cambridge, and the collection was probably substantially complete by the autumn of 1530. His efforts to secure the royal divorce, of which the *collectanea* forms a small part, were rewarded with the bishopric of Hereford in 1535. The document supports a view of monarchy and episcopacy which gave more to the king than Stephen Gardiner and his conservative colleagues were prepared to admit. Far from deriving episcopal power directly from God, the manuscript proposed in its choice of documents texts which suggested that episcopal authority was derived from the king. While Gardiner sought to make the

---

[2] Tyndale, W., *The Obedience of a Christian Man*, ed. Loveitt, R., Religious Tract Society Christian Classics Series vol. V (London, no date), pp. 90, 92.
[3] Marsilius of Padua, *The Defender of Peace. Volume II: The Defensor pacis*, trans. Gewirth, A. (New York, 1956), p. 92.
[4] *Ibid.*, p. 100.
[5] BL Cotton ms Cleopatra E.vi. fols.16–135. A detailed study of this document, to which the present work is indebted, is to be found in Nicholson, G.D., 'The Nature and Function of Historical Argument in the Henrician Reformation', Cambridge PhD, 1979.

power of the bishops independent of any earthly power, the argument of the *collectanea* was that the bishops of the English Church were entirely dependent upon the king for the exercise of their office. The episcopal *potestas iurisdictionis* was entirely of human origin, and was understood in various ways as emanating from or being delegated by the king to the bishops. Fox reworked the texts, expanding some of the sources, into a treatise first published in 1534, *Opus eximium, de vera differentia regiae potestas et ecclesiasticae*.

The *collectanea* manuscript served primarily as a vehicle for expressing the authenticity of the claims of the king to possess headship of the Church, and as a means for defining the nature of that headship. The manuscript was presented to the King, and bears copious annotations in his own hand. Essentially, it presented historical arguments which support the claim that divinely ordained power is ultimately vested in the Crown, which has no superior other than God. This authority had from time to time been 'lent' to the clergy, though without the loss of the Crown's ultimate rights over it; the power of the priesthood was derived from the king. It included the teaching of the medieval author Gervase of Tilbury, whose principal (and only surviving) work is the *Otia Imperialia*, which he completed between 1214 and 1218. This work begins with a discussion of the *sacerdotium* and the *regnum*; the intention of the author was to define the sphere of each. God is the author and protector of both spheres, and neither one is greater than the other.[6] The *collectanea* manuscript includes from Gervase the argument that when Moses anointed Aaron, he was acting as a type or figure of a king, and that the laws of God were declared to the people of Israel not by the high priest, but by Moses as king. This was followed by a similar argument derived from the 'Donation of Constantine', which still had considerable authority despite having been discredited as an historical document by Lorenzo Valla almost a century earlier. It was cited as evidence for the opinion that Pope Sylvester's authority had originally been vested in the Emperor Constantine, and was therefore not his solely by divine right.

Fundamental to the arguments for the royal supremacy over matters spiritual as well as temporal in England was the concept that the power of the Emperor had been 'diffused' in some sense amongst the diversity of princes who held sway over Christendom by the first years of the sixteenth century. If the realm of England is an empire, then according to the arguments of the *collectanea*, ultimate authority over matters spiritual and temporal rests in the king by virtue of the *imperium* which he possesses. Much of the manuscript was concerned with

---

[6] Richardson, H.G., 'Gervase of Tilbury', in Thrupp, S., ed., *Change in Medieval Society* (London, 1965), pp. 89–102.

demonstrating that such indeed is the case. *Imperium* is vested in the Crown, which is possessed by the king; his authority is not a personal attribute, but is derived from his possession of the Crown. The notion of *imperium* was central to the 1533 Act in Restraint of Appeals. The Act's preamble begins with a clear statement of the Crown's historical claims over both temporal and spiritual authority in terms which seem to have been derived from the texts of the *collectanea*:

> Where by divers sundry old authentic histories and chronicles, it is manifestly declared that this realm of England is an empire, and so hath been accepted in the world, governed by one Supreme Head and King, having the dignity and royal estate of the imperial Crown of the same, unto whom a body politic, compact of all sorts and degrees of people, divided in terms, and by names of spiritualty and temporalty, be bounden and owe to bear, next to God, a natural and humble obedience:[7]

The idea of an ancient and pure ideal of a personal royal supremacy protected from foreign interference by the king's right of empire had an important influence on the early drafts of this Act. In the original drafts of the Act, the supremacy was qualified as being 'derived and depended of the Imperiall crown of this realme'; the words were suppressed in its final revision.[8]

The temporal possessions of the Church were a major preoccupation of the *collectanea*. The transfer of goods from prince to Church was seen as having a role in the devolution of God-given powers of jurisdiction and authority. The suggestion that all ecclesiastical endowment was derived from kings and nobles found a place in the Act in Restraint of Appeals, which affirmed that

> the King's most noble progenitors,and the antecessors of the nobles of this realm, have sufficiently endowed the said Church, both with honour and possessions.

This allowed for the reconciliation of the full and final power of the king in all matters spiritual and temporal with a church 'sufficient and mete in itself'.[9] This preoccupation recurs in Edward Fox's *Opus eximium*, where support for the royal origin of the temporal goods of the Church was sought in Christ's injunction to 'render unto Caesar the things that are Caesar's' (Matthew 22). All dominion, authority, honour, nobility and freedom, as well as the power of coercion and restraint are derived from

---

[7] Act in Restraint of Appeals, 1533 (24 Henry VIII, c.12), in Gee, H., and Hardy, W.J., *Documents Illustrative of English Church History* (London, 1921), p. 187.
[8] Elton, G., 'The Evolution of a Reformation Statute', *English Historical Review* 64 (1949), pp. 174–97.
[9] Gee and Hardy, *Documents*, p. 188.

the person of the king. The spiritual and temporal spheres are distinguished by the Apostles' commission to minister, not to exercise power which had been given to the secular prince.[10] The royal supremacy over the episcopate was also supported by Stephen Gardiner's 1535 *De vera obedientia*. In a discussion of statutes made by kings which affected the Church, he asserted that the king's dignity was seen as always having been above that of the greatest bishops of England ('certe concedatur necesse est regiam dignitatem summis in Anglia episcopis semper praefuisse'[11]). Kings were seen to have acted as defenders of the Church, which they did 'quomodo caput tuetur corpus'.[12] A logical consequence of the supremacy was the closure of the faculties of canon law at the universites; if the King is supreme head of the Church, and all law flows from the King, then the law of a foreign bishop has no binding force in his realm and threatens to undermine his royal authority.[13] Cromwell's oration to the bishops assembled in Convocation in 1537 demonstrates the exercise of the king's supremacy over matters of doctrine. Indeed, the very fact of Cromwell's authority over the Church derived from the King and devolved to a layman, was a visible expression of the Henrician concept of the supremacy in action. On that particular occasion the bishops had been called by the King 'to determine certain controversies, which at this time be moved concerning the christian religion and faith, not only in this realm, but also in all nations throughout the world'. The bishops were to put forward their opinions, with the King as final arbiter; 'much less will [his majesty] admit any articles or doctrine not contained in the Scripture'.[14] By that date, clearly, the King had determined that his headship over the Church extended not only to matters of jurisdiction and administration, but to matters of doctrine. Further to this, the King had set himself up as the ultimate interpreter of Scripture. The emphasis on the place of Scripture as the touchstone of orthodoxy, even perhaps above the King's authority as supreme head, reflects the influence of Reformed thought upon Cromwell. This is particularly true in the insistence upon *sola scriptura*, even in matters touching the supremacy.[15]

[10] Fox, E., *De vera differentia regiae potestatis & Ecclesiasticae, & quae sit ipsa ueritas ac uirtus utriusque. Opus Eximium* (London, 1538), fol.63.
[11] Gardiner, S., *De vera obedientia*, in Janelle, P., ed., *Obedience in Church and State* (Cambridge, 1930), p. 118.
[12] *Ibid.*, p. 118.
[13] Logan, F.D., 'The First Royal Visitation of the English Universities, 1535', *English Historical Review*, 106 (1991), p. 867.
[14] (Foxe, J.), *The Acts and Monuments of John Foxe*, ed. Cattley, S.R., 8 volumes (London, 1837–39), vol. V, p. 379.
[15] The title page of the 1541 Great Bible represents clearly, in an image intended for wide public display, the role of the King as the Head of the Church in doctrinal matters as well as jurisdictional; a very similar image of his son, Edward VI, was

Royal exercise of the newly established supremacy began in earnest in 1535 after a series of Acts which had confirmed in statute the King's claims over the English Church. Early that year, the bishops in office were required to submit their papal bulls of appointment to the King; the first submissions, from Cranmer, Gardiner and Clerk, took place on 10 February, the last, from Standish, on 1 June. Only those of of Fisher, Athequa, and the absentees Campeggio and de'Ghinucci were never submitted. The bishops then petitioned, successfully, for commissions under the King's seal re-appointing them to their sees, and granting them the right to perform certain episcopal functions. These included the right to ordain those born in their diocese, if suitable, to holy orders; to grant probate of wills where the estate was under £100; to carry out visitations, with the qualification that they could do so only so far as the laws of the realm should allow; to punish crimes and excesses found out in those visitations. In essence, the King returned to the bishops all those things which had formerly pertained to their office in terms of jurisdictional power, but with the new proviso that such jurisdiction was by virtue only of the King's supremacy and at his good pleasure.[16] Control of the diocese, and maintenance of standards, was exercised through a combination of the ordinary business of ecclesiastical courts, and regular visitation by the bishop or his delegate. The actual extent to which this was practised during the late Middle Ages varied widely from one diocese to another, and while exemptions and conflicting jurisdictions could interfere with the efficient carrying out of the visitation, the

equally widely disseminated as the frontispiece to Cranmer's *Cathechismus*; see Plates III and IV.

[16] *Licentia regia concessa domino episcopo ad exercendam iurisdictionem episcopalem*, in Hughes, P., *The Reformation in England*, 3 volumes (London, 1950–54), vol. I, pp. 272–3. A number of scholars have suggested that Henry considered himself to be a lay bishop able to delegate his powers to whomever he chose (see, for instance, Claire Cross, 'Churchmen and the Royal Supremacy', *Church and Society in England: Henry VIII to James I* (London, 1977), ed. Heal, F., and O'Day, R., pp. 15–34); hence the appointment of the layman Cromwell as vicegerent, and the return of episcopal powers to the bishops at the King's pleasure. None of his bishops, not even Cranmer, seem to have agreed with this interpretation, and it is more likely that the King himself actually considered the Crown to hold within itself all the rights and powers of both the spiritual and temporal spheres. Indeed, it is a moot point whether an anointed king can be properly considered to be a layman at all, and many of the actions of the coronation service and the vesture of the newly crowned king have close parallels in ordination rites and the sacred vestments of the clergy. Perhaps the king is neither lay nor clerical, but of another estate which contains within itself elements of the other two. Others, of course, would have argued that the clergy differed from the laity only in terms of the office they held, and that the distinction stood only as long as the office was held or exercised, as the ability to exercise the office came from the common priesthood of all the faithful, the permission to exercise it from the holding of the office.

14

principle and practice was understood and accepted. Visitation of the diocese was in theory carried out every three years, though the practice varied widely from diocese to diocese. An extension of visitation by the Ordinary or his delegate was the visitation of an entire archdiocese by the metropolitan or his commissary, during which all lesser jurisdictions were suspended. The royal visitation of the entire realm was a logical consequence of locating the source of all ecclesiastical jurisdiction in the person of the King. Cromwell, by his authority as the King's vicegerent, vicar general and official principal, issued an inhibition which forbade all bishops from exercising their episcopal office for the duration of the 1535 visitation. Many bishops complained of the inhibition to Cromwell, as the King had deprived them of all their power and authority, taking it into his own hands.[17] Whatever the situation might have been before-hand, it became clear by the end of the 1530s that the bishops had become entirely dependent on the King for the exercise of their power.

In January 1536 the King wrote to all the bishops concerning contentious preaching, seeking to eliminate both teaching which sup-ported papal supremacy and the disturbing novelties of progressive reformers. In April the Archbishop of York, Edward Lee, wrote to Cromwell to complain of preachers who having been inhibited by the Archbishop claimed to hold licences from the Archbishop of Canterbury. The conservative Lee was unprepared to accept the authority of the other primate to license preaching in his diocese, but was forced to accept the King's authority (exercised personally or vicariously through Cromwell) in the matter; these preachers

> saie theye have licence of my lord of Cantorborie: but I trust
> theye have no suche, and if they have, none shalbe obeyde here,
> but onlie the kinges and youres.[18]

The ancient rivalry between the primatial sees of England had survived the introduction of the royal supremacy.

The bishops were required to exercise their authority, which they now held at the King's pleasure, in the establishment of the doctrine of the supremacy among their subjects. The first royal injunctions of 1536 (issued by Cromwell in the King's name) had the prime intention of establishing throughout the realm the King's authority over the Church.[19] Episcopal visitation followed over the next few years, with the bishops repeating in their injunctions the principal points regarding

---

[17] Strype, J., *Ecclesiastical Memorials* (Oxford, 1822), vol. I, part 1, p. 322.
[18] Duffy, E., *The Stripping of the Altars. Traditional Religion in England, c.1400–c.1580* (New Haven, CT, and London, 1992), p. 388.
[19] Frere, W.H., and Kennedy, W.M., eds., *Visitation Articles and Injunctions of the Period of the Reformation*, vol. II, *1536–1558*, Alcuin Club Collections, XV (London, 1910), pp. 1–11.

the supremacy along with other areas of concern related to the specific situation. Edward Fox's 1537 injunctions for Wigmore monastery and Cranmer's 1541 set for All Souls' College Oxford were the result of visitations carried out to address specific complaints of unsatisfactory behaviour by the members of the two institutions.[20] A series of diocesan visitations followed the second royal injunctions of 1538 with the intention of enforcing the promulgation and acceptance of the supremacy. In some cases, the injunctions clearly state that they are given by the authority given to the bishop 'of God and the King'.[21]

Another insight into the conservative Henrician episcopate, from two of its leading members, may be found in a letter to Reginald Pole from Cuthbert Tunstall, Bishop of Durham, and John Stokesley, Bishop of London, probably written early in 1537 and published in England in 1560.[22] The letter is probably a response to Pole's treatise on the unity of the Church *Pro ecclesiasticae unitatis defensione* of May 1536 which he had written in response to the recent events of the Henrician schism. Both Tunstall and Stokesley had been reluctant supporters of the break with Rome, and it may be that they felt particularly vulnerable to attack from a source both close to, and firmly supportive of, the papal supremacy to which they had subscribed only a few years earlier. They may also have felt it necessary to defend themselves against accusations from within; both bishops were, after all, close friends of John Fisher who had lost his life for opposing the royal supremacy only eighteen months or so before. The arguments they used to support the role of the King in the English Church appear to be drawn from the same source as the teaching of the Bishops' Book, published in 1537 and in the process of compilation at the very time their letter was written. That book, in discussing the sacrament of order, placed the teaching and sacramental ministry of the Church alongside 'the civil powers and governance of

---

[20] *Articles and Injunctions*, pp. 30–3, 70–81.

[21] Shaxton's injunctions for Salisbury diocese, 1538, *Articles and Injunctions*, p. 53; likewise Veysey's 1538 set for Exeter, *ibid.*, p. 61, and Bonner's of 1542 for London, *ibid.*, p. 82.

[22] *A letter written by Cutbert Tunstall late Byshop of Duresme, and John Stokesley somtime Byshop of London, sente unto Reginalde Pole, Cardinall, then beynge at Rome, and late byshop of Canterbury* (London, 1560). The letter must have been written after Pole became a cardinal on 22 December 1536 (there are several references to the red hat), and before Stokesley's death on 8 September 1539. There is internal evidence supporting the view that this is a reply to Pole's *Pro ecclesiasticae unitatis defensione*; see, for instance, sig.C.iii, which refers to letters of Pole 'sente hither' concerning the primacy of the bishop of Rome. This is certainly the view of A.B. Emden (*A Biographical Register of the University of Oxford to AD1500*, 3 volumes, Oxford, 1957–59), who describes the letter as a 'remonstrance', while C. Höllger ('Reginald Pole and the Legations of 1537 and 1539: Diplomatic and Polemical Responses to the Break with Rome', Oxford DPhil, 1989, p. 15) believes it to have been written between 16 and 20 January 1537.

kings and princes' as a parallel jurisdiction and power. The limits of the office were clearly set out. The office of ministry in the Church was

> to administer and distribute unto the members of Christ's mystical body spiritual and everlasting things, that is to say, the pure and heavenly doctrine of Christ's gospel, and the graces conferred in his sacraments[23]

The role of the secular ruler in this process was limited. While it was accepted that the authority of Christian kings and princes was over and above all other authority in the rule and government of their subjects, the principal duty of the secular ruler was

> to defend the faith of Christ and his religion, to conserve and maintain the true doctrine of Christ, and all such as be true preachers and setters forth thereof, and to abolish all abuses, heresies, and idolatries, which be brought in by heretics and evil preachers, and to punish with corporal pains such as of malice be occasioners of the same . . .[24]

In this there was no particular innovation; under all the English medieval heresy legislation, the convicted heretic was passed over to the secular magistracy for execution of sentence. However, the teaching of the book reflected the changing situation of the English Church resulting from the break with Rome. The final office of the secular ruler was

> to oversee and cause that the said priests and bishops do execute their said power, office, and jurisdiction truly, faithfully, and according in all points as it was given and committed unto them by Christ and his apostles.[25]

The secular ruler was excluded from any preaching or sacramental function; any notion of the king being in some sense a lay bishop was out of the question. Equally, the holders of ecclesiastical office were excluded from temporal power, except to the extent that this was delegated by the secular ruler.[26] The image of the two swords of spiritual and temporal power appears in a number of contemporary writings. The image was a useful one in defining, or attempting to define, the limits of kingly power over the Church and ecclesiastical power in the civil sphere. The *collectanea* manuscript had described the royal and ecclesiastical powers as 'gladii duo'.[27] This separation of the two swords of temporal and spiritual power recalls the teaching of Martin Luther, and suggests

---

[23] Lloyd, C., ed., *Formularies of Faith Put Forth by Authority during the Reign of Henry VIII* (Oxford, 1866), p. 102.
[24] *Ibid.*, pp. 120–1.
[25] *Ibid.*, p. 121.
[26] *Ibid.*, p. 119.
[27] BL Cotton ms Cleopatra E.v. fol.60r and following.

some influence upon the English episcopal Reformers. It is known that he and Edward Fox (one of the chief compilers both of the *collectanea* and of the Bishops' Book) were on good terms.[28] Luther's teaching, expressed in the 1523 treatise, *Von weltliche Oberkeit, wie weit man ihr Gehorsam schuldig sei*, was that secular and ecclesiastical authority are distinct and must not be confused, and that many of the Church's troubles had arisen as a result of such a confusion.

In 1540 seventeen questions on the sacraments were sent to a commission of bishops and other leading ecclesiastics and theologians. Cranmer's own answers survive intact, while the other replies exist in a composite where differences of opinion are illustrated by marginal or other notes. Furthermore, the King's own annotations survive on the documents, giving an insight into his own understanding at that time of the episcopal office and its relationship to his own supreme headship. The three sets of composite answers appear to represent three stages of collation; the first bears copious royal notes, while on the second (which appears to be a fair copy of the first) fewer annotations appear. The third contains much more detail, stating clearly who held what opinion. The documents are valuable in that they preserve the opinions of the majority of the bishops of the day, as well as those of several future bishops, on a number of topics relating directly to the episcopal office. Certain questions deal with the place of the bishop in the Church's ministry, others with the relationship of the kingly office to the episcopal, and others enquire of the extent and limits of ecclesiastical authority.[29] Six of the 1540 questions on doctrine referred to the role of the Christian prince. Cranmer stressed his firm support of the king's supremacy by copying out before his signature, in his own hand, the final sentence of the text of his answers:

---

[28] See, for instance, Rupp, E.G., *Studies in the Making of the English Protestant Tradition* (Cambridge, 1949), p. 115, citing a letter from Luther to Fox dated 12 May 1538, four days after the latter's death from the stone, the ailment which he shared with Luther and which formed the basis of the cordial relationship which developed between the two men.

[29] BL Cotton ms Cleopatra E.v. fols.36–47, 53–9. Apart from a number of bishops of the day, the following (most of whom later became bishops) are noted in the documents as members of the commission: Richard Cox (Bishop of Ely, 1559); John Crayford, Master of Clare College, Cambridge; Hugh Coren (Archbishop of Dublin, 1555; Bishop of Oxford, 1567–68); George Day (Bishop of Chichester, 1543–51, 1553–56); Roger Edgeworth, Oriel College, Oxford; Edward Layton, Archdeacon of Salisbury and Dean of York; Owen Oglethorpe (Bishop of Carlisle, 1556–59); John Redman, Fellow of St John's College and Lady Margaret Praelector, University of Cambridge; Thomas Robertson, Archdeacon of Leicester; one Symons; William Tresham, later Vice-Chancellor of the University of Oxford and canon of Christ Church. Thomas Thirlby was at the time of the commission bishop-elect of Westminster, and is noted throughout the responses as such.

> T. Cantuarien. This is myn opinion & sentence at this present, which nontheles I do not temerariously defyne, but referre the iugement therof holly vnto your maiestie.[30]

The document addresses the matter of the power to ordain, in particular the source of episcopal authority in relation to the making of priests. It also considers whether the Apostles, as they had no Christian king, made the first bishops by necessity or by divine authority. The choice is here between two options; either the Apostles, lacking a higher authority, were able to appoint their successors in an extraordinary way, a situation which was to continue until a Christian prince rose up with the ordinary power to appoint bishops which he could then devolve to the Apostles' successors; or the authority to appoint their successors was directly given to the Apostles from God, with the consequence that their successors also could be argued to have direct divine authority to ordain others to their office. The commissioners were also asked to consider whether the New Testament required the consecration of a bishop or a priest, or whether appointment alone was sufficient, a matter of singular importance to the English Church of 1540. The king appointed the bishops; if appointment were sufficient to make a bishop, then the lay head of the English Church has the power to create bishops, and is the ultimate source of the power of order. It is important to note that they were asked to consider the question of the appointment of both bishops and priests. If the episcopate alone were under consideration, then it might be argued from a sound and traditional viewpoint that appointment to that office stirred up and made active the fullness of the priesthood which had already been received sacramentally in priestly (presbyteral) ordination. The inclusion of the making of priests in this question colours it differently, as it would seem that an affirmative in this case gives the secular appointing power full control over the raising of a layman to spiritual office. This was certainly the opinion of Marsilius, who argued from Scripture and by reasoning that

> in perfect communities of believers, the election, assignment, and presentation of persons to be promoted to ecclesiastic orders pertains only to the human legislator or the multitude of the believers in that place over which the minister is to care; and that no bishops or priests, individually or collectively, are allowed to appoint men to such orders without the permission of the legislator or of the ruler by its authority.[31]

Most of the bishops and divines asserted that some form of consecration in addition to appointment was necessary. William Barlow answered that

[30] *Ibid.*, fol.59v.
[31] *Defensor pacis*, p. 259.

bishops have no authority to make priests without the authority of the Christian prince, though the rest of the commissioners except Cranmer believed that the bishop's authority to ordain comes from God, though some added the condition that the permission of the prince was necessary for the bishop to exercise this power. Barlow and two of the theologians asserted that lay men could make priests and bishops, using as an example the action of Moses (see Exodus 40:1–16) who 'by a privilege givin hym of god made Aron his brother preiste', though some restricted the exercise of this right to emergency situations only. Apart from Barlow and Cranmer the other bishops opposed this view.[32] Cranmer's opinion differed considerably from the replies of the others:

> A Busshop may make a prieste by the scripture, and so may princes and gouerners also, and that by the authoritie of godde committed theym, and the people also by thair election, ffor as we rede that bisshops haue don it, so christen Emperours and prynces vsuallye haue don it, and the people bifore christen princes were comonly did electe thair busshopps and preistes.[33]

He added further that there is no basis in Scripture for a separate consecration:

> In the new testament he that ys appoynted to be a Bisshop or a preiste nedeth noo consecration by the scripture, ffor election or appoyntyng therto ys sufficient.[34]

This could be interpreted as a clear statement by Cranmer that the role of the bishop in the process of making other bishops and priests was, in effect, utterly redundant, that the very act of appointing was enough to make a man a priest or a bishop. It is very important here to be careful over the meaning of 'election or appoyntyng' in this context. It would be all too easy to equate this with the legal process by which bishops are made. Looking at the other answers, an alternative explanation of appointing in this sense is presented. Barlow asserted that 'onely the appoyntyng' was required; the text continues immediately, as if in agreement, with the opinion of another of the commissioners that 'onlie the appoynting cum manuum impositione [by the laying on with hands] is sufficient withoute consecratio'. Most of the other commissioners were clear 'that consecration is requisite . . . [it] hath ben receyuid frome the appostells tyme, and institute of the hoile goste to conserve grace'. Nicholas Heath and two of the divines were of similar mind, believing that

---

[32] BL Cotton ms Cleopatra E.v., fol.45v.
[33] *Ibid.*, fols.58v–59r.
[34] *Ibid.*, fol.59r.

> prestehode ys giuen cum manuum impositionem [with the laying
> on of hands], and that by scripture, and that Consecration hath
> ben of long tyme receyvid in the churche.[35]

It is important to understand what is meant in this context by
'consecration' and 'appointment'. It has been suggested that Cranmer
may have understood 'consecrating' as the use of ceremonies such as
anointing and the *traditio instrumentorum*, while 'appointing' refers to
the act of laying on of hands with prayer.[36] Indeed, this opinion seems to
have been shared by Barlow, who considered that consecration as such
was not necessary to the making of a bishop, that appointment alone
sufficed. In 1536, a number of articles had been sent to Cromwell by
Rowland Lee, Bishop of Coventry and Lichfield and Lord President of
the Marches of Wales, against Barlow and a preacher named Tally. The
charges against the Bishop were based around a sermon which he had
given on 12 November 1536; in the course of that sermon

> he affirmed and sayde that . . . if the kinges grace being supreme
> hedd of the churche of Englande did chuse denomynate and
> electe any laye man (being lerned) to be a Bisshopp, that he so
> chosen without mencyon made of any orders, shulde be as goode
> a bisshopp as he is or the best in Englande.[37]

This extreme example of a possible consequence of erastianism in action
in the making of bishops was not without precedent. William Warham
had asserted in 1532 (in his defence against an action of praemunire) that
a man becomes a bishop not by consecration but by pronouncement in

---

[35] *Ibid.*, fol.46r.

[36] Bradshaw, P.F., *The Anglican Ordinal*, Alcuin Club Collections, LIII (London,
1971), p. 15. The *traditio* or *porrectio instrumentorum* was the handing over of the
instruments or vessels to be used by the ordinand in his new office. Different objects
symbolized the order, both minor and major, being conferred. The action was seen by
the majority of Scholastic theologians as the matter (the essential outward action) of
the sacrament of order. This question is discussed at length in Carleton, K.W.T., 'The
traditio instrumentorum in the Reform of Ordination Rites in the Sixteenth Century',
in Swanson, R.N., ed., *Continuity and Change in Christian Worship*, Studies in
Church History vol. XXXV (Woodbridge, 1999).

[37] BL Cotton ms Cleopatra E.v., fol.415. See also Strype, *Ecclesiastical Memorials*,
vol. I, part 2, p. 273. Barlow was the principal consecrator at Matthew Parker's
consecration as Archbishop of Canterbury in 1559; the fact that no records are extant
of Barlow's own episcopal consecration led to a considerable controversy in the
nineteenth century over the validity of Parker's consecration and therefore that of all
subsequent Anglican orders. While this is not the place to enter into that debate
afresh, it might be noted that it was Barlow who as early as the year of his first
episcopal appointment was arguing against the necessity for formal consecration for
the validity of the episcopal order, and whose receiving of that consecration is most
in doubt.

Consistory. It remains only to substitute the action of the king for that of the pope to arrive at Barlow's conclusion.

The commission dealt also with the question of excommunication, in particular whether God's law allowed the power and authority to excommunicate to those other than bishops and priests. Cranmer firmly supported a form of devolved authority which the bishops received from the Crown, not unlike the concept of devolved papal authority found in the later Middle Ages. The principal difference between Cranmer's concept and the late medieval teaching was that for Cranmer, the Church's minister could only excommunicate lawfully when permitted to do so by the civil law, and then only under the circumstances defined by that law. In addition, the power to excommunicate (being derived from the secular arm) could also be exercised by duly authorized laymen.[38] The other bishops and divines were divided on the issue. While some, including Lee and Tunstall, believed that the power of excommunication was given only to the apostles and their successors (implicitly, therefore, to the bishops alone), others argued that laymen who had been appointed to the task by the lay ruler were also able to excommunicate; the power belonged to the Church 'and vnto suche as the churche shall institute'.[39]

Most of the questions posed to the commission dealt with the usual situation of the Church. Two of the questions dealt with the extra-ordinary situations which the Church might face, either in a foreign land where Christianity had not yet been planted, or in the unlikely event of the extinction of a hierarchy within a realm, and whether in those circumstances the Christian prince could preach the word of God himself, and even make bishops and priests to supply the lack.[40] If the conferring of holy order were understood to be a sacrament, then the affirmative in this case would imply that the king, by virtue of his office, was an extraordinary minister of that sacrament, giving him the same power (*potestas ordinis*) as any bishop (which would, of course, include the pope, whose place in the hierarchy of *potestas iurisdictionis* the king had taken). Cranmer was unequivocal in his support of the king's power to accomplish this:

> It ys not againste goddis lawe, butt contrarye thei ought in ded so
> to doo, and therbe histories that witneseth, that some christen
> princes and other lay men unconsecrate haue don the same.[41]

It does not follow from this that Cranmer believed the king to be a 'lay bishop'. The king was not seen as some form of senior ecclesiastic with

---

[38] BL Cotton ms Cleopatra E.v. fol.59v.
[39] *Ibid.*, fol.49r.
[40] *Ibid.*, fol.59r.
[41] *Ibid.*, fol.59r.

dormant powers which were activated only in the case of necessity. Rather, the essential act in conferring the office of bishop lay, for Cranmer, in the appointment itself. The doctrine of the royal supremacy over matters spiritual extended to the supplying in the Church whatever might be lacking, even under certain circumstances to include supplying its ministers. The other commissioners agreed that where ordinary ministers of God's word were lacking, then it was the duty of lay men to undertake preaching and teaching.[42] They were divided, however, over the matter of the making of priests by laymen. Around half the commissioners were very clear that laymen could 'in nowise' make priests, having no authority whatsoever to do so. The others supported the view that, in certain special circumstances, laymen have the authority to minister the sacraments and to make priests. The division over this matter broadly reflected the difference of conservative opinion against the more progressive views of around half the commissioners. It is noteworthy that the otherwise conservative Tunstall and Thirlby joined with Barlow and seven others in support of the progressive view, though this may reflect their legal training against the theological backgrounds of those like Lee and Oglethorpe who held to the conservative line. Bonner was among those who suggested that God would inspire the prince by direct inner illumination 'as he did S. paule', giving him direct divine authority to exercise a ministry within the Church in the special circumstances. This answer is sufficiently ambiguous to avoid either granting or specifically denying to the king any sacramental power or authority over the Church, even in such extraordinary circumstances. The need for sacraments does not of itself validate such efforts to recreate the Church's ministry by any means; 'Necessitas non habet legem.'[43]

By the year 1540, the bishops and leading divines of the English Church had reached a turning point in the relationship of ecclesiastical ministry to civil authority in the person of the king. It was becoming clear that the breach with Rome was, if not final, at least some way from healing, and that many leading churchmen considered that it was not England but Rome which would have to change in order to heal the rift. The bishops no longer looked to a foreign power for the source of their authority to govern the Church. The gap left by the pope was amply filled by the supremacy, which by 1540 was consolidating its position as the source of power both temporal and spiritual. Many of the bishops refused to concede actual sacramental power to the person of the king, though the doctrine held by Cranmer and Barlow at least pointed at once to both a high doctrine of kingship and a relative secularization of the

---

[42] *Ibid.*, fol.46r.
[43] 'Necessity does not have [the force of] law.' *Ibid.*, fol.46.

episcopal office in the sacramental sphere, just as the use of bishops as senior civil servants in the late Middle Ages had led to a secularization of their role within the temporal sphere. The uncertainty over the place of the laity in general, and whether duly authorized laymen could perform non-sacramental episcopal functions such as excommunication was compounded by the position of Cromwell within and above the clerical hierarchy. The bishops who inclined towards the lay performance of functions normally reserved to those in episcopal office tended to be those who held more Reformed views of Order, treating it less as a sacrament (or wholly non-sacramentally) and more as an office to be held for a time, the order becoming extinct in the individual when the office ceased to be held, a doctrine which may be found in the early writings of Martin Luther.[44] However, at no point did Luther concede to the secular ruler such powers as were granted to the King as supreme head of the Church in England.

The King's Book of 1543 was the final official word in the reign of Henry VIII on the relationship between the secular ruler and the office of bishop. The very fact that the book was promulgated by the King's authority alone emphasizes the extent to which the royal supremacy had taken on significant responsibility for the maintenance of orthodoxy in the Church, a function which most usually attached to the episcopal office. The book extended the King's authority over the Church's ministry beyond the position reached by its predecessor, the Bishops' Book of 1537. The means by which the Church's ministry was maintained and continued in any realm was the responsibility of the secular ruler.[45] Further, ministry within the Church could only be exercised with the consent and authority of the secular ruler; priests and bishops may not 'exercise and execute any of the same offices, but with such sort and such limitation as the ordinances and laws of every Christian realm do permit and suffer.'[46] The King had effectively taken on all responsibility for the continuation and maintenance of ecclesiastical office in the English Church by virtue of his supreme headship.

The exercise of the supremacy under Edward VI continued in the same fashion. On the death of Henry VIII, the bishops' commissions under the late King's seal lapsed and they were required to petition once again for the licence to exercise episcopal office. Likewise, all ordinary episcopal jurisdiction was suspended for the general visitation of 1547, which was carried out by a commission of both clerics and laymen. Subsequent episcopal visitations were carried out by bishops in their capacity as

---

[44] The principal statement of Luther's teaching on the Church's ministry is found in his 1520 treatise *De Captivitate Babylonica Ecclesiae*.

[45] Lloyd, *Formularies*, p. 278.

[46] *Ibid.*, p. 279.

royal commissioners, and any injunctions issued were supplementary to those of the royal visitors of 1547.[47] Further, a Royal Proclamation of 24 April 1548 inhibited all preaching in the realm without licence from the King, the Protector (Somerset) or the Archbishop of Canterbury; all other bishops were included in its terms. This meant that no bishop had the right to preach, or to license another to preach in his diocese, without first seeking that right from the King. The general visitation of 1547 was designed primarily to promote preaching of an approved sort throughout the realm, and was carried out quite independently of the bishops. The Edwardian bishop was wholly dependent for the exercise of his office on the royal supremacy; this suspension of ordinary episcopal jurisdiction continued until the reconciliation with Rome in 1554 when the pre-1535 situation with regard to episcopal power was restored and royal visitations were discontinued.[48]

The Reformed Ordinals of 1550 and 1552 made little reference to the place of the king in the making of the Church's ministers. All candidates for the three orders of deacon, priest and bishop, were required to swear an oath of the king's supremacy. The form of the oath required the candidate to renounce the Bishop of Rome, to acknowledge the king as only supreme head in earth of the Church of England, and to undertake to uphold and maintain the laws relating to the king's authority and the repudiation of the pope. The Litany and Suffrages included three petitions for the king, and only one each for the ministers of the Church and for those being ordered or consecrated. In the order for consecrating archbishops or bishops, the king's mandate for the consecration was to be read before the administration of the oath of supremacy. There was no other reference to the king's role in either Ordinal, and the remainder of the rites allowed and even encouraged an interpretation that what was being done came directly from God through the Church. Alternative interpretations of the role of the supreme head could be placed on the rite. The conferral of the Church's orders could be the result of immediate divine action, through the bishop as minister, with the permission of the king (and the implication that such permission was not necessary for valid reception). The other interpretation which

---

[47] This is clearly expressed in the first of Robert Holgate's injunctions for York Minster, 1552; *Articles and Injunctions*, p. 310.

[48] Davies, E.T., *Episcopacy and the Royal Supremacy in the Church of England in the Sixteenth Century* (Oxford, 1950), pp. 78–9, where it is also noted that after the final cessation of royal visitations in 1559 the bishops began to regain their power as Ordinaries. See also the discussion in Bowker, M., 'The Supremacy and the Episcopate: The Struggle for Control, 1534–1540', *Historical Journal*, 18 (1975), pp. 227–43, and Strype, *Ecclesiastical Memorials*, vol. II, part 1, p. 142, where he mentions having seen licences to the bishops of Exeter (dated 1551), Lincoln and Chichester (both dated 1552).

the rites allow is for the king, as head, to be the channel of the divine ordering action, ministered through the bishops acting as the king's commissaries. The latter interpretation would also hold true if the act of conferring orders were seen in the same light as an appointment to secular office, carried out by the king's agent but with his authority and on his behalf. Those who understood ordering as a purely non-sacramental, administrative act, with the office ceasing when the office-holder ceased to practise an active ministry, would be able to accept that interpretation. In terms of the relationship of the king to the orders of the English Church, at least, the Ordinals were sufficiently ambiguous not to rule out by that fact alone their validity from a Catholic understanding of the Church's ministry.

For John Hooper, Christ as the true head of the Church was not only its true Priest and Bishop, but also its King, Emperor and Protector.[49] Many of the problems faced by the Reformed Church of England were derived from the confusion of roles between the king and the bishops. Too many bishops had been servants of the state, more concerned with personal advancement than with the flock committed to their charge, and Hooper believed that they should not hold civil and ecclesiastical office simultaneously.[50] The office of bishop had degenerated from its scriptural origins, especially in the letter to Titus (1:5–9), principally through the growth of riches in the Church, such that 'bishops became princes, and princes were made servants'.[51] Every man should do the works required by his own vocation, and not meddle in the labours of others, just as the prophet Jonah had been sent to Nineveh to preach, not to take part in government.

> It is not the office of the bishop to play the king and lord, nor the king's part to play the bishop: for the king's office is enough for a king, and the bishop's office enough for a bishop.[52]

Hooper was prepared to concede responsibility in matters of religion to the Crown under certain circumstances; it is notable that the context of this admission was an apology he was forced to make for his position after reports that he had cursed or encouraged others to curse Queen Mary. He seemed to be advocating the doctrine of royal supremacy

[49] 'A Declaration of Christ and his Office' (1547), *Early Writings of John Hooper, D.D.*, ed. Carr, S., Parker Society (Cambridge, 1843), p. 78.
[50] 'A Declaration of the Ten Holy Commandments' (1549), *Early Writings*, p. 398.
[51] 'A Declaration of the Ten Holy Commandments' (1549) (on the eighth commandment, 'Thou shalt not steal'), *Early Writings*, p. 396.
[52] Hooper, Sermons upon Jonas: third sermon, 5 March 1550, *Early Writings*, pp. 506–7.

which Edward VI and his father had held and exercised, and which the Queen was seeking to disregard in her actions:

> God doth not bid the king and queen commit matters of religion to the bishops; neither doth he will them to give bishops power to condemn when they lust, and so afterwards commit such as they have condemned to the secular powers: but doth command all princes to be learned themselves, to hear them, and to judge themselves such doubtful and weighty causes by the word of God.[53]

John Ponet, from his exile at Strassburg, went further than any other English Reformer before him in advocating that, under certain circumstances, a bad king might be legitimately removed from office and even killed. *A shorte treatise of politike power, and of the true obedience with an Exhortacion* was published by him in 1556; it seems to have been based largely on Melanchthon's 1539 tract *On the Office of Princes*.[54] The beginnings of the theory of legitimate tyrannicide amongst the English Reformers reflects a similar development in the teaching of Martin Luther, from the idea of the tyrant as God's scourge to his understanding of the right of an inferior magistrate to resist an unjust ruler.

The dependence of the exercise of the episcopal office upon the royal pleasure, established by Henry VIII and continued by Edward VI, was revoked by Mary. The Queen believed that ecclesiastical power was wholly independent of the civil.[55] As a consequence, a set of Articles was sent to all the bishops 'by the Queen's Majesty's commandment' in March 1554 which commanded that

> no bishop, or any his officer or other person aforesaid, hereafter in any of their ecclesiastical writings in process, or other extrajudicial acts, do use to put in this clause or sentence *Regia auctoritate fulcitus*.[56]

From this point onwards, the authority of the Marian bishops was no longer sustained or upheld by the Queen's authority. Technically, until the reconciliation of the realm with the see of Rome which took place in November that year, their authority and jurisdiction was not derived from the pope either. As a result, for all practical purposes the bishops were, for that period, acting on the sole authority of their episcopal order alone.

---

[53] 'Apology [against reports that Hooper had cursed the Queen]' (published 1562), *Later Writings of Bishop Hooper*, ed. Nevinson, C., Parker Society (Cambridge, 1852), p. 559.
[54] Dickens, A.G., *The English Reformation*, Second Edition (London, 1989), pp. 342–3.
[55] Mary to Pole, 28 October 1553, in Pole, R., *Epistolae Reginaldi Poli*, ed. Quirini, A.M., 5 volumes (Brescia, 1744–57) iv, 120.
[56] 'Sustained by the Queen's authority'; *Articles and Injunctions*, p. 325.

The validity of holy orders conferred during the period of schism, and particularly those conferred using the rites of the 1550 and 1552 Ordinals, came frequently under question and often proved to be a source of some considerable confusion. All clergy ordained by the rites of the Reformed Ordinals were obliged to seek reconciliation before they were permitted to exercise their office under the restored Catholic rites. Bonner's articles for the visitation of the diocese of London, which took place between 3 September 1554 and 8 October 1555, asked

> Whether such as were ordained schismatically, and contrary to the old order and custom of the Catholic Church . . . being not yet reconciled nor admitted by the ordinary, have celebrated or said either Mass or other Divine Service within any cure or place in this city or diocese?[57]

A study of the episcopal register for this period of Bonner's episcopate shows that large numbers of candidates were admitted to first tonsure and minor orders, compared with the numbers of those admitted to major orders. The omission of those grades of order in the Edwardian rites would seem to have been remedied in this way, and one may presume that it was by these means that irregularly ordained clergy were reconciled and enabled to carry out their ministry within the restored Catholic Church.[58] Reconciliation of clergy who had taken advantage of the 1549 Act to take away all positive Laws against Marriage of Priests (2 and 3 Edward VI, c.21), repealed in 1553 by Mary's First Statute of Repeal (1 Mary, Stat.2, c.2), held more difficulties. By the Queen's Injunctions of 1554, secular priests deprived for marriage who had done penance and undertaken to live apart from their wives were permitted to receive a benefice in another place. Former religious, having taken a solemn vow of chastity, were to be treated more seriously, with a formal pronouncement of divorce and some form of punishment to be administered.[59] Evidence from the diocese of York for the period suggests that the majority of deprivations took place on account of marriage.[60] After his deprivation from the see of Chester in 1554 on account of marriage, John Bird acted as suffragan to Bonner in London diocese, despite

---

[57] *Articles and Injunctions*, p. 337.

[58] Register of Edmund Bonner, Guildhall Library, MS9531/12 Part 2, fol.28r. and following. A study of the names of the individuals involved would confirm or deny this, though the high number of candidates presenting themselves in the period just before Christmas 1554 adds weight to this argument.

[59] Dickens, A.G., and Carr, D., *The Reformation in England to the Accession of Elizabeth I*, Documents of Modern History (London, 1967), pp. 143–7.

[60] Dickens, A.G., *The Marian Reaction in the Diocese of York*, Part 1, *The Clergy*, Borthwick Institute, St Anthony's Hall Publications vol. 11 (York, 1957), p. 16.

falling into the category of a married ex-religious (Bird had been a Carmelite friar).

Mary seems not to have been thoroughly consistent in her attitude towards the Crown's power of deprivation from ecclesiastical benefices, especially from the episcopate. Henry VIII never exercised the right of deprivation that he believed he possessed. The bishops deprived under Edward VI, both those appointed under the royal supremacy such as Bonner and Day, and those who were in office before the schism from Rome, Gardiner in 1551 and Tunstall in 1552, were removed by Royal Commission. When, after Edward's death, the case of Winchester was examined in August 1553, the deprivation was described as 'pretensed', and Ponet said to have 'intruded' into the see. The restorations of Bonner and Day took place at the same time on the same grounds suggesting that Mary did not believe the Crown to possess the power of deprivation, even in those cases where appointment had first been made by the Crown. Despite this, seven bishops, all of whom had been appointed by the action of the royal supremacy, were deprived by Royal Commission in March 1554. The vacancies thus created were filled by appointment under the former (and, at the time, still the legally correct) means of *congé d'élire*. Further, the appointments were secretly passed to Cardinal Pole for confirmation, an action which strictly breached the statute of praemunire.[61] The confirmation was made from Brussels, Pole having received a special dispensation to enable him to effect this 'mission at long range'.[62] Tunstall's deprivation was reversed by the legal re-erection of the see of Durham, which had been divided by Act of Parliament in March 1553, though it would seem that the Queen, in her dealings with the Bishop, simply ignored the dissolution.[63]

In a few years, the English episcopate under Mary moved from an order entirely dependent upon the royal supremacy, through a period of autonomy when it depended entirely upon the authority inherent in the office of bishop itself, to end in the same relationship with Rome and the papacy from which the Church had split some thirty years earlier. It may be that this experience coloured the views of the bishops, to the extent that, almost to a man, they were unable to accept the reimposition of a royal supremacy after the accession of Queen Elizabeth. When the Uniformity bill was passing through Parliament in 1559, Mary's Bishop of Chester, Cuthbert Scott, spoke in the Lords against the whole idea of the imposition of faith by statute; 'if it shall hang upon an act of parliament we have but a weak staff to lean unto'.[64]

---

[61] Loades, D.M, *The Oxford Martyrs* (London, 1970), pp. 113–15.
[62] Loades, D.M., *The Reign of Mary Tudor* (London, 1991), p. 127; Register of Reginald Pole, fols.7v–13v.
[63] Loades, *The Reign of Mary Tudor*, p. 103.
[64] Haigh, C., *English Reformations*, pp. 240–1.

There are indications that, in the early years of the sixteenth century, an opinion was being advanced in many quarters that the Church would benefit from an increase in the authority of the bishops. The intention seems to have been to restore the situation to that which existed before the growth of the cardinalate and the development of religious orders directly subject to the pope and exempt from episcopal control. During the Fifth Lateran Council (1512–17), two Venetians, Tommaso Giustiniani and Vincenzo Quirini, who had recently entered the new austere order of Camaldolese monks, presented to Pope Leo X a voluminous work on the reform of the Church which was more far-reaching than anything which had been produced since the conciliar period. The degree of frankness in this document was to be found again in the report of the 1536 commission of cardinals to Pope Paul III, and it would not be inappropriate to suggest that the presence on that commission of Gasparo Contarini, close friend of the two Camaldolese from his youth, provided a link with this work.[65] Contarini's treatise on the episcopal office, *De officio viri boni ac probi episcopi*, was published in 1517, the year in which the Lateran Council was concluded. It derives much from the example of Pietro Barozzi, Bishop of Padua from 1487 to 1507, whom Contarini knew, as well as drawing on the ideas of his friends Guistiniani and Querini. There may also be an influence drawn from the sermons of Savonarola, which Contarini had read during the summer of 1516.[66] Barozzi was one of a number of notable reforming bishops who held office during the fifteenth and early sixteenth centuries. Among his contemporaries noted for their pastoral zeal, for carrying out visitations and for holding synods must be included Lorenzo Giustiniani, Patriarch of Venice, Antonio Bertini, Bishop of Foligno, Gian Matteo Giberti, Bishop of Verona, and Antonino Forciglioni, Archbishop of Florence. The *Repertorium totius summe* by Antonino of Florence includes a chapter on the office of bishop which draws on the Pastoral Epistles and the Fathers. The tone is pastoral; the bishop is the spiritual father of his diocese, whom spiritual sons should imitate as natural sons imitate their natural father. A copy of the work was bequeathed to Hereford Cathedral Library by Charles Booth, Bishop of Hereford. In that copy, in the chapter on the episcopal office, are underlined the words *non est facile stare in loco petri et pauli*. Booth was probably about seventy years old at the time of the break with Rome, a civil lawyer by training (including a spell in Bologna where he obtained his doctorate),

---

[65] 'Libellus ad Leonem X', in Mittarelli, J.B., and Costadini, A., *Annales Camalduenses*, vol. IX (Venice, 1773), pp. 612–719; Jedin, H., *A History of the Council of Trent*, trans. Graf, E., vol. I (London, 1957), pp. 128–9.
[66] Gleason, E.G., *Gasparo Contarini: Venice, Rome, and Reform* (Berkeley and Los Angeles, 1993), p. 93.

and bishop for nearly twenty years during a difficult time for the higher clergy of the English Church. It is tempting to suggest that Booth himself may have underlined this phrase.[67] In France, Francois d'Estraing, Bishop of Rodez (1504–29), promoted the instruction of the laity and the formation of his clergy, reformed his cathedral chapter, and carried out visitations of his diocese. Guillaume Briçonnet, Bishop of Meaux, sought to reform his diocese through preaching, upsetting the Franciscans who saw their privilege of freedom from episcopal control being attacked. In Germany and Spain, too, bishops held reforming synods and were noted for their energetic pastoral activity.[68] The Pastoral Epistles and the early Church Fathers were held up to bishops as 'mirrors of the virtue of their state'. Popular works included the *Regula pastoralis* of Gregory the Great, *De officiis* of Ambrose, Gregory Nazianzen's *Apologia*, and the works of John Chrysostom on the priesthood.[69] This type of work, often referred to as the 'mirror of bishops' literature, covered the theological and legal dimensions of the episcopal office as well as its pastoral and administrative functions.

Central to Continental reform of the episcopate in the fifteenth and early sixteenth centuries was the requirement of residence in the diocese. A Bull of Pope Alexander VI, *In apostolicae sedis specula*, included chapters on the nomination of bishops and their duty of residence which were of great importance to the Church for the reform of its members; unfortunately, the Bull failed to address the heart of the matter, reform of the head. Cardinal Cajetan, Thomas de Vio, was the first to maintain (in his commentary on the *Summa Theologiae* of Thomas Aquinas, 1517), that the episcopal duty of residence rested on a direct divine ordinance, with only the most weighty motives able to excuse from it. Every memorial dealing with reform from the Council of Basle to the Council of Trent, including the important *Consilium . . . de emendanda ecclesia* demanded that bishops comply with the duty of residence.[70] The successful pastoral action of the exemplary bishops noted above was only possible because each was resident in his diocese and took a personal role in its activity.

In England, too, in the late fifteenth and early sixteenth centuries, there were moves to encourage reform of the episcopal office by its holders. John Colet's 1512 sermon to Convocation at Canterbury

---

[67] 'It is not easy to stand in the place of Peter and Paul.' Antoninus Forciglioni, Archbishop of Florence, *Repertorium totius summe*, 3 volumes (Basle, 1502). The copy at Hereford Cathedral is shelved at K.2.X–XII; the date in the accessions catalogue is given as 1511, while the colophon reads '15011'.

[68] Jedin, Vol.1, pp. 149–54. Nicholls, D., 'France', in Pettegree, A., ed., *The early Reformation in Europe* (Cambridge, 1992), pp. 123–4.

[69] Jedin, vol. I, p. 163.

[70] Jedin, vol. II, p. 321.

attacked clerical abuses and advocated reform of the Church from within, calling upon the bishops to lead the process. The Church was to be reformed not by the passing of new laws but by the enforcement of existing ones. Bishops, especially, were to be chosen not for their worldly abilities but for their spiritual life, while candidates for ordination should be subject to more rigorous examination.[71] In the fifteenth century, even in the better-regulated dioceses both in England and on the Continent, the examination of candidates by the bishop or his deputy was inadequate or perfunctory.[72] The years leading up to the convocation of the Fifth Lateran Council saw a general call for reform of clerical selection and training, a part of which was the desire for reform of the English clergy expressed by Colet. William Melton, Chancellor of York from 1498 to 1523, who had been Fisher's tutor at Michaelhouse, Cambridge, published with Colet's approval a sermon to ordinands which expressed the same concern with the quality and number of those entering holy orders, intending that the sermon should be read to candidates during the weeks leading up to their ordination.[73] Thomas More, whose spiritual mentor was John Colet, also advocated the introduction of much stricter standards of selection for the priesthood; in *A Dialogue Concerning Heresies*, which dates from around 1528, he proposed this as a first step towards dispelling the truth of the proverb that 'yf a preste be good than he is olde', alluding in particular to the negligence of chastity amongst the clergy.[74]

Many theologians distinguished the episcopal office from the ordinary priesthood (presbyterate) in terms of jurisdiction only. They believed that the power to govern was received by the bishops in episcopal consecration, and this power alone separated them from priests of lower rank. In essence, all bishops were priests, but only bishops had the power *ex officio* to govern the Church (the power of jurisdiction, generally referred to as *potestas iurisdictionis*). The sacramental power (*potestas ordinis*) of holy order, and the priesthood in particular, was held equally by bishops and priests, while the ordinary exercise of certain aspects of that power was restricted to the episcopate. Priests were considered to be extraordinary ministers of the sacrament of Confirmation by many authorities, and there are a few isolated cases of abbots, not having received consecration as bishops, validly ordaining their subjects to major orders, even to the priesthood, the necessary condition

---

[71] Colet, Convocation Sermon, in Williams, C.H., ed., *English Historical Documents, 1485–1558* (London, 1967), pp. 656–7.

[72] Hay, D., *The Church in Italy in the Fifteenth Century* (Cambridge, 1977), p. 53.

[73] Swanson, R.N., 'Problems of the Priesthood in Pre-Reformation England', *English Historical Review*, 105 (1990), pp. 861–2; Melton, W., *Sermo Exhortatorius* (London, c.1510)

[74] Fox, A., *Thomas More, History and Providence* (Oxford, 1982), p. 169.

for validity being specific papal authority to confer those orders. It was not unusual for religious superiors to administer the tonsure or minor orders, but what amounted to presbyteral ordination is documented in only a few cases. Much of the argument centred around the interpretation of the teachings of St Jerome in the fourth century, who in response to a particular situation in the Church at Rome gave the opinion that priest and bishop were originally the same, and that the distinction between the two offices grew up later. The argument was set out by Thomas Aquinas in his *Summa Theologiae*:

> Jerome says, Formerly, presbyter and bishop were the same thing. Then he adds, Consequently, just as priests know that by custom in the Church they are subject to those placed over them, so also bishops should know that they are superior to priests more by custom than by disposition of the Lord and they should govern the Church in common.[75]

This text and others similar were frequently cited to support the fundamental equality of the episcopal and sacerdotal or presbyteral office. The counter argument to this is also found in Aquinas, and points towards his only qualified acceptance of the concept. According to this argument, the presbyter and bishop were not distinguished at first by name. St Augustine, in *De Civitate Dei*, had explained that bishops were so called because they superintend (*superintendunt*), and that in Greek, presbyters were called *elders* (*seniores*).

> Thus St Paul commonly used the name *presbyters* as referring to both, as when he says, *The elders who do their work well while they are in charge are to be given double consideration.* The same is true of the name *bishops*, as is stated in *Acts* in reference to the presbyters of the church of Ephesus, *Take heed to yourselves and to the whole flock, wherein the Holy Ghost hath placed you bishops, to rule the Church of God.*[76]

In practice, however, Aquinas believed there had always been a distinction between them, even from apostolic times. In support of this he cited Bede's commentary on the gospel of Luke in the *Glossa ordinaria*, which refers to the commissioning of the seventy-two in Luke 10 as the first occasion of the ordination of presbyters:

> *As the apostles are the prototype of bishops, so the seventy-two disciples are the prototype of presbyters of the second rank.* but later, to avoid schism, it was also necessary to distinguish them

---

[75] Aquinas, T., *Summa Theologiae*, vol. XLVII, ed. Aumann, J. (London 1973), 2a2ae. 184, 6, p. 41, quoting from St Jerome's Commentary on the Epistle to Titus.
[76] *Summa*, 2a2ae. 184, 6 ad 1, p. 43, citing 1 Timothy 5:17 and Acts 20:28.

by name, so that higher prelates were called bishops and those of inferior rank were called presbyters.[77]

Finally, Aquinas stated that Augustine had listed among heretical doctrines the teaching of the Arians that a presbyter should not be distinguished in any way from a bishop.[78]

The study of scholastic theology ceased in the English universities in the mid-1530s, forming no part of the syllabus for higher studies in theology from that time. However, many of the bishops in the earlier part of this study had been trained in the law rather than in scholastic theology, while the later Henrician theologian bishops and their successors had been brought up in the period of reaction against medieval theology in the universities brought about by the spread of Reformed ideas. Of those who had undergone a traditional theological education to the highest level, John Fisher stood out most clearly amongst his contemporaries as one most concerned to defend traditional notions of the office and function of the bishop. He is alleged to have assisted in the composition of Henry VIII's *Assertio septem sacramentorum*, and published a defence of that work, the *Defensio Regiae Assertionis*, the greater part of which was an attack of Luther's eucharistic doctrine. One chapter only discussed holy order, and included also a discussion of the sacrament of matrimony. Two works by Fisher set out his theology of the episcopal office most clearly. His *Assertionis Lutheranae confutatio* taught the separation of the pastoral function from the sacramental, and maintained the medieval distinction between the power of order (*potestas ordinis*) and the power of jurisdiction (*potestas iurisdictionis*) in the office of a bishop or priest. Distinction within the hierarchical grades was a matter of differences in the power of jurisdiction. So far as the power of order was concerned, the pope was no different from any other bishop; the distinction between the two was one of jurisdiction, the power for which flowed ultimately from the pope as vicar of Christ on earth, through bishops and priests and then to the rest of the Church; 'have we not observed', he asked, 'that Christians are born of priests, priests of bishops and that bishops are generated by the sovereign pontiff (as often as it be necessary)?'[79]

---

[77] *Summa*, 2a2ae. 184, 6 ad 1, p. 43, referring to the *Ecclesiasticae Hierarchia* of Pseudo-Dionysius, and citing *Glossa ordinaria*, Bede, *In Lucam*, III.10.

[78] *Summa*, 2a2ae. 184, 6 ad 1, p. 45, citing Augustine *De Haereses* 53.

[79] Fisher, J., *Assertionis Lutheranae confutatio* (Antwerp, 1523); Gogan, B., 'Fisher's View of the Church', in Bradshaw, B., and Duffy, E., eds., *Humanism, Reform and the Reformation* (Cambridge, 1989), p. 138. See also Rex, R., *The Theology of John Fisher* (Cambridge, 1991), pp. 107–8, where this passage is discussed. Dr Rex expands Gogan's argument that Fisher demonstrates a lack of scholastic precision in this passage by confusing *potestas ordinis* and *potestas iurisdictionis*. Dr Rex also makes a distinction between 'sacramental and universal' power to baptize, 'sacra-

It would not be correct, however, to proceed from here to the assumption that Fisher considered bishops and priests to be essentially the same. In the *Sacri sacerdotij defensio contra Lutherum*, a reply to the Reformer's 1522 *De abroganda Missa privata* and written alongside the *Assertionis Lutheranae Confutatio*, he explored the teaching of Jerome, coming to the ultimate conclusion that there was a fundamental distinction, a conclusion which he was able to make as a result of the clear separation of the powers of order and jurisdiction. In the letter to Evagrius, for instance, Jerome seemed to Fisher to be arguing for the identity of the presbyteral and episcopal offices, though Jerome's commentary on Acts 20 suggested a different view. The essential difference between the presbyter and the bishop rested on their relative powers over the *corpus Christi reale*; while the presbyter possesses the sacerdotal power to confect the eucharist, it is the bishop only who possesses additionally the power to bestow the sacerdotal power of consecration, through the conferring of the sacrament of order. Fisher's interpretation placed bishops as superior to priests by virtue not only of jurisdictional power but also of their ability to bestow upon others the sacramental power to celebrate mass and to transubstantiate bread and wine into the true body and blood of Christ.[80] He was fully in accord with the fifteenth-century emphasis on the close relationship between the sacrament of order and the sacrament of the altar. As a theologian by training rather than a lawyer, his distinction between bishop and priest rested on more than the exercise of authority in the external forum. Bishop and priest are both *sacerdotes*; each is equally able to offer the sacrifice of the Mass. Only the bishop, however, has the power to pass on that ability. It is not surprising, therefore, to find in Fisher a great devotion to the eucharist, and unlike many of his brother bishops, a personal practice of daily celebration of the Mass.

mental and episcopal power' to ordain, and the papal appointment of bishops 'who, like priests, were of course *ordained* by other bishops'. The majority of scholastic theologians denied the sacramental nature of the consecration of bishops, though it was affirmed overwhelmingly by post-Tridentine theologians, who were supported in particular by the definition of the Council of Trent in 1563 (Ott, L., *Fundamentals of Catholic Dogma*, [1952], trans. Bastible, J., Cork, no date, p. 433; Council of Trent, Twenty-third Session, 15 July 1563, in Alberigo, J., *et al.*, eds., *Conciliorum oecumenicorum decreta* (Bologna, 1973), pp. 742–4; Schroeder, H.J., trans., *Canons and Decrees of the Council of Trent*, Rockford, IL, 1978, pp. 160–3. Rather than any confusion on Fisher's part, or an expression of a 'highly clerical mentality', it seems more likely in the context of his remarks that he was advocating an organic unity within the Church which included pope and ordinary Christian in a single inter-connected whole. As Professor J.J. Scarisbrick has pointed out, Fisher did not repudiate scholasticism, but relegated it respectfully to second place to patristic scholarship in his mature thought; 'The Conservative Episcopate in England, 1529–1535', Cambridge PhD, 1955, p. 349.

[80] Fisher, J., *Sacri sacerdotij defensio contra Lutherum* (Cologne, 1525).

As might be expected from one trained in the law, Stephen Gardiner's doctrine of episcopacy rested much more firmly on the idea of authority and jurisdiction. His 1535 treatise *De vera obedientia* was an attempt to set episcopal authority in England on a sound footing in the light of the separation from the see of Rome and from the papal power of appointment of bishops. It set out a doctrine which merged royal and episcopal authority, and at the same time delineated their relative spheres of influence and activity. Oversight of the Church is vested primarily in the bishop, though without prejudice to the right and duty of the parish clergy to rule their flocks. Further, the superior authority of the archbishop does not nullify the ordinary jurisdiction of the diocesan bishop over his subjects. Higher in dignity than any bishop, however, has always been the king, acting as the Church's defender just as the head watches over or defends (*tuetur*) the body. Despite this headship role, Gardiner would not allow that episcopal power was, or even could be, channelled through the king. Every bishop (including the bishop of Rome) derived his authority directly from the Word of God 'in sua diocesi plebem diuini uerbi, et sacramentorum ministratione alant'.[81] The bishop did not depend on the king for the power and authority to exercise his office. Equally, his episcopal power was not dependent on the pope, who was seen as no more than one of the many bishops of the Church, with no more authority over the Church in England than any other foreign bishop. At the time of writing the treatise, it was most important for Gardiner to establish the independence of the episcopal office from the papal power. Failure to do so would have rendered the situation of the Henrician Church unworkable. The means which Gardiner chose, a demonstration of the ultimate dependence of the bishop's power on God alone, successfully eliminated the role of the pope. It also excluded the king as a replacement channel for episcopal power after the removal of the pope.

Edward Fox's *De vera differentia* made a subtle distinction between the sources of episcopal power. While he believed that clergy received divine authority to govern the Church, the coercion which made their authority effective came from the prince.[82] He used Jerome to support the view that there was no primitive distinction between the office of bishop and priest, but that the difference entered the Church through the influence of the devil.[83] Fisher had interpreted Jerome as allowing for a distinction between the episcopal and presbyteral offices from the beginning. Fox, however, came to the conclusion that Jerome taught no distinction between the two offices in the primitive Church. The first

---

[81] *De vera obedientia*, pp. 102, 118, 128.
[82] *De vera differentia*, fol.22.
[83] *De vera differenta*, fols.25v–26r.

bishops were simply the senior presbyters, elected in the local churches from among their number. The practice had grown as a result, he believed, of the need to provide an individual who could be a focus of unity in the face of schism.

Fox also made a major contribution to the compilation of the *Institution of a Christian Man*, usually known as the Bishops' Book, which was completed in 1537. It was commended by the King for study by the clergy, but never received his authority nor that of Parliament. The book taught that the bishop and priest were of the same office, and that this had been the case since the beginning of the Church, as in the New Testament there is 'no mention made of any degrees or distinctions in orders, but only of deacons or ministers, and of priests or bishops'.[84] A thorough revision of the Bishops' Book was presented to Convocation in 1543 under the title *The Necessary Doctrine and Erudition of a Christian Man*, and was much more conservative in its doctrine. It was issued with a preface by the King, and with his full authority, and came to be known more usually as the King's Book. The book's teaching on the identity of bishop and priest was the same as its predecessor; Scripture expressly mentions 'these two orders only, that is to say, priests and deacons'.[85] This doctrine, expressed in the two major doctrinal statements of the Henrician Reformation, had an impact beyond the English Church's understanding of the nature of its episcopal office. It affected the place of the minor orders, and of the subdiaconate, within the Church's ministry. If they were not scriptural in origin, then they must be of human origin. If this were to be the case, then they could be dispensed with in any further revision of the ministerial office. The next official statement of the English Church's doctrine of ministry and order, the 1550 Ordinal, quietly and completely omitted the subdiaconate and the minor orders.

The 1537 letter of Tunstall and Stokesley to Cardinal Pole agreed in essence with the teaching on the episcopal office of the Bishops' Book, which was probably in the process of compilation at the time their letter was written. They argued in favour of the equality of all the bishops, and against the notion that one bishop, the pope, had some form of supremacy amongst the episcopate. Cyprian had claimed in his *De simplicitate clericorum* that the apostles were endowed with 'lyke equalitie of honoure and power'. From Jerome, *Contra Iouinianum*, they derived the view that all the apostles, and not only Peter, had been given the keys of the kingdom of heaven. In addition, Jerome's commentary on the Epistle to Titus was also taken, as it had been by Fox, to support the opinion that bishops and priests were fundamentally of the same office.[86]

[84] Lloyd, *Formularies*, p. 105.
[85] *Ibid.*, p. 281.
[86] Tunstall and Stokesley, *Letter*, Sig.B.i.

The bishops and divines of the 1540 doctrine commission were asked to consider the relationship between bishops and priests. Its members were divided over the question of whether the bishop or the priest existed first in the Church, or if the two orders came into existence simultaneously. Some (including Barlow and Thirlby) held that bishops and priests were originally a single order, while others (including Lee, Bonner, Heath and Oglethorpe) belived that a distinction existed from the beginning. Amongst the latter, one group saw the Apostles as the first priests, later becoming bishops when the power to ordain others as priests was given to them. Others held that the Apostles were the first bishops, and that the seventy-two disciples sent out by Jesus (see Matthew 26:20 and Luke 10:1) were the first priests. The majority held that the Apostles were made bishops from the first, and that they made others bishops and priests.[87] Cranmer, in his answers to the same questions, was of the opinion that bishops and priests were at one time not two, but one office 'in the begynnyng of Christs Religion'.[88] This was entirely consistent with Cranmer's other writing on the subject, and with the known opinions of other Reform-minded individuals.

Around the same time, Cranmer was collecting Patristic and other texts which were to influence his later thought. The manuscript known as his 'Commonplace Book' includes a substantial section of references relating to the Church's ministry from Scripture and the Fathers. It is important to exercise caution in the use of this document. While it may not represent Cranmer's own opinions, it indicates some of the sources of his own doctrine on the ministry. In particular, he records a number of texts from Jerome which support the view that bishop and priest were one office in the primitive Church, alongside others from Chrysostom, Ambrose and Basil.[89]

The first Ordinal of the Reformed Church of England, published in 1550, was chiefly the work of Cranmer but was accepted by the majority of bishops (Nicholas Heath, by this time translated to Worcester refused to assent to it, and as a result was committed to the Fleet on 4 March, 1550).[90] In the Preface to the Ordinal, three orders of ministers – deacon, priest and bishop – were listed as having existed in the Church since the

---

[87] BL Cotton ms Cleopatra E.v. fol.45.

[88] *Ibid.*, fol.58v.

[89] BL Royal ms 7.B.xi, fols.178ff. The collection was probably completed by 1543; Bradshaw, *The Anglican Ordinal*, p. 12. It should not be seen as a complete statement of Cranmer's thinking on the matter, but the selection of texts gives an insight into both the sources available to him and the general directions of his reflection which resulted in his mature thought. This would be expressed in his later writings and in the doctrinal and liturgical projects (the Ordinals of 1550 and 1552, for instance) in which he played a major part.

[90] Bradshaw, p. 18.

time of the Apostles. Entry to the first two orders is by admission; the episcopal order is received by consecration.

> And none shalbe admitted a Deacon, except he be xxi yeres of age at the least. And euery man, which is to be admitted a Priest, shalbe full xxiiii yeres olde. And euery man, which is to be consecrated a Bishop, shalbe fully thyrtie yeres of age.[91]

There was a suggestion here that in the distinction between the 'admitting' of deacons and priests, and the 'consecrating' of bishops, no new order was conferred on the bishop, but that he was a priest set apart for certain special tasks within the Church. This was supported by certain features of the rites themselves. The epistle at each service was 1 Timothy 3, though a different section of the text was to be read at each. For the consecration of bishops, the lesson was to begin at the first verse ('This is a true saying, if a man desire the office of a Bisshoppe, he desireth an honest woorke') and be read to the end of verse seven ('He must also haue a good report of them whiche are without, leste he fall into rebuke and snare of the euil speaker'). The epistle at the ordering of deacons began at the eighth verse ('Likewyse muste the ministers be honest . . .') and continued to the end of the chapter.[92] At the ordering of priests, the whole chapter was to be read, almost as if the order of priest was understood to contain within itself both the ministry of service of the primitive deacon and the duty of oversight of the bishop. The alternative lesson appointed for the ordering of priests was the twentieth chapter of the Acts of the Apostles, frequently to be found supporting the view that bishops and priests were one order, in which St Paul gave instructions to the elders of the Church at Ephesus as to how they should exercise their ministry of oversight. Its use in this context would suggest a desire on the part of the compilers of the Ordinal to express and affirm the fundamental equality of the two offices.

Perhaps the clearest distinction between the three offices, as conferred in the 1550 Ordinal, was to be found in the prayers which accompany the laying on of hands, and which may be seen as the central rite of the service. The bishop alone was to lay hands on the deacon, in accordance with ancient custom, saying

> Take thou aucthoritie to execute the office of a Deacon in the Church of God committed unto thee: in the name of the father, the sonne, and the holy ghost. Amen.[93]

---

[91] *The First and Second Prayer-Books of King Edward the Sixth*, Everyman edition (London, 1910), p. 292.
[92] *Ibid.*, pp. 299, 304–5, 313.
[93] *Ibid.*, p. 301.

For the ordering of priests, it was the bishop together with all the priests present, who 'lay theyr handes seuerally upon' the head of the ordinand, while the bishop alone says

> Receiue the holy goste, whose synnes thou doest forgeue, they are forgeuen: and whose sinnes thou doest retaine, thei are retained: and be thou a faithful despensor of the word of god, and of his holy Sacramentes. In the name of the father, and of the sonne, and of the holy gost. Amen.[94]

This was no innovation, but rather was a continuation of the traditional practice whereby the unity of the college of presbyters with their bishop was most visibly expressed. The order for the consecration of bishops was expressed in such a way as to suggest that his order was not necessarily something new, received from outside him, but that the act of consecration was intended to draw out or activate something which he already possessed, namely the priesthood to which he had formerly been ordained. The actual words used in the prayer are derived from 2 Timothy 1:6–7; the key phrase is here italicized:

> Take the holy gost, and remember that thou stirre up the grace of god, *whiche is in thee*, by imposicion of handes: for god hath not geuen us the spirite of feare, but of power, and loue, and of sobernesse.[95]

In the Litany during the rites for ordering priests and deacons, the congregation are commended to pray

> That it may please thee, to blesse these men, and send thy grace upon them, that they maye duelye execute the offyce nowe to be commytted unto them, to the edifyinge of the Churche, and to thy honoure, prayse, and glorye.[96]

In the consecrating of bishops, the prayer omits the reference to an office about to be conferred, suggesting that the bishop-elect already held the office in some way, the congregation being bidden to pray for him to be given the grace to exercise the office:

> That it maye please thee to blesse this our brother elected, and to sende thy grace upon him, that he may duely execute the office wherunto he is called, to the edifying of thy Churche, and to the honour, prayse and glory of thy name.[97]

It was a short step from the opinion that consecration was merely the completion of a process which had been commenced by appointment to

[94] *Ibid.*, p. 311.
[95] *Ibid.*, pp. 316–17.
[96] *Ibid.*, p. 295.
[97] *Ibid.*, p. 314.

the one which was actually held by several of the bishops of the period under study, that consecration itself was unnecessary. It is also significant that these words had been first addressed by St Paul to Timothy after he had commenced his apostolic ministry. Episcopal consecration completes and fulfils that which the bishop-elect already possesses within himself. This illustrates a nice ambiguity; on the one hand, the bishop-elect may be consecrated so that he can exercise the fullness of the priestly office to which he has already been admitted; on the other hand, the consecration may be simply a setting-apart of one who is already a bishop by reason of his appointment. The latter alternative would certainly fit more comfortably into Cranmer's ideas about the necessity for episcopal consecration as expressed in his answers to the King's questions on doctrine ten years earlier. It also appears to be a departure from medieval tradition. Only one medieval English pontifical contains the formula *accipe Spiritum sanctum* as the form of episcopal consecration, though 'take the holy gost' in 2 Timothy 1:6–7 was generally interpreted in scholastic theology as referring to Timothy's consecration to the episcopate.[98] The 1552 Ordinal, while removing some features of the first work such as certain of the vestments and the giving of the chalice to the newly ordained priest, retained the doctrine of the 1550 Ordinal concerning the relationship between the three orders of deacon, priest and bishop.

The Reformed Ordinal was set aside with the restoration of Catholicism under Queen Mary. The official teaching, set out in a series of sermons by Thomas Watson, Bishop of Lincoln, in 1558, held the bishop to possess the priestly office in its fullness. In his homilies the sacrament of order is inextricably bound up with the eucharist, as Fisher had taught thirty years before. The sacrament of the altar is the highest sacrament, and therefore the priesthood is the highest order; the other orders were ordained by God to assist the priest, especially at the altar. Bishops,

> as the successours of the Apostles haue hier dignitie and distinct offices and aucthoritie aboue other inferiour Priestes, for the perfection of the people in Christes Religion, haue power to geue the holy Ghoste for the confirmation of them that be baptised, and by imposition of their handes to ordeyne Priestes and other ministers of Gods holye woorde and Sacramentes.[99]

---

[98] Brightman, F.E., *The English Rite*, 2 volumes (London, 1921), vol. I, p. cxli; sources cited by Brightman for the rite in the English pontificals include *Glossa ordinaria*, Aquinas, Nicholas of Lyra and Erasmus.

[99] Watson, T., *Holsome and Catholyke doctryne concerninge the seuen Sacramentes of Chrystes Church, expedient to be knowen of all men, set forth in maner of shorte Sermons to bee made to the people* (London, 1558), fol.clvii.

They also have the power of jurisdiction, which they must use to keep the Church free from 'all errours, Scismes, disobediences, and vngodly lyuynge'. The episcopate was the fullest expression of the priesthood which was possessed to a lesser degree by the presbyterate, and the Church's ministry was one in which diversity was manifested.[100] This argument was to be used later in the definition of the Church's ministry by the Council of Trent (Twenty-third Session, 15 July 1563). There were defined seven sacramental grades of order; four minor orders, and three major, subdiaconate, diaconate and priesthood. Their relationship to each other was one of service to the highest of those grades, the priesthood, and all other grades were seen as being steps on the way to it. This priesthood was possessed in its fullness by bishops, who formed the highest of the three hierarchical grades of order (the others being ordinary priests and ministers). The ordinary power to ordain and confirm was given to the highest hierarchical grade only, and it was to that grade that ordinary jurisdiction also belonged.[101]

[100] *Ibid.*, fol.clv.
[101] Session XXIII, Canons on the sacrament of order. See especially Canons 2, 6, and 7 (*Conciliorum oecumenicorum decreta*, pp. 743–4; *Canons and Decrees of the Council of Trent*, pp. 162–3).

Chapter Two

MODELS OF EPISCOPAL OFFICE

Three passages from the Pastoral Epistles, 1 Timothy 3:1–7 and 4:14, 2 Timothy 1:6–7, and Titus 1:7–9, appear again and again in discussions of the office of bishop during the period of the Reformation in England. They also find their place in all the rites of episcopal consecration, and are often quoted in prayers central to the action of consecrating. Subject to varying interpretations, they supported a number of conflicting definitions of the essence of episcopacy. Amongst the Church Fathers, the writings and example of Augustine and Cyprian seem to have been most important as model bishops in the movement of reform which was centred around the episcopal office. Several bishops are known to have possessed the works of Augustine, while the works of Cyprian were less widely known; his *De unitate ecclesiae* was not published in England until the seventeenth century, a Latin edition in 1632 with the first English translation not published until 1681. On the other hand, manuscript copies of the Fathers, especially of Augustine, circulated widely in England in the fifteenth century, and a number of foreign printed editions were available by 1520. Erasmus had brought out his own editions of Jerome in 1516, of Cyprian in 1520, and of Augustine in 1529, and it seems likely that the significant number of bishops in the English Church who had been touched in some way by Erasmian reform would have been aware of this work and indeed, Augustine appears to have been the principal patristic influence upon John Fisher.[1]

---

[1] Charles Booth, Bishop of Hereford, bequeathed *Plura ac diversa diui Aurelij Augustini Sermonum* (Basle, 1494) to his Cathedral library in 1535; he also left Antoninus Forc+glioni (fifteenth-century Archbishop of Florence), *Repertorium totius summe* . . . (3 volumes, 1502), which draws on Augustine in its twentieth chapter 'De statu episcopos'. Richard Fox gave Augustine's *Confessiones* (Milan, 1475), and *In librum Psalmorum* (Venice, 1493) to Corpus Christi College, Oxford, and *Expositio de Sermone in Monte* to the collegiate church of Bishop Auckland, Durham. Manuscript copies and early printed editions of Cyprian's *Opera* were in circulation in the period, and it is most likely that they were freely available to the bishops. See also Scarisbrick, 'The Conservative Episcopate in England', p. 353, where Augustine is described as Fisher's 'guiding light through the ways of Revelation'.

In many writings of the period under study, however, a single model of the ideal bishop was pervasive in its influence. Christ himself provided the fundamental model for episcopal office for many of those who exercised that office in the Church. Two bishops in particular, one a conservative appointed before the break with Rome, the other an Edwardian appointee noted for his commitment to radical reform, wrote extensively around this idea (though the concept of Christ as a model for the episcopate pervades almost all contemporary thinking on the idea of the office of bishop). John Longland's Good Friday sermon of 1538, given before Henry VIII, must be seen in its context. Not only was it an exposition of Christ as the true model bishop, but it also contained a clear polemical message against the pope, who appears frequently throughout the sermon as an antitype for the true Christian bishop.[2] Longland considered the name 'bishop' to have been derived from the term used in the Old Testament for the high priest who enters the sanctuary, citing Numbers 19. In that chapter, the Hebrew *hakohen* (translated in the Greek Septuagint as *arch-hiereus*) refers to a member of the hereditary priesthood who, by family descent, had the right and duty to enter the sanctuary and offer sacrifices; the term is rendered by the Vulgate as *pontifex*. Longland saw this entering of the sanctuary as 'a manyfest figure . . . of the Passyon of our sauyour Chryst'. Christ may properly be called '*Summus pontifex*, the hyghest bushop'. Longland quotes Hebrews 4:14: 'Habemus pontificem magnum qui poenetrauit coelos, IESVM filium dei' [We have a great high priest who has entered the heavens, JESUS the son of God] with a marginal note 'Magnus Episcopus noster christus est'; this verse is one of several in that letter where the term *arch-hiereus* is used to describe Christ. A long discussion of the ways in which the Bishop of Rome failed to imitate this model begins with the exhortation 'Let all earthly bushops lerne of this heuenly bushop Chryst'; the bishop should be merciful, ready to forgive, not cruel, not vengeful, but full of pity. 'The verye offyce of a bushop is *predicare, orare, & sacrificare sive offerre*. To preache, to praye, to doe sacrifyce and to offer.' It is the property of a good bishop to offer sacrifice for his people. Longland asks how the bishops shall answer Christ on the day of judgement; the way his question is phrased shows clearly that the main target of his attack is the bishop of Rome:

> How dyddest thou enter into thy bushopryke? by me or by the worlde? unlawfully or lawfully? by simonye or freely? by labour by paction, or called of god? How dyddest thou rule thy cure?

---

[2] Longland, J., *A Sermonde made before the Kynge, his maiestye at grenewich, upon good Frydaye. The yere of our Lorde God M.D.xxxviij* (London, [1538?]).

thy diocese? dyddest thou pray for thy people? dyddest thou preache me to thy diocesans? dyddest thou gyue them goostly and bodelye foode? dyddest thou minyster spirytuall and goostly salues (the sacramentes I meane) to heale the soores of theyr soules? Howe dyddest thou lyue? dyddest thou caste awaye the cure the glorye and pompe of the world? dyddest thou folowe me in humilyte, in charyte, in compassion, in pouertye, in clennes, & in chaaste lyuynge? . . . Howe dyddest thou gouerne thy diocesans? dyddest not thou make of all thynges that thou dyddeste medle with a money matter? in sellynge that whiche was not in the to sell nor giue, that that thou calleddest thy pardons, thy commyssyons, thy breeues, thy delygaces, reseruacions, exemptions, appellacyons, bulles and dyspensacions?

The ideal bishop is one who responds to a call to the pastoral office of Christ; who, like Christ, prays for his flock, and feeds them not only with spiritual food through the preaching ministry but also with bodily food by the exercise of hospitality. The spiritual welfare of the flock is served by the dispensing of the sacraments, means whereby the soul wounded by sin is healed and strengthened, and by the example of the bishop who follows Christ in poverty and humility, not in vain glory and fine living. The Bishop of Rome is taken as a perfect example of the direct opposite of this model, and, by implication, as the very opposite of Christ himself; the specific identification of the Pope with the Antichrist is not far below the surface of the text.

The sermon continues with a discussion of the second office of a bishop according to the model of Christ. Prayer forms the link between the bishop as preacher and as sacrificer. Prayer informs and directs the intellect of the preacher, and makes him depend not on his own ability but on the inspiration of Christ, who offered up for his people 'prayers and supplicacyons with a hudge crye'. The sermon concludes with an exposition of other characteristics of the bishop, leading to a final condemnation of the Bishop of Rome. Hebrews 7:26 describes Christ as 'also, *Pontifex sanctus, innocens, impollutus, segregatus a peccatoribus* . . .' ['. . . a high priest, holy, blameless, undefiled, separated from sinners']. *Impollutus* is defined as meaning 'all chaaste and immaculate', while *segregatus a peccatoribus* means 'segregate from them, not from theyr companye – Math 9'; the latter passage includes the calling of Matthew the tax collector, and would suggest that Longland interpreted the phrase as meaning that while the bishop should not avoid the company of sinners, he should remain free from the stain of sin. This accords with the statement earlier in the sermon that the bishop should take a leading part in the dispensing of sacraments as means of healing the wounds of sin. However, while Christ is rightly called '*Magnus episcopus, magnus sacerdos*', no other bishop or priest in this world is worthy to be called great, nor ought to take the name *magnus* upon him. The Bishop of Rome wrongfully encroaches upon Christ by taking upon himself not only the title *magnus*,

> but addeth more *videlicet Maximus, Summus, Sanctus, Beatissimus, Vniuersalis*, and soche other . . . The bushop of Rome and all other bushoppes are but underlynges and vnworthy suffragans vnto this bushop Chryst.[3]

Longland was expounding a position which had been taken by all the bishops in the previous year, in the publication of *The Institution of a Christian Man* (the Bishops' Book). The idea of Christ as the great Bishop was set out in an observation on the sixth article of the Apostles' Creed, that Christ ascended into heaven and sits on the right hand of God the Father.[4] The King's Book of 1543, *A Necessary Doctrine and Erudition for any Christian Man*, took up the same theme in its discussion of the same article of the creed; Christ is

> the only eternal Priest and Bishop of his said church, that is to say, the only Mediator between God and mankind, the Redeemer, Intercessor, and Advocate for the remission of sins . . .[5]

It was the high priestly role of Christ, and his headship of the mystical body of the Church, which were the key doctrines associated with his place as the Church's great high bishop, recalling Longland's Good Friday sermon of 1538.[6] The principal scriptural sources for the discussion of the sacrament of order are the Pastoral Epistles, specifically 1 Timothy 1, 4 and 5, and Titus 1 and 3. The Henrician Catholic bishop was the head of his diocese, which was a type of Christ's mystical body; he was expected not only to preach but to pray and offer sacrifice (specifically, the sacrament of the altar) for it.[7] Shortly after the accession of Edward VI, Gardiner emphasized this role of the bishop, affirming that Christ 'was the bishop that offered for our sins, and the sacrifice that was offered . . .'.[8] The same model was to be found in the restored Catholicism of Queen Mary's reign, where in 1554 the future successor to Longland in the diocese of Lincoln declared it to be 'playne

---

[3] 'Greatest, highest, holy, most blessed, universal'; *A Sermonde made before the Kynge*.
[4] Lloyd, *Formularies*, p. 69.
[5] *Ibid.*, p. 237.
[6] *Ibid.*, p. 278.
[7] See, for instance, the Bishops' Book on the sacrament of orders, where the Church's ministers are understood fundamentally to be preachers and dispensers of the sacraments. Lloyd, *Formularies*, p. 102.
[8] Paul's Cross sermon, St Peter's Day (29 June) 1548, in Blench, J.W., *Preaching in England in the Late Fifteenth and Sixteenth Centuries* (Oxford, 1964), p. 251.

by Saynte Paule, that euery Byshoppe and priest is ordeined to offre sacrifice'.[9]

Taking Christ as the model for an ideal bishop was not confined to the conservative episcopate under Henry VIII. John Hooper's thought was influenced chiefly by the work of Zwingli (whom he never met) and Bullinger.[10] The work which Hooper wrote a few years before he attained episcopal office in England, *A declaration of Christ and his office*, is almost identical in framework to the exposition in Longland's 1538 sermon. Hooper declared that Christ's office or role was fourfold; to teach the people, to pray and make intercession for them, to offer sacrifice to God, and to sanctify the believers. This exactly parallels Longland's definition of the bishop as one called 'to preache, to praye, to doe sacrifyce and to offer' after the example of Christ. Central to both discussions is the idea, found in Hebrews 5, of Christ as the high priest appointed by God to enter the sanctuary. Hooper saw the first office of Christ, that of preacher and teacher, as consisting the essence of episcopacy. The office of all bishops and priests is 'to preach and pray', and teaching is 'the chiefest part of the bishop's office'.[11] Unlike Longland (and the other conservative bishops), Hooper restricted the essential role of the ministerial episcopate to this first office of Christ. The second office of Christ, to pray and make intercession for his people, served as a model for the whole Church, not merely the bishops. It was the whole Christian people whom Christ expressly bound 'unto this intercession and prayer' in his name.[12] The sixth chapter of Hooper's discourse is headed 'The third Office of Christ is concerning his priest-hood, to offer sacrifice unto God, and by the same to purge the world from sin'. This office in particular was restricted to Christ alone, the emphasis being on the unique place in salvation occupied by the sacrifice of the cross.[13] Hooper, in common with the doctrines of the other major Reformers, desired to separate the sacrifice of Christ from any ministerial function, particularly that of the offering of the sacrifice of the Mass central to the idea of episcopal office of conservative bishops such as Longland or Fisher.[14] The fourth office of Christ, 'to consecrate and

[9] Watson, T., *Twoo notable Sermons . . . concerninge the reall presence of Christes body and bloude in the blessed Sacrament; also the Masse, which is the sacrifice of the newe Testament* (London, 1554), sig.Q.i,r.

[10] He was not personally acquainted with Calvin, and seems never to have visited Geneva; West, W.M.S., *John Hooper and the Origins of Protestantism*, dissertation der theologischen Fakultät der Universität Zürich zur Erlangung der Doktorwürde (Teildruck, private publication, 1955), p. 5.

[11] 'Fifth Sermon upon Jonas' (March 1550), *Early Writings*, p. 507; 'A declaration of Christ and his office' (1547), *ibid.*, p. 19.

[12] *Ibid.*, pp. 33–4.

[13] *Ibid.*, p. 48.

[14] For instance, Zwingli: 'Christ, having sacrificed himself once and for all, is for all

sanctify those that believe in him', was mediated through the sacraments, which Hooper defined as a ceremony instituted in the law of God to be a testimony of God's promise to all who believe.[15] The Church could be defined by reference to the first and fourth offices of Christ; at this stage, Hooper understood the two marks of the true Church to be 'the pure preaching of the gospel, and the right use of the sacraments', a definition closely associated with the teaching of Calvin.[16] Within three years, he had added the use of discipline to the proper function of bishops and priests, whose true vocation consisted in studying and preaching the word of God, administering the sacraments ('christianly'), and correcting the faults of the indurate with severity.[17] By the accession of Queen Mary, he was using language which more clearly reflected that of John Knox's threefold marks of the Church: the Word preached, the sacraments christianly administered, and the discipline.[18] The latter had been elevated to an essential feature of the Church's nature from its place in Calvin's theology as an important feature of its organization. In his Apology to the King and Queen, he wrote of the office of bishops and clergy that they could do no more than preach God's Word, minister his sacraments, and pronounce excommunication.[19]

Hooper also spoke against the external trappings of episcopacy as practised at the commencement of the reign of King Edward. The Answer to the Bishop of Winchester's Book identified clerical vesture of the period (including the tonsure as well as distinctive clothing) with the corruptions introduced by the Papacy. 'What devil hath made a crown, a long gown, or a tippet, to be a thing necessary for a bishop? Restore it to Rome again, from whence it came.'[20] Despite this plea at the commencement of the reign, it would appear that the tonsure continued

eternity a perpetual and acceptable offering for the sins of all believers, from which it follows that the mass is not a sacrifice, but is a commemoration of the sacrifice and assurance of the salvation which Christ has given us.' Sixty-seven theses, 27 January 1523; Potter, G.R., *Huldrych Zwingli*, Documents of Modern History (London, 1978), pp. 22–3. Also Calvin: '. . . it is most clearly proved by the Word of God that this Mass, however decked in splendor, inflicts signal dishonor upon Christ, buries and oppresses his cross, consigns his death to oblivion, takes away the benefit which came to us from it, and weakens and destroys the Sacraments by which the memory of his death was bequeathed to us . . .' *Institutes of the Christian Religion* (Library of Christian Classics vols. XX and XXI, ed. McNeill, J.T., Philadelphia, 1960), IV.xviii.1; vol. XXI p. 1429.

[15] *Early Writings*, pp. 71, 76.

[16] 'We have laid down as distinguishing marks of the church the preaching of the Word and the observance of the sacraments.' *Institutes*, IV.i.10, p. 1024.

[17] Fifth Sermon on Jonas, March 1550, *Early Writings*, p. 504.

[18] After his release from captivity on the French galleys in 1549 Knox became an influential figure in Reformed circles around the court of Edward VI.

[19] *Later Writings*, p. 559.

[20] *Early Writings*, p. 245.

along with traditional episcopal habits at least until the beginning of 1550. Hooper's first sermon of a Lent series on Jonah, given before the King in that year, called for bishops and ministers of the Church to be known from ministers of the devil by their preaching, 'not by shaving, clipping, vestments, and outward apparel'.[21] In the third sermon he complained of a number of features of the new ordinal which seemed to him to be later innovations which contradicted the scriptures, particularly the vestments which he saw as those rather of 'Aaron and the gentiles, than of the ministers of Christ'.[22] Given his opinions on the matter, Hooper was put into a difficult position when offered the see of Gloucester by the King at Easter 1550. Apart from his objections to swearing by the saints (the oath being amended to omit the offending phrase) he objected to 'those Aaronic habits which they [the bishops] still retain in that calling, and are used to wear, not only at the administration of the sacraments, but also at public prayers'. At first he declined the King's offer, but after a spell in prison and an agitated meeting with the Council on Ascension Day 1550, he was consecrated according to the new Ordinal in the traditional vesture of an English bishop, 'a long scarlet chimere down to the foot, and under that a white linen rochet that covered all his shoulders. Upon his head he had a geometrical, that is, a four-squared cap, albeit that his head was round.'[23] Hooper's stand received a varying amount of support from other Reformers. Peter Martyr agreed in principle with Hooper's objections, but saw in the distinctive vesture nothing fatal nor contrary to the word of God. Martin Bucer found in it nothing intrinsically evil, though desired its abolition due to the danger of superstitious use. For Nicholas Ridley, vestments were an indifferent matter; it was lawful to wear them when instructed to do so by the King, and he sought to convince Hooper of the folly of refusing to wear them. However, John a Lasco was fully in support of Hooper's position.[24] Hooper himself may well have served as a model for Northumberland in his idea of the bishop as supervisor and preacher, worthy of a reasonable hire, a model which he attempted to apply to episcopal appointments during his protectorate, not always successfully; no less a figure than John Knox was offered the bishopric of Rochester by him in October 1552.[25]

[21] 'First Sermon upon Jonas' (19 February 1550), *Early Writings*, p. 449.

[22] 'Third Sermon upon Jonas' (5 March 1550), *Early Writings*, p. 479.

[23] Hooper to Bullinger, London, 29 June 1550, Robinson, H., ed., *Original Letters Relative to the English Reformation*, Parker Society, 2 volumes (Cambridge, 1846/7), vol. I, p. 87; *Acts and Monuments*, vol. VI, p. 641.

[24] Bradshaw, *The Anglican Ordinal*, p. 37. Strype, *Ecclesiastical Memorials*, vol. II, part 2, pp. 351–2.

[25] Heal, F., *Of Prelates and Princes*, p. 144; Guy, J., *Tudor England* (Oxford, 1988), p. 219.

Longland's threefold model for the bishop is echoed in an earlier work by the Swiss reformer Heinrich Bullinger. *De episcoporum . . . institutione et functione* of 1536, dedicated to Henry VIII, also commends a threefold model for the bishop: '. . . so we believe that the office of the chief evangelical teachers and ministers is to teach, to pray, and to administer the sacraments'.[26] It is certain that the King knew the work; the presentation copy (now in the British Library) bears his manuscript additions.[27] It is unlikely, therefore, that Longland, one of the few theologians among the bishops in 1538, was not aware of it. It is even less likely that Hooper, given his close relationship with Bullinger, was unaware of the work. There is evidence that Bullinger's *De episcoporum* was known to Cranmer, who is said to have read the entire book before presenting it to the King.[28] In addition, Bullinger was reported in 1548 to have sent a letter to Cranmer containing 'a grave and learned admonition as to his episcopal duties' and words on the eucharist, though the date of the letter was not mentioned; it was said to be 'constantly being copied'.[29]

Much debate ensued in the latter part of the reign of Edward VI over the name 'bishop' itself as an appropriate term for the office. The term which was put forward in its place, 'superintendent', was considered a more suitable rendering of the Greek *episkopos*, its original meanings of oversight and supervision having been overlaid by centuries of development of the ecclesiastical episcopal office. The 1552 Ordinal retained the term 'bishop', though in the King's memorials from that year onwards, it began to be replaced by 'superintendent', perhaps as a result of Continental influences.[30] The two terms were interchangeable in Bucer's treatise *De ordinatione legitima*.[31] The English Reformers' arguments were summarized by John Ponet, Bishop of Winchester, writing in 1553:

> Who knoweth not that the name *bishop* hath been so abused, that when it was spoken, the people understood nothing else but a great lord, that went in a white rochet with a wide shaven crown, and that carried an oil-box with him, wherewith he used once in seven years, riding about, to *confirm* children, &c. Now, to bring the people from this abuse, what better means can be devised than to teach the people their error by another word out

---

[26] Bullinger, H., *De episcoporum . . . institutione et functione* (Zürich, 1536), fol.80r.
[27] See Plate VIII.
[28] Nicholas Partridge to Bullinger, 17 September 1538, *LP*, XIII, part 2, 373.
[29] John ab Ulmis to Bullinger, from London, 18 August 1548, *Original Letters*, vol. II, p. 381.
[30] Strype, *Ecclesiastical Memorials*, vol. II, part 2, p. 141.
[31] See, for instance, the ending of the treatise in Whitaker, E.C., *Martin Bucer and the Book of Common Prayer*, Alcuin Club Collections no. 55 (Great Wakering, 1974), p. 183: '. . . when anyone is ordained Superintendent, that is, bishop . . .'.

of the Scripture of the same signification. Which thing, by the term *superintendent*, would in time have been well brought to pass: for the ordinary pains of such as were called super-intendents, to understand the duty of their bishops, which the papists would fain have hidden from them; and the word *super-intendent* being a very Latin word, made English by us, should in time have taught the people, by the very etymology and proper signification, what thing was meant, when they heard that name, by which this term *bishop* could not so well be done; by reason that bishops, in time of Popery, were *overseers* in name, but not in deed.[32]

A similar view of the holders of episcopal office had appeared a few years earlier in England in Ponet's translation of Bernardino Ochino's *A tragoedie or Dialoge*. It put forward the bishops of the early Church as models for the bishops of the day. Those godly bishops had been replaced by

> suche as were most worldely, most ambitious and craftie, seking more their owne glory and lucre then the auauncement of goddes glorye, and the excercise of their office, rather pluckyng from the shepe their mylke, than fedyng them with good pastures. So that the name of a Byshop now, is no more the name of a verye paynfull office as it was in tymes past, but of a great pompe & dignitie.[33]

Furthermore it may be deduced from this passage that the image of the bishop as shepherd, most appropriate for a pastoral office, was being proposed as a suitable model for the Reformed episcopate.

Another model for the bishop was derived from the image of the Church as Christ's mystical body. The letter of Tunstall and Stokesley to Cardinal Pole, written in the later 1530s, argued against the supremacy of the Pope. In taking on a headship role, the Pope was attempting to exercise a function not proper to a bishop in the Church, headship and episcopal office being incompatible.

> The office deputed to the Byshops in the mistical body, is to be as eies to the whole bodye, as almightye God saieth to the prophete Ezechiel: *Speculatorem te dedi Domui Israel.* I have made the an ouerseer ouer the house of Israel. And what byshope so euer refuseth to use the office of an eye in the mysticall body, to shewe vnto the bodye the righte waye of liuinge,whiche appertayneth to the spirituall eie to do, shal shew him selfe to be a blynde eye: and

[32] Strype, *Ecclesiastical Memorials*, pp. 141–2.
[33] Ochino, B., *A tragoedie or Dialoge of the vniuste vsurped primacie of the Bishop of Rome, and of all the just abolishing of the same*, trans. Ponet, J. (London, 1549), sig.B.iv,v–sig.C.i.,r.

if he shall take other office in hande then appertayneth to the righte eye, shall make a confusion in the bodye, takynge vpon him an other office, then is geuen to him of God.

Therefore, the eye cannot take on the office of the whole head, 'for it lacketh brayne'.[34] The image of Christ's mystical body was used again, at the restoration of Catholicism under Mary, as a justification for harsh measures taken against heretics; the bishops were seen as the physicians and surgeons of the body, who as a last resort have to cut out incurable wounds when the 'sweete medycines of Gods worde and his holye Sacramentes' are unable to cure the soul's disease.[35]

Some individuals were held up as models. Peter Martyr found the ideal bishop in the person of Martin Bucer. On meeting in Strassburg shortly before they proceeded to England to take up their chairs at Oxford and Cambridge respectively, Martyr expressed his delight at discovering in the person of Bucer, 'bishops upon the earth . . . which be truly holy'.

> This is the office of a pastor, this is the bishoplike dignity described by Paul in the Epistles unto Timothy and Titus. It delighteth me much to read this kind of description in these Epistles, but it pleaseth me a great deal more to see with the eyes the patterns themselves.[36]

At the same time, Bucer himself was far from content with the state of the English episcopacy. On Whit Sunday 1550 he wrote to Calvin that, to the bishops, 'the idleness and luxury of antichrist is more agreeable than the cross of Christ'.[37] The principal argument throughout Bullinger's *De episcoporum* was for a return to primitive apostolic simplicity, both in the method of consecrating bishops and in the way the episcopal office ought to be exercised. At the installation (by proxy) of Nicholas Ridley as Bishop of London in 1550, William May, Dean of St Paul's, had prayed

> O Lord, Almighty God, we beseech thee, grant to thy servant Nicolas, our Bishop, that by preaching and doing those things which be godly, he may both instruct the minds of his diocesans with true faith, and example of good works: and finally, receive of the most merciful Pastor the reward of eternal life.[38]

From time to time, a particularly outstanding bishop would present himself as a model for the episcopal office. One such, from the period

---

[34] Tunstall and Stokesley, *Letter*, sig.C.iv.,v.

[35] Watson, *Holsome and Catholyke doctryne*, fol.clxiii, v.

[36] *Martyrs divine epistles*, appended to Peter Martyr, *Common places*, tr. Anthony Marten (1583), pp. 62–3, cited in Collinson, P., *The Religion of Protestants* (Oxford, 1982), pp. 22–3.

[37] *Original Letters*, vol. II, p. 547.

[38] Strype, *Ecclesiastical Memorials*, vol. II, part 1, p. 339.

under study, was the Bishop of Rochester, John Fisher. Fisher was known throughout Europe even in his own lifetime to be the model of a perfect bishop. Erasmus described him as a 'divine prelate' in a letter to Wolsey, while in 1520 he wrote to Reuchlin of him that there is in England 'no man of more learning, nor a prelate more holy, than that bishop'.[39] Had he not obtained the privilege of dedicating his edition of the Greek New Testament to Pope Leo X, Erasmus would have dedicated the work to Fisher.[40] Such was the extent of Fisher's moral authority in 1527 that the King sought his support from the start of his divorce proceedings. Despite the increasing demands on his time and energies from this date, Fisher continued to be attentive to all the demands of his episcopal ministry; neither the public side of divine worship, preaching and involvement in the campaign against heresy nor his private devotion were allowed to suffer.[41] Much contemporary praise of Fisher was centred around the model of an ideal bishop in 1 Timothy 3:1–7.[42] Reginald Pole, in *Pro ecclesiasticae unitatis defensione*, which was addressed to Henry VIII, asked

> What other have you, or have you had for centuries, to compare with Rochester in holiness, in learning, in prudence and in episcopal zeal? You may be, indeed, proud of him, for, were you to search through all the nations of Christendom in our days, you would not easily find one who was such a model of episcopal virtues.[43]

Later, to the imprisoned Cranmer, Pole described Fisher as the holiest and most learned of men.[44] Fisher served as an inspiration to contemporary bishops such as Johann Fabri of Constance, himself a noted preacher and reformer, and later holders of the office like Carlo Borromeo, for whom Fisher was an example of episcopal virtue to the extent that his portrait was included in Borromeo's private gallery of exemplary bishops along with his predecessor at Milan, St Ambrose.[45]

The residence of the bishop in his diocese was taken to be so necessary

[39] Bridgett, T.E., *Life of Blessed John Fisher* (London, 1888), p. 53.
[40] *Ibid.*, pp. 93–4.
[41] Bradshaw, 'Bishop John Fisher 1469–1535: The Man and his Work', in Bradshaw and Duffy, p. 10.
[42] Thompson, 'The Bishop in his Diocese', in Bradshaw and Duffy, p. 67.
[43] Surtz, E., *The Works and Days of John Fisher* (Cambridge, MA, 1967), pp. 385–6; Bridgett, *Life*, p. 445; Thompson, 'The Bishop in his Diocese', p. 67.
[44] 'Cardinalis Poli ad Cranmerum epistola', undated ms (possibly later copy), Lambeth Palace Library ms 2007 fol.247r.
[45] Rex, *Fisher*, pp. 8, 29; Bradshaw, 'Bishop John Fisher 1469–1535: The Man and his Work', p. 4; Thompson, 'The Bishop in his Diocese', p. 67; Prosperi, A., 'Clerics and Laymen in the Work of Carlo Borromeo', in Headley, J.M., ed., *San Carlo Borromeo* (Washington, 1988), p. 120.

to the right exercise of the episcopal office that it is scarcely able to qualify as a model, in the sense of an ideal to which one might strive, as one might, for instance, seek to imitate Christ through being fully aware that one's efforts will certainly fall short of the ideal. Perversely, the absolutely fundamental requirement for episcopal residence was more often met in the breach than in the observance. Before the first beginnings of the English Church's break from Rome, canon law was quite specific in requiring bishops to visit their cathedral churches at the very least in Lent and at Easter.[46] The most notable absentees were those Italian bishops who resided in Rome, and whose English sees were their payment for handling the King's dealings with the Holy See, the practice having commenced under Henry VII. Campeggio's interest in his diocese of Salisbury has been said to derive more from the prospective income from his see than from any genuine pastoral interest, and while he seems never to have visited his diocese despite visiting England as Legate, on at least one occasion he sent his brother Marcantonio there as his proctor.[47] He justified this practice in a letter to his brother where he stated that it was necessary and permissible for him to govern his see *in absentia* as a cardinal bound to reside in the papal *Curia*.[48] As a member of the 1539 Reform commission, he opposed Carafa's resounding condemnation of pluralism, only to be opposed by Pole, Contarini and Quinones.[49]

The most notorious absentee bishop must surely have been Cardinal Wolsey, who in sixteen years as Archbishop of York never once visited his cathedral city, and only entered his diocese at the end of his career after his fall from royal favour. His pluralism, the cause of much absenteeism on the Continent, was very rare for a bishop of the English Church. His absence, however, should not be equated with an inability to exercise control. In addition to his own sees, Wolsey controlled Salisbury and Worcester, with also, perhaps, Llandaff for the Queen's chaplain Athequa, and Bath and Wells for the absent Clerk, employed by Wolsey on diplomatic missions.[50] The requirement that bishops should attend to matters of state took many away from their dioceses for long periods, leaving temporal matters in the hands of commissaries or vicars general, and spiritual matters in the hands of whatever suffragans they were able to employ. Despite this, a number of bishops managed to maintain a high standard of residence in their sees, often undertaking spiritual duties such as ordination personally. Fisher embodied his own attitude to residence in the statutes for St John's

[46] Lyndwood, W., *Provinciale* (London, 1679), Bk.III, Tit.4, Ch.1; Thompson, 'The Bishop in his Diocese', p. 70.

[47] Wilkie, W.E., *The Cardinal Protectors of England* (Cambridge, 1974), p. 158.

[48] 27 January 1537, *LP*, XIII, part 1, 255; Wilkie, *Cardinal Protectors*, p. 231.

[49] Wilkie, p. 235.

[50] *Ibid.*, p. 147.

College, considering it suitable for the head to be associated and joined with the members. He believed that when bishops were absent from their dioceses, souls fell to the devil. It appears that he was able and willing to put his teaching into practice; his record of residence seems to have been better than that of most of his contemporaries.[51] John Veysey seems to have spent most of his time away from his diocese in his native Sutton Coldfield, where he was a great benefactor to the town.[52] John Clerk spent much time away from his diocese of Bath and Wells, being employed on embassies to Rome and France by Wolsey and on state affairs by Cromwell. In his absence, three suffragans performed his spiritual duties while his brother Thomas took charge of the episcopal estates.[53] While Henry VIII demanded the attention of his bishops on matters of state, the regime under his son moved away from this; both Somerset and Northumberland believed that the bishops should be active in their own jurisdictions rather than in government.[54] A logical consequence of this conviction was the dissolution of the see of Westminster in 1550. The third decree of the 1555–56 national synod was directed against 'the great abuse' of absentee bishops 'which thing has been the cause of almost all the evils that afflict the Church', echoing the strictures against non-residence from the Sixth Session of the Council of Trent (13 January 1547).[55]

Renewal of the episcopal office had been a cornerstone of Catholic Reform from the beginning of the sixteenth century, and continued throughout the period of post-Tridentine Reformation. A number of English and Welsh bishops were directly or indirectly influenced by this movement in the models for their own conduct of the episcopal office. One of the principal Catholic Reformers who had an influence on the development of the office of bishop in the English Church, particularly in the period of Reform under Mary, was the close friend and associate of Reginald Pole, Gasparo Contarini. While still a layman, Contarini had written a treatise for a friend, Pietro Lippomano, who in 1516 had just been appointed Bishop of Bergamo. *De officio episcopi* was modelled on the practice of Pietro Barozzi, Bishop of Belluno and Padua whom Contarini had known while a student at the University of Padua, though many of the ideals presented in the work were derived from patristic sources. Foremost amongst the bishop's qualities was the need for him to be a model in the Christian life for all the souls under his care. This high

[51] Thompson, 'The Bishop in his Diocese', pp. 70–1.
[52] Strype, *Ecclesiastical Memorials*, vol. II, part 1, p. 423. It appears that his benefactions were largely funded from the revenues of his diocese.
[53] Hembry, P., *The Bishops of Bath and Wells, 1530–1640* (London, 1967), p. 42.
[54] Heal, *Of Prelates and Princes*, p. 139.
[55] Hughes, P., *Rome and the Counter-Reformation in England* ([London], 1942), p. 78.

calling of the episcopal office required the bishop to raise himself 'above the human rank to a participation in the angelic nature'.[56] The reality of the episcopate, however, represented a considerable departure from this ideal. For Contarini, the greatest evil was the failure of the bishop to reside in his see, handing over the work to others while retaining the revenues for himself and taking no interest whatsoever in the people over whom they were set. Only under exceptional circumstances, and for the highest reasons, should the bishop reside away from his see.[57] Contarini's record of residence as Bishop of Belluno, coming several years after the writing of the treatise, demonstrated the difficulty of bringing together theory and practice in this matter. During the five years of his episcopate, he made only one visit to his diocese as bishop in the summer of 1538. However, in accordance with his views on the matter, he appointed capable vicars general to oversee the diocese in his absence.[58] There was also a certain irony in Contarini's later papal provision to the bishopric of Salisbury on the death *in curia Romana* of its Bishop, deprived in English law but whose deprivation was not recognized by the pope; Contarini was unable to take possession of his see.

Given the presence of the bishop in his see, Contarini set out a number of specific duties which pertain to the office. First among them he set the conduct of divine worship, and recommended the practice of frequent, if not daily, celebration of the eucharist by the bishop.[59] He related how he had been present at the daily celebration of Mass by Pietro Barozzi in his private episcopal chapel at Padua, and how most good bishops had done the same. There is evidence to suggest that Cuthbert Tunstall was resident in Padua while Barozzi was bishop, and it is interesting to note that Barozzi's practice of daily celebration was later mirrored in England in the practice of Tunstall's friend John Fisher.[60] For Contarini, the frequent celebration of Mass was the source of the bishop's under-

---

[56] Contarini, *De officio episcopi*, in Olin, J.C., *The Catholic Reformation: Savonarola to Ignatius Loyola* (Westminster, MD, 1969), p. 94.

[57] *Ibid.*, p. 95.

[58] Gleason, *Contarini*, p. 179. Dr Gleason makes a valid point in reminding the modern reader of the different processes of thought which separate the middle of the sixteenth century from the end of the twentieth. Bishops like Contarini, Carafa and Pole could separate the reality of the Church's (and their own) practice from the theory of how things ought to be. While working for the reform of the Church, they were able, without perceiving hypocrisy in themselves, to remain within its structures and indeed be supported financially by them.

[59] *De officio episcopi*, p. 97.

[60] Tunstall was Doctor of Civil and Canon Law of the University of Padua, probably taken between 1505 (when he is recorded as being at Rome) and 1508 (the date of his appointment as Chancellor and Auditor of Causes to William Warham, Archbishop of Canterbury). Pole was also to be found in Padua some years later, arriving in April 1521; Schenck, W., *Reginald Pole, Cardinal of England* (London, 1950), p. 7.

standing of the Scripture and his ability by regular preaching to incite his flock to follow the Christian life and its moral precepts. He also reproved those bishops who spent the revenues of their sees on magnificent dinners and great feasting while neglecting the needs of the poor; hospitality to the needy and the avoidance of gluttony were important features of the daily life of the bishop. Beyond his own household, the bishop should make the improvement of the standard of his clergy an important priority in his ministry. Careful examination of candidates for ordination was highly recommended, as the bishop who chose his clerics well would have little work to do in governing the clergy, and it was important to be able to select candidates who had been well educated from an early age. While the study of theology was important, particularly that of the Fathers, the study of sacred Scripture 'which at length brings to perfection all the studies of the cleric' was to be preferred above all.[61]

The duty of the bishop to preach frequently, even daily, to the people during Mass, was among the first duties of the bishop towards all his people. An ancient custom faithfully observed, the bishops of Contarini's day had allowed the religious to take over this role on account of their slothfulness. He recommended that the custom should, at least in part if not entirely, be revived and that the bishop should preach before all the people. If this should be too much, then a sermon to the clergy should through them be carried to all. 'By no means should the good Bishop, in my opinion, fail to observe this obligation.'[62] He should also be diligent in seeking out and eradicating heresy, being particularly watchful for heretical books imported into his diocese. 'For there is no deadlier disease nor anything which more easily opens the window to atheism than heresy which, when it destroys the foundations of faith, also suddenly overturns all public order.' In this, too, lies a certain irony; Contarini had died while under suspicion of heresy from a pope, his former colleague Carafa, then Paul IV, whose opposition to the heterodox was considerably more radical than Contarini's own.[63]

Shortly after his arrival in Venice in 1532, Pole was recommended to Gian Pietro Carafa by Gian Matteo Giberti, the Bishop of Verona.[64] Giberti, who had been an advisor to Pope Clement VII, represented the practical working-out of the model of an ideal bishop set out by Contarini in *De officio episcopi*, and his work was influential in the forming of Pole's seminary legislation.[65] Central to Giberti's plan for the reformation of the clergy of his diocese was residence in his see. Bishop

---

[61] *De officio episcopi*, p. 102.
[62] *Ibid.*, p. 104.
[63] *Ibid.*, p. 105.
[64] Fenlon, D., *Heresy and Obedience in Tridentine Italy* (Cambridge, 1972), p. 29.
[65] *Ibid.*, pp. 251, 256.

from 1524 to his death in 1543, he took up residence after the sack of Rome in 1527 and immediately commenced his rigorous programme of reversal of the general religious decline in his diocese. Visitation and examination of the clergy combined with education and the spread and encouragement of preaching were the principal means he employed. A contemporary writer commented

> The priests in this diocese are marked men; all are examined; the unworthy or unsuitable suspended or removed from their offices; the gaols are full of *concubinarii*; sermons for the people are preached incessantly; study is encouraged; the bishop, by his life, sets the best example.[66]

Giberti was a member of the commission (which included also Contarini, Carafa and Pole) which Pope Paul III had summoned to Rome in 1536.[67] After three months of deliberations they presented their report, the *Consilium delectorum cardinalium et aliorum prelatorum de emendanda ecclesia*. The bishop was presented throughout this document as the means by which the Church could be reformed. In order to eliminate the abuse of the ordination of unsuitable candidates to holy orders, the bishops were recommended to establish the means for their examination. Further, it was suggested that each bishop should have a teacher in his diocese to instruct clerics in minor orders, a suggestion which ultimately evolved into the Tridentine seminary. The bestowal of benefices on foreign clerics who would be unable to perform the duties of the cures attached was condemned:

> A benefice in Spain or Britain then must not be conferred on an Italian, or vice versa. This must be observed both in appointments to benefices vacated through death and in the case of resignations, where now only the intention of the person resigning is considered and nothing else.

---

[66] Marino Sanuto in his *Diarii* in late 1527, in Olin, *The Catholic Reformation*, p. 134.

[67] The other members of the commission were Jacopo Cardinal Sadoleto, Federigo Fregoso, Archbishop of Salerno, Jerome Aleander, Archbishop of Brindisi, Gregorio Cortese, Abbot of San Georgio Maggiore in Venice, and Tommaso Badia, Master of the Sacred Palace. The commissioners sought advice from other learned individuals in their deliberations, and Peter McNair has suggested that Contarini may have invited Peter Martyr Vermigli to Rome in 1536 to be consulted by the commission. Martyr was then a noted Hebraist and reformer who had been a Lateran Canon at Padua at the same time that Pole was at the University there, and was probably well known to him, perhaps through the humanist circle around Pietro Bembo. See McNair, P., *Peter Martyr in Italy* (Oxford, 1967), pp. 96–7, 133–4. Pole's association with Martyr, who fled to Protestantism in 1542, and others who trod the same path, was a major factor contributing to his later troubles as legate to England during the pontificate of Paul IV, who as Cardinal Carafa was a co-member of this commission.

Despite this, Contarini later accepted Salisbury without hope of residence, though, it ought to be added, with as little hope of financial benefit. On residence, the report added that the offices of cardinal and bishop were incompatible; the role of the cardinal was to assist the pope in the government of the Church, while the bishop's duty was to tend his own flock. The abuse of the preaching office, particularly by unsuitable or unqualified friars, was to be corrected by the bishops who were urged to examine and license all preachers, either personally or through capable deputies. Control over the printing of books and over what was taught in schools were two other ways in which the bishops were encouraged to correct abuse and impose reform.

Carafa, twenty-four years Pole's senior, had been a co-founder of the Theatine Order with Gaetano da Thiene. The Theatines had a particularly rigorous vow of poverty, and concentrated particularly on pastoral work among the poor, in preaching, catechizing and administering the sacraments. The order proved to be a training ground for many future bishops, and the name 'Theatine' came to be applied colloquially to other orders and individuals as a label indicating the practice of an austere style of priesthood heavily influenced by the Counter-Reformation. Many Theatines were prepared to accept appointment to sees with low levels of episcopal remuneration where they undertook reform of their charges primarily through their position as resident bishops. Formed in Rome where the order received the approval of Pope Clement VII in 1524, the small circle of early members of the Theatines moved to Venice after the sack of Rome in 1527. There they established close ties with Contarini, Giberti and others of their circle of Reformers. Pole had considered entering the order, and Thomas Goldwell, later Marian Bishop of St Asaph, made his profession in 1550.[68] Goldwell had met Pole in Padua in 1532, where he joined his household. After nine years as administrator of the English Hospice of St Thomas (later the English College) at Rome he entered the Theatine novitiate in 1547. He interrupted his novitiate to enter the 1549 conclave with Pole as the latter's attendant. Having accompanied Pole to England as papal legate in 1554, he was provided to St Asaph in 1555. Goldwell supplies another link between Borromeo and the English episcopate. After his deprivation from St Asaph, he was Borromeo's Vicar General for the diocese of Milan from December 1563 until his return to Rome in 1565. Another connection between the English episcopate and the reforming Bishop of Milan was Pole's assistant in England, Niccolo Ormaneto, who had been in Giberti's household before entering that of Pole. Under Pole, Ormaneto worked at Oxford for four years to improve discipline and the intellectual life of the University. In 1558 he was called to Rome to

---

[68] Hughes, *Rome and the Counter-Reformation*, p. 93.

undertake reform of the see on behalf of the Pope, and from there was sent to Milan by Borromeo on the latter's appointment as Bishop to prepare the way for similar reform. Reform in Milan proceeded along similar lines to Pole's programme for England, using provincial and national synods to respond to local needs and to prepare articles for episcopal visitations. Ormaneto was later appointed Bishop of Padua, another see with important English episcopal connections.[69] It therefore becomes possible to draw a line of descent from the early Catholic reform of the episcopal office in Giberti and Barozzi, through English bishops like Fisher and Pole, then back into the mainstream of the post-Tridentine Catholic Reformation through Ormaneto and Goldwell to the model see of the Counter-Reformation, the Milan of Carlo Borromeo.

The models which individual bishops adopted for the exercise of their office varied considerably throughout the period. Most of the models for episcopal office referred back in one way or another to the scriptures. While the passages from St Paul discussed above were frequently employed, the models were also derived from the image of Christ as High Priest described in the Epistle to the Hebrews, and from Old Testament models of hereditary sacrificing priesthood. Certain contemporary works sought to provide an ideal to follow, and practical suggestions for putting that ideal into practice. There existed also a handful of outstanding bishops whose practice set them apart from their brothers, and who came to represent the achievement of an ideal, men such as Barozzi, Giberti and Fisher, and even John Hooper whose model of a Reformed episcopate was highly influential to those of a similar disposition. For most of the bishops, however, the daily reality of their task was conditioned by external factors: royal or papal requirements, canon or civil law directly and indirectly related to the exercise of the office, and very often the prevailing ethos amongst the other holders of the office and the bishop's immediate predecessors in his see. It was against this background that a small number of individuals stood out and were subsequently adopted as models of episcopal office for both Catholic and Reformed traditions.

---

[69] Wright, A.D., *The Counter-Reformation* (London, 1982), p. 188; Tucker, M.A., 'Gian Matteo Giberti, Papal Politician and Catholic Reformer', *English Historical Review*, 18 (1903), p. 458.

Chapter Three

BISHOPS OF THE ENGLISH CHURCH
1520–1559

During the period from 1520 to 1559, key changes of episcopal personnel took place which provided successive monarchs with the opportunity to change the character of the bench of bishops according to the needs of religion or state, or to reward royal servants for their part in their ruler's designs. The first decade, from 1520 to 1530, was a time of comparative stability, with few vacancies occurring for the appointment of new diocesan bishops. The second decade, particularly around the years 1532–36, was one in which most dioceses had a change of bishop. Even disregarding the few deprivations for political reasons in the early years of the 1530s, the decade is clearly one of change to an unusual extent. Whether this contributed to the nature and spread of the Henrician Reformation is a matter for some debate. Even in the latter part of the 1540s, when religious change was at its most rapid with the accession of Edward VI, changes to the episcopal bench were relatively few. It was by chance, rather than by design, that Henry was able to appoint known supporters of his supremacy to high office in his Church, though the influence of Anne Boleyn in putting forward her chaplains at a key period of change should not be forgotten.[1] The period from the accession of Queen Mary in July 1553 to the deprivation of all but one of her bishops in the first year of the reign of Queen Elizabeth was the most unstable for the episcopate of the English Church throughout the whole early modern period up to the Civil War.

The growth of papal power in the later Middle Ages had led to a situation where, by a succession of papal enactments in the fourteenth century, control over episcopal appointments was in the hands of the pope. The rights of ordinary episcopal electors, the cathedral chapters, were taken over by the papacy, while the rights of secular rulers over episcopal appointment were, in effect, revived. The secular ruler found it

---

[1] As Diarmaid MacCulloch has pointed out in his contribution to Pettegree, A., ed., *The Early Reformation in Europe* (Cambridge, 1992), p. 167.

easier to deal with the papacy than with the web of complex vested local interests in a cathedral chapter; the pope required the consent of the local ruler for his power to be effective.[2] Papal provision to English benefices, usually of a royal nominee, increased markedly in the period between the accession of Edward III and the election of Pope Clement VI in the middle of the fourteenth century.[3] From the time of Henry VII provisions were obtained by the agency of a succession of senior churchmen in the Roman *Curia*, an arrangement which continued up to and including the appointment of Thomas Cranmer as Archbishop of Canterbury in February 1533. In receiving the pallium from Rome at his consecration on 30 March, Cranmer was receiving a symbol not only of his authority as metropolitan but also of the absolute dependence of that authority upon the see of Rome and its bishop. The pallium represented the devolution of papal authority to the archbishop, and the ultimate dependence of episcopal authority on papal. The translation of papal power to the king was symbolized in the retention of the bestowal of the pallium by Cranmer as the King's agent on at least two occasions: on the newly consecrated Archbishop of Dublin in 1536, and in 1544 upon Robert Holgate as part of his admission to the Archiepiscopate of York. The garment survives in English archiepiscopal heraldry long after its final demise as an item of vesture.[4]

The same devolution of authority was to be found in the fact that the archbishops of both Canterbury and York were, by virtue of their office, papal legates. The authority of such a *legatus natus* could only be overridden by the special appointment by the pope of a *legatus a latere* or *de latere* (the phrase varies). After Cardinal Wolsey's appointment as legate *a latere*, William Warham, Archbishop of Canterbury, found his metropolitical authority to be continually inhibited. On one occasion it led him to complain, in a letter to Wolsey or to the King (it is unclear which),

> I am informed that youre grace intendithe to interrupte me in the vse of the prerogatiues in the whiche my predecessors and I in the righte of my churche of Canturbery hathe been possessed by priuilege, custume and prescription tyme out of mynde . . . I shulde haue nothinge lefte for me and my officers to do but shulde bee as a shadoo and ymaige of an archiebisshop and

[2] Southern, R.W., *Western Society and the Church in the Middle Ages*, The Pelican History of the Church, vol. II (Harmondsworth, 1970), pp. 158–59.
[3] Heath, P., *Church and Realm, 1272–1461* (London, 1988), p. 127.
[4] MacCulloch, *Thomas Cranmer*, p. 338. The pallium, a narrow strip of white lamb's wool joined front and back and embroidered with black crosses, appears as a 'Y' shape when worn over both shoulders. It appears as such in the arms of all Archbishops of Canterbury, and continues to be central to the arms of that see to the present day; see Plates I and II.

Legate voide of auctoritie and iurisdiction. Whiche shulde bee to my perpetuall reproche and to my churche a perpetuall preiudicie.[5]

Warham's attempts to prevent Wolsey's attempts to subject the jurisdiction of the province of Canterbury to his legatine authority were supported by three of his suffragans, Robert Sherburne, Bishop of Chichester, Richard Nykke, Bishop of Norwich, and John Fisher, Bishop of Rochester.[6] In 1527, Tunstall complained that his ordinary authority as Bishop of London had been overridden by Wolsey, who had set up by legatine commission an episcopal tribunal in Westminster Abbey to try the heretics Thomas Bilney, Thomas Arthur and Richard Foster.[7]

Warham's successor as archbishop, Thomas Cranmer, renounced the title of *legatus apostolice sedis* in Convocation in 1534.[8] It seems that the title fell out of use in the Northern Province during the same year. Edward Lee, who had been appointed to York in 1531, is described as 'Eboracensis archiepiscopi anglie primatis ac ap[ostol]ice sedis legati' in the entry for 20 December 1533 in his ordinations register. The entry for 19 September 1534 describes him as 'Ebor[acensis] archiepiscopi anglie primatis et metropolitani'.[9] When in 1557, Reginald Pole's legation *a latere* was revoked by Pope Paul IV, he retained the status of *legatus natus* by virtue of his office as Archbishop of Canterbury.

Due to an unusual number of deaths and a number of deprivations and resignations, twelve new bishops were appointed between 1532 and 1536, including key Reformers and supporters of the royal supremacy such as Cranmer, Edward Fox, Hugh Latimer and William Barlow. Gardiner had been appointed to Winchester in 1531, while Nicholas Heath had to wait until 1540 before he was rewarded with the bishopric of Rochester. Credit for their advancement has been claimed in a number of cases for Queen Anne, whose own advancement had been made possible by the break from Rome. Her former chaplain, William

---

[5] BL Cotton ms Cleopatra F.ii fol.167. The intended recipient of the letter is unclear, referred to throughout as 'youre grace' or 'youre good grace'. While this may indeed refer to Wolsey himself, the title could also be applied to the King. The same confusion exists in the later manuscript tables of contents of the entire manuscript Cleopatra F.ii, one claiming the letter to be to Wolsey, the other that it is a letter to 'KH8'. On balance, however, the likelihood is that the letter is to Wolsey, as it was he whose officers were inhibiting Warham's jurisdiction.

[6] Guy, J.A., 'Henry VIII and the *praemunire* Manoeuvres of 1530–1531', *English Historical Review*, 97 (1982), p. 483.

[7] Brigden, S., *London and the Reformation* (Oxford, 1989), p. 161.

[8] Churchill, I.J., *Canterbury Administration* (London, 1933), vol. I, p. 157.

[9] Borthwick Institute, Register 28 (Lee), fol.188.

Latimer, attributed to her specifically the advancement of Cranmer, Latimer, Shaxton, Goodrich and Skip.[10]

At the end of 1533, three sees – Ely, Coventry and Lichfield, and Bangor – were vacant as a result of the deaths of their bishops. The pope, acting normally on the king's own recommendation, had up to that date provided bishops to vacant English and Welsh sees, though he reserved the right to provide his own nominee under certain conditions, principally where the bishop of the diocese had died while present in Rome. During the period of the Reformation Parliament, five sees – Canterbury, London, Winchester, York, and Durham – were filled by papal provision. The last to be filled, that of Canterbury, was effected with all the requisite bulls being sought and received from Rome. The statutory adoption of royal sufficiency in matters spiritual represented by the Act in Restraint of Appeals led to a crisis of authority in the matter of the appointment of bishops, since in addition to the vacancies at Ely, Coventry and Lichfield, and Bangor, two sees, Salisbury and Worcester, were held by absentee Italians. Lorenzo Campeggio was Bishop of Salisbury at the time when, with Wolsey, he was appointed as a papal legate in the case of the King's divorce. The revenues from the see were a reward for the services he rendered on behalf of the King and the English Church, particularly in the matter of the appointment of bishops, in the Roman *Curia*. Geronimo de'Ghinucci, Bishop of Worcester, had served the King as ambassador in Spain and with Campeggio in the *Curia*. A bill of deprivation directed at them was drafted by Cromwell, or at his direction, during the fifth session of the Reformation Parliament. It cited existing statutes concerning residence, the appointment of aliens to benefices and the export of revenue without royal licence. The bill became law on 21 March 1534.[11] The two bishops were given four months from Easter 1534 to return to England and to take the Oath of the King's Supremacy.

A licence to elect Rowland Lee as Bishop of Coventry and Lichfield had been sought by the dean and chapter as early as January 1532, and Nicholas Hawkins had been nominated to the see of Ely in June 1533, to be replaced as bishop-designate by Thomas Goodrich on his death in 1533 or early in 1534, while John Salcot was elected Bishop of Bangor in January 1534. The king's right to govern the English Church without foreign interference led to the adoption of legislation setting out a new process for the appointment of bishops without reference to the papacy. The 1534 Act in Absolute Restraint of Annates and concerning the Election of Bishops (25 Henry VIII, c.20) provided for vacant sees to be

[10] Dowling, M., ed., 'William Latymer's Cronickille of Anne Bulleyne', *Camden Miscellany XXX*, Camden Fourth Series, vol. XXXIX (London, 1990), p. 59.
[11] 25 Henry VIII c.5; Wilkie, *Cardinal Protectors*, pp. 216–17.

filled by election on the part of the dean and chapter of the king's nominee notified to them by letters missive. Failure to do so would result in the direct appointment of the royal candidate by letters patent. The process of appointment was completed by the outcome of the election receiving the Royal Assent. Between 1534 and Henry's death in 1547 twenty-seven new bishops were appointed and six sees were filled by translation; at the accession of Edward VI, only four bishops, Cranmer, Gardiner, Veysey and Tunstall, remained in the sees to which they had been appointed before the break with Rome.

The bishop as servant of the court, with only secondary responsibility for his diocese, was a consequence of the growth of late medieval papal *plenitudo potestatis* which made the bishop no more than a channel of the pope's authority within his diocese. It is in this context that the English bishop as a channel of the king's authority within his diocese must be understood. The rights of overseeing a diocese by virtue of the possession of episcopal office (the Greek word *episkope* signifying such oversight or supervision) had been assumed by the pope; the local bishop had become merely his agent, and jurisdiction was exercised by papal delegation. It was natural, therefore, that certain elements of episcopal jurisdiction could be further delegated, to a vicar general or commissary, who need not be a bishop, nor even, indeed, a cleric. The appointment of a layman, Thomas Cromwell, as Henry's vicar general and vicegerent in matters spiritual was a logical extension of this principle. The regular liturgical and spiritual functions reserved to the consecrated bishop (the power to ordain to major orders, to confirm, to consecrate churches and so forth) were often carried out by assistant or auxiliary bishops, termed suffragans. The original (and correct) use of the term 'suffragan' when applied to a bishop defines the relationship of an ordinary diocesan bishop to his metropolitan. The sees of the southern province are suffragan to the see of Canterbury, and those of the northern province, to York. The Latin participle, *suffragans*, from which the noun *suffraganeus* is derived, refers both to voting and to assisting; the original suffragan may well have been a bishop within a province having the right to elect the metropolitan. By the later Middle Ages the term had come to refer to assistant bishops whose functions were primarily liturgical. Such suffragans were often members of religious orders who had been appointed by papal provision to defunct sees, in Africa or the Moslem-occupied Holy Land (*in partibus infidelium*), since it had been considered essential from the earliest times that episcopal functions could only be exercised by bishops appointed to specific sees, and that each see should have only one bishop. The requirement for each bishop to have his own diocese was met in many cases by the expediency of defunct or tiny sees. In England by the beginning of the sixteenth century, a considerable number of suffragan bishops were employed, some of whom were consecrated to titles *in partibus*, others absentee bishops of Irish sees, all of whom played an important part in bearing the burden of the diocesan bishop's sacramental responsibilities. With the ending of papal provision to English dioceses in 1533 came the consequent ending of papal provision of English candidates to distant or defunct sees. The Suffragan Bishops Act of 1534 (26 Henry VIII c.14) was designed to meet the need for continued episcopal assistance in England and Wales. The work of suffragans was still seen as important and complementary to that of diocesan bishops. Twenty-six towns, many of which were the sites of defunct Saxon sees, were named in the Act as places to be 'taken and accepted for sees of bishops suffragan'. The new suffragans were to be given the same degree of authority and honour 'as to suffragans of this realm heretofore has been used and accustomed'. They were to be licensed by their diocesan bishop, who would determine the limits of their ordinary jurisdiction and of the exercise of their episcopal power. Two of the new suffragan sees, Gloucester and Bristol, later in the reign went on to achieve full diocesan status.[12]

Very soon after the King had established the independence of the English Church from the see of Rome, he began to plan for a thorough reorganization and rationalization of the English sees. A manuscript in the King's own hand, now in the British Library, contains detailed plans for the alteration and creation of dioceses. It would seem from the places listed that the King's intention was to convert many of the major monastic houses into cathedrals. The document implies that the decision to dissolve the principal monasteries had been taken, though this does not necessarily suggest a date after the 1539 Act suppressing the major houses.[13] The far-reaching nature of the proposals was never carried into effect, though if it had there would have been a very significant change in the religious map of England. 'Plasys to be altheryd acordyng to our devyse whyche haue sees in them' (Canterbury, Winchester, Ely, Durham, Rochester, Worcester, Carlisle and Norwich) were listed alongside thirteen counties or pairs of counties where new bishoprics were to be made. A number of proposed foundations came to nought; new sees were to be set up at Waltham for Essex; St Albans for Hertfordshire; Dunstable, 'nowenham' [Newnham?] or 'elwestowe' [Elstow?] for Bedfordshire and Berkshire; Leicester for Leicestershire and Rutland; Fountains for Lancashire and the Archdeaconry of Richmond; Bury [St Edmunds] for Suffolk; Shrewsbury for Staffordshire and Shropshire; Welbeck, Worksop or Turgarton for Nottingham and Derby; Launceston, 'bedmynne' [Bodmin] or 'wawather' [Lostwithiel?] for Cornwall.

---

[12] Gee and Hardy, *Documents*, pp. 253–6.
[13] Strype gives a date of 1539 for the document; *Ecclesiastical Memorials*, vol. I, part 1, p. 540.

Four of the six sees created between 1540 and 1545 are also listed, 'osnay and tame' to serve Oxford and Berkshire, 'peterburrow' for North-ampton and Huntingdon, Westminster for Middlesex and 'saynt peters' [Gloucester] for 'Gloccstershyre'.[14] After the dissolution of the greater monasteries, the eight former monastic foundations were refounded with a dean and chapter, and over a period of time six new sees were created. The short-lived diocese of Westminster was created in 1540, its territory consisting largely of the county of Middlesex with the abbey church of St Peter, Westminster, as its cathedral church. It was dissolved by letters patent in 1550 when Nicholas Ridley became Bishop of London; its only Bishop, Thomas Thirlby, was translated to Norwich. The dioceses of Chester and Osney were created in 1541, the latter see being transferred to Oxford in 1545; Peterborough Abbey gained cathedral status in 1542, along with Gloucester and Bristol, the two latter having been set up as sees of bishops suffragan under the Suffragan Bishops Act. Thus, by the end of the reign of Henry VIII, the number of sees in England and Wales had risen to twenty-seven.

A number of changes were proposed or effected during the reign of Edward VI. The dissolution of the see of Westminster has already been noted. Nicholas Heath was imprisoned in February 1550 as the result of a conflict over the new Ordinal, and in 1552 his see of Worcester was given to John Hooper, Bishop of Gloucester since 1550, who then became bishop of the two sees combined. In 1552 Cuthbert Tunstall was deprived, and his see of Durham dissolved to be replaced by Act of Parliament in March 1553 with two new bishoprics. When Edward VI died on 6 July 1553, only two of the English and Welsh dioceses were vacant. John Scory had been translated to Chichester from Rochester in the preceding year, and Arthur Bulkeley, Bishop of Bangor, had died in March 1553 after twelve years in office. Worcester and Gloucester had been combined under John Hooper in 1550 as a single diocese, and although Durham had been dissolved by Act of Parliament in 1552, this was entirely disregarded by Mary, who treated him as if the dissolution had never taken place. The translation of Ridley from London was also halted by the death of the King. Though the legal effects of the dissolution of Durham were soon reversed by Parliament, at the end of Edward's reign the total number of dioceses recognized in English law was twenty-four.[15]

---

[14] BL Cotton ms Cleopatra E.iv fol.304v, where they are set out in parallel columns, on the left of the folio the counties with the proposed new sees, and on the right the list of existing cathedral foundations. The same list is set out in Strype, *Ecclesiastical Memorials*, vol. I, part 2, p. 275, with minor differences in spelling. Strype adds a footnote: 'So they stand in the King's MS. according to the placing and spelling: not so correct in the transcript therof, in the Hist. of the Reformation, vol.i. p. 262.'

[15] 1 Mary Stat.3 c.2.

If Durham is excluded from the calculation, then of the twenty-two bishops in full legal possession of their sees, only one, Cranmer, had been appointed before the Henrician schism from Rome. The bishops in office at Mary's accession included many who were later to be condemned as heretics and ejected from their sees, some to suffer death, others exile. Furthermore, a significant number of episcopal appointees died between 1553 and 1558, a period of major and radical change in the composition of the bench of bishops in the English Church. Within a year of Mary's accession there were eleven episcopal deprivations, followed by a twelfth in 1555, compared with only four deprivations and two resignations in the whole of Edward's reign. By the spring of 1556, four of the twelve, Cranmer, Ridley, Hooper and Ferrar had been executed for heresy (Latimer, famously executed alongside Ridley, was at this time not a holder of episcopal office, having resigned his bishopric in 1539), while others like Barlow, Ponet and Scory had gone into exile on the Continent. In little over a year more than half the sees of England and Wales had to be filled. The difficulties were compounded by the deaths of eleven bishops in the second half of the reign, and of four more between the premature death of Mary in November 1558 and the end of the year. Thirteen of the fourteen diocesan bishops who survived into the first year of Elizabeth's reign were deprived. Only one, Anthony Kitchin, took the oath of supremacy, and he remained Bishop of Llandaff until his death in 1566.[16]

Having lawfully established her accession to the throne against the claim of Jane Grey, one of Mary's first priorities was to reconcile the realm with the see of Rome. This necessarily involved the replacement of the Protestant settlement worked out under Edward and the restoration of Catholicism. An important early manifesto for this restoration was set out by the Master of Balliol College, Oxford, and future Bishop of Gloucester, James Brooks, in his sermon at Paul's Cross in London given on 12 November 1553 and published shortly afterwards with a number of additions. He took as his text the passage from the gospel of the day on the raising of the daughter of Jairus (Matthew 9:18–26):

> Domine, filia mea modo defuncta est, sed ueni impone manum tuam super eam, et uiuet. O Lorde my daughter is euen now disceassed and deadde, but come, laie thy hand on her, and she shal liue.[17]

He explained that it was his intention to apply the text in a mystical sense, though without prejudice to the original meaning. The daughter in

[16] Stanley Thomas, Bishop of Sodor and Man, took the oath and remained in office until 1570; see Appendix IV.
[17] Brooks, J., *A sermon very notable, fruictefull, and godlie, made at Paules crosse the xii daie of Nouebre, . . . 1553* (London, 1553), sig.A.ii.

the passage stood for the Church of England, the spiritual daughter 'of our mother the holy catholyke church', which was spiritually dead. He likened the English Church to an erring daughter, for which the Catholic Church had motherly compassion, even though the daughter be dead through her separation from the rest of the Church. The Catholic Church cannot be divorced from Christ its spouse, for 'whomthe holie ghoste hath ones coupled and ioigned together in Matrimonie, whoe can afterwarde sunder, and seperate againe'.[18] He continued at some length to cite the evidence for his assertion that the Church of England was dead like the daughter of Jairus: the abundance of heresies, especially about the eucharist; the ambitious conduct of clergy seeking high office; the inhibition of godly preaching and the shunning of the canonical hours of prayer; the marriage of the clergy. Then followed the central hinge of the whole sermon:

> Now that you haue heard the death of thys doughter, firste by defection from her mother, then after by misbeleuyng, and last of al by misliuyng, now shal you heare brieflye, the laiyng on of the hand of God, for her resuscitacion and reuiuing again.[19]

The hand of God was laid upon spoilers, tyrants and persecutors of the Church, from Heliodorus (2 Maccabees 3) and Nebuchadnezzar to Montanus and other heretics. It was to be laid upon the Church of England through the Queen, whose accession showed God's judgement and mercy in setting over the realm 'suche a merciful, and faithful: such a gracious, and verteous: suche a goodly, and godlie gouernesse, and ruler . . . to thende she might execute iudgement, and iustice'. The Queen was likened to Judith and Esther:

> Suche a Mary, as by her pure virginitie, and chaste continency, should confound thunchast incontinencie of al soche as saie, thei canne not liue chastlye, and continentlye'.

She was likened also to Queen Helena, whose finding of the true cross had made her 'an earnest restorer of the crucifixe of Christe' just as Mary was an earnest restorer of his Church.[20] Just as the divorce of Henry VIII from Queen Catherine had been the original cause of the breach of all good order, all good living, all good believing, godliness, and goodness, so the restitution of her daughter, Queen Mary, would be the occasion of

---

[18] *Ibid.*, sig.A.v.

[19] *Ibid.*, sig.I.i.

[20] Saint Helena was, of course, the mother of Constantine the Great, from whom, in a very doubtful fashion, Henry VIII (and therefore his daughter) claimed descent. The *collectanea* manuscript was neither the first nor the least of the sources gathered during his reign in support of this descent, which was important for the King's claim of Empire for the English Crown.

restoring the same. Looking forward to the reconciliation of the realm with the Catholic Church, he concluded

> after her grace hathe here plaied her part a while (as she hath alredy moste graciouslie began) God shal then extende his most gratious hande, ouer this ded doughter this realme, and shal say to her, as he said to the daughter of Jairus, in the dependaunce of the Gospel of this day, Puella tibi dico, surge. Thou damoysell Englande, to the, I saie, arise. Arise England . . . .[21]

The first stages in the full reconciliation of the English Church to Rome and Catholicism took the form of a restoration of religion as practised in the last years of Henry VIII. As a key feature of this process, the bench of bishops was first purged of dangerous heretics (who were generally treated as intruders), and in their place, where possible, the previous holders of the dioceses were appointed to their former sees. Once the episcopate had taken on its former Henrician hue, the next stage could begin, with the arrival of Pole as papal legate and his consecration as Archbishop of Canterbury in place of the deprived and condemned Cranmer. This was followed by a steady stream of new appointments, men who were both known conservatives and consistent supporters of the Catholic cause, even to the extent of having suffered personal exile in many cases. The death of Mary before the completion of the renewal of the body of bishops left a number of sees vacant or in the process of being filled. It is notable that the commitment to the Catholic cause of those Marian bishops who were in office on the accession of Elizabeth led to their almost unanimous rejection of the Protestant settlement which came quickly to be set in place.[22]

The holders of episcopal office in England and Wales during the period from 1520 to 1559 came from a variety of educational and career backgrounds, though few bishops of the period came from noble families. A small number of families supplied more than one bishop to the Church. Geoffrey Blyth, Bishop of Coventry and Lichfield, had an elder brother John who was Bishop of Salisbury from 1494 to 1499; Edward Lee, Archbishop of York 1531–44, was a kinsman of Rowland Lee, Bishop of Coventry and Lichfield 1533–43; Richard Pates, appointed to the Bishopric of Worcester by the pope in 1541 but taking formal possession only in 1555, was a nephew of John Longland, Bishop of Lincoln. It seems that few, if any, cases of episcopal preferment in the period were a result of nepotism. Dates of birth survive for just under half the bishops covered by this study. Given that there is

[21] *Ibid.*, sig.I,v.

[22] For a discussion of the surviving Marian bishops after the accession of Elizabeth, see Carleton, K.W.T., 'English Catholic Bishops in the Early Elizabethan Era', pp. 1–15.

an even distribution across the whole period of bishops for whom this figure is available, it is possible to analyse the average ages of these bishops on their first appointment as diocesans. The average age across the whole period was forty-nine. This can be broken up into shorter periods which show a remarkable degree of consistency. The bishops in office in 1520, those appointed between that date and the break with Rome, Henrician appointments after that point, and the Marian bishops raised to the office during that reign were of the same average age on appointment as for the period as a whole. The only exception was the average age on appointment of those bishops appointed during the reign of Edward VI, where the figure increased to fifty due at least in part to the appointment of Miles Coverdale at the age of sixty-three and the slightly lower number of new appointments to the episcopal bench in the reign.[23] The consistent average age of new bishops throughout the period is even more worthy of mention when it is compared with the figures given by Kenneth Fincham for later Tudor and early Stuart bishops. The average age of late Elizabethan bishops at consecration was still forty-nine; only for Jacobean bishops did this average age rise to fifty-one.[24] Dr Fincham's figures are based on consecration, an act which took place as part of the process of first appointment to episcopal office in that period. Only three suffragan bishops were appointed in the Elizabethan period, and none in the Jacobean, so the figures are consistent with the present study in which the date of first appointment, rather than consecration, has been chosen. The figures are not thereby distorted through changes in the availability and appointment of suffragan bishops.

A number of bishops in office during the period from 1520 to 1559 had commenced their ecclesiastical careers as members of religious orders. The appointment of bishops from the ranks of the regular clergy was not unknown before the sixteenth century, though it was never particularly common. Most bishops came from the secular clergy, having been trained in administrative matters and often with an academic background in law rather than theology. Those regulars who were appointed to the episcopal office tended to become suffragan bishops, often with a particular commission to their own subjects in their order in which they frequently held senior office. The dissolution of the monasteries in the latter half of the 1530s meant that former religious were treated on the same basis as the secular clergy. A number of former religious who

---

[23] See Prosopography (Appendix I). The four Italian bishops, Campeggio, de'Ghinucci, de'Gigli and de'Medici have been disregarded for this analysis, leaving eighty-four bishops of whom the dates of birth of thirty-eight are known or may be conjectured with a reasonable degree of reliability, a sample of forty-five per cent. In each of the periods mentioned in the text, at least one-third of all episcopal appointments made were of men for whom such dates are available.
[24] Fincham, K., *Prelate as Pastor*, p. 19.

attained episcopal office in the period in question, however, had left the observance of their rule some time before their houses were dissolved. Out of the eighty-eight bishops who had legal possession of their sees in England and Wales between 1520 and the death of Queen Mary, twenty-five had been professed members of religious orders. Ten were from monastic orders following the Benedictine rule, including three Cistercians and one Cluniac. Nine friars and former friars included five Dominicans, one Carmelite, one Augustinian friar and two Franciscans, the Observant William Peto and the notorious Conventual friar Henry Standish. Five had been Canons Regular, including the former provincial of the Bonshommes, a Gilbertine Canon, and three Augustinians, who had the misfortune of belonging to one of the least well regarded of the orders in the late medieval Church.[25] Only one bishop in the study belonged to a new order, the Theatine Thomas Goldwell, Marian Bishop of St Asaph.

While in many cases a background in a religious order had little positive influence on the later episcopal careers of these bishops, some individuals seem to have taken something of the ideals of their professions into their new state. The influence of the Theatine ideal on Goldwell as a bishop is an obvious case, though it also left its mark on others, such as Reginald Pole who at one time had contemplated joining the order. The former Cistercian, John Hooper, while leaving aside his religious profession and despite his saturation with Zwinglian reform, may well have been influenced by the austerity of his former life when setting up his episcopal household at Gloucester. The former Augustinian friar Miles Coverdale had been resident at the house of his order in Cambridge in the early 1520s; the prior of that community from 1523 was Robert Barnes, the noted Reformer and leading promotor of Lutheran ideas in the university town, who was burned in 1540 as a relapsed heretic. From exile in Zürich about the year 1541, Coverdale published a defence of Barnes against a *post mortem* attack.[26]

It has been suggested that the teaching of Luther had a particular appeal to members of religious orders. Luther himself was a monk who had followed the rule of St Augustine, and it may be no coincidence that his most devoted follower was the Augustinian Barnes, and that former religious numbered highly amongst the more Reform-minded bishops of the English Church.[27] On the other hand, there were others who were less committed to the ideals of either the religious life or of the Reformation. John Salcot seems not to have been fully committed to the stability

[25] Wright, *The Counter-Reformation*, p. 198.
[26] Coverdale, M., *A confutacion of that treatise which one J Standish made agaynst the protestacion of D. Barnes in M. D. XL.* (Zürich, 1541?)
[27] Huelin, G., 'Martin Luther and his Influence on England', *King's Theological Review*, vol. 9, no. 1 (1986), p. 11.

characteristic of the Benedictine rule, holding the abbacies of both St Benet's Hulme, Norfolk, and of Hyde Abbey, Winchester, during a period in which he was also Bishop of Bangor. Bangor seems to have been considered compatible with the holding of abbacies *in commendam*; indeed, it has been said that the diocese was not merely neglected but virtually deserted by its bishops.[28] Salcot's predecessor, the Cistercian Thomas Skevington, was abbot commendatory of Beaulieu in Hampshire throughout his episcopate, while John Penny, who preceded Skevington as Bishop, was an Augustinian Canon who held the abbacy of St Mary de Pré, Leicester, *in commendam* from 1505 to 1508, but relinquished it on his translation to Carlisle. The three other Augustinians, two Canons and one Friar, who became bishops during the period under study, were all notable for their contributions to the establishment of the Reformation in England. Robert Ferrar was burned for heresy in 1555; William Barlow survived to be Elizabethan Bishop of Chichester; the former friar Coverdale was responsible for a significant proportion of the biblical translation and editing of the period. Barlow and Coverdale took part in the consecration of Matthew Parker as Archbishop of Canterbury on 17 December 1559; the other consecrators were the former Dominican John Scory, who preached the sermon (on 1 Peter 5:1), and John Hodgkin, the suffragan Bishop of Bedford appointed under Henry VIII.

Ten of the former religious were appointed to Welsh dioceses, suggesting a continuation of the use of these sees to provide revenues for bishops whose main functions were elsewhere. Bangor was held *in commendam* by a succession of abbots up to the dissolution. Llandaff was held by the Spanish Dominican George Athequa, confessor to Catherine of Aragon, from 1517 to his resignation in 1537, to be succeeded by the Gilbertine Canon, Robert Holgate, who became Archbishop of York in 1545. Holgate was followed by the former Benedictine Anthony Kitchin, who held possession throughout all the changes of the next twenty years, and having taken the Oath of Supremacy under Queen Elizabeth died in 1566 as Bishop of Llandaff. St Asaph was held throughout the forty years before the death of Queen Mary by a succession of religious and ex-religious. The Franciscan Standish was followed by Barlow for a few months, to be succeeded by the Cluniac Robert Warton; his translation to Hereford in 1554 was followed by the appointment of the Theatine Goldwell. Barlow and Ferrar provided an unbroken succession of former Augustinian Canons at St Davids from 1536 to 1555.

Four of the twenty-five bishops were former provincials of their orders, John Bird of the Carmelites, Paul Bush of the Bonshommes,

---

[28] Scarisbrick, 'The Conservative Episcopate', p. 43.

John Hilsey of the Dominicans, and Henry Standish of the Conventual branch of the Franciscans. The Benedictine John Chambers was abbot of Peterborough Abbey for twelve years before the dissolution, and was appointed first bishop of the new diocese of Peterborough. Robert King was commendatory abbot of the Cistercian Abbey of Osney for the last two years of its existence, having acted for ten years before that as a suffragan bishop to John Longland in Lincoln Diocese, where the Abbey was situated. After the surrender of Osney, King was appointed first bishop of the new diocese centred there, and which in 1545 was moved the short distance to Oxford. Henry Holbeach became dean of the new cathedral foundation at Worcester after the dissolution, having formerly been prior of the Benedictine community attached to the cathedral. At the same time he was appointed to the newly created suffragan see of Bristol, from which he was moved in 1544 to the diocese of Rochester in succession to Nicholas Heath, whose predecessor in the see, John Hilsey, was another former religious who also had connections with Bristol. Hilsey had been prior of the Dominican Convent at Bristol in 1533, and from there was appointed prior provincial of England in 1534 by Cromwell. The Dominican connection with Rochester established by Hilsey was continued by the appointment of Maurice Griffith as Bishop in 1554. Griffith, another Dominican friar, was appointed Hilsey's Chancellor in 1535, and became Archdeacon of Rochester in 1537, a post he held until his own episcopal appointment under Mary. Griffith's immediate predecessor in office, and under whom he served as archdeacon, was yet another former Dominican friar, John Scory, the last of three Edwardian bishops of Rochester.

In the thirteenth century, when university education effectively commenced, thirty-six per cent of the bishops had been graduates. This figure rose to just over sixty per cent in the fourteenth century, while by the fifteenth century some ninety-one per cent of bishops held university degrees.[29] To this should be added the unknown number of bishops who had enjoyed some benefit of study at university without proceeding to a degree. The great majority of diocesan bishops of the English Church in the first half of the sixteenth century had the benefit of a university education, a fact which set them apart from the majority of the parish clergy. It is important to bear this in mind when considering the provision made by the bishops for the education of their clergy throughout the period under study. Clerical education was the sole preserve of the universities, of which only a small proportion of clergy were able to take advantage. The problem of inadequately trained clergy was one which recurred throughout the period of the Reformation in England, and many bishops addressed it in a variety of ways. The

[29] Heath, *Church and Realm*, p. 158.

ultimate solution for Catholic Reform, the college of future priests in each diocese where through prayer and study the priestly life would grow 'as if in a seed-bed' ('tamquam ex seminario'), was proposed in England in the 1550s during the reign of Queen Mary, and adopted in Continental Europe as a key feature of the Counter Reformation, though never in England. The Elizabethan Settlement brought reform of the universities, and new colleges for the training of godly preachers, but nothing quite like the Catholic seminary. Despite these apparent shortcomings, a number of colleges at the universities had been newly created in the late fifteenth and early sixteenth century where the main purpose was to train men for the priesthood, an important example being Michaelhouse at Cambridge, the college in which John Fisher was educated.

After initial studies of a more general nature leading to the degree of Bachelor of Arts, it was usual to specialize in one subject or another, which could lead to the higher degrees of Bachelor or Doctor in a particular subject. However, it was quite a usual occurrence in the period to follow a specific course of study without taking a degree at the end. The majority of bishops appointed in the first half of the sixteenth century took higher degrees in civil or canon law, or in theology. The changing pattern of subjects studied by the bishops during the period under scrutiny reflects the changing perceptions of episcopal office, and its function within the commonwealth, among the bishops themselves and those responsible for their choice and appointment. The picture is often painted of an episcopate heavily weighted in favour of lawyers at the beginning of the 1520s.[30] In his study of the pre-Reformation English Church, Christopher Harper-Bill argues that a training in law was a more suitable preparation for pastoral activity, with its emphasis on equity and compassion in interpretation, and that the canonist had a better appreciation of the problems of the ordinary Christian than the theologian whose training had been in abstract intellectual concepts.[31] Half of the sixteen bishops appointed during the reign of Edward IV had been doctors of law, and only six were theologians, while under Henry VII, sixteen of the twenty-seven episcopal appointments were of lawyers, and only six of theologians. John Guy has suggested that this represents a deliberate policy on the part of Henry VII to appoint bishops who

---

[30] See, for instance, Bowker, M., *The Henrician Reformation: The Diocese of Lincoln under John Longland, 1521–1547* (Cambridge, 1981), p. 10, discussing the English bishops of the southern province in the early 1520s; Wolsey, despite his grace to proceed to the degrees of Bachelor and Doctor of Theology in the University of Oxford, is not included among the theologians by Dr Bowker, who also disregards Drs Atwater, Audley and Fitzjames, presumably on account of their deaths in the first half of the decade, and Dr Standish as Bishop of a Welsh diocese.

[31] Harper-Bill, C., *The Pre-Reformation Church in England, 1400–1530* (Harlow, 1989), p. 28.

would be able servants of the state, even if this were to the detriment of the Church.[32] The situation began to change with episcopal appointments made under Henry VIII. Seven of the bishops in office in 1520 are known to have studied theology at Cambridge or Oxford, of whom six had proceeded to the degree of Doctor by 1501; six others held the degree of Doctor of Civil Law, and two degrees in both Civil and Canon Law. One bishop, Robert Sherburne, was a Bachelor of Medicine. At least a third of the bench of bishops, on the eve of the Reformation in England, were demonstrably competent theologians. Ten years later, at the beginning of 1530, the picture was almost exactly the same. Of those whose subject of higher study is known, six bishops were theologians, nine were civil or canon lawyers, and one was a Bachelor of Medicine, out of a total of twenty. By the end of 1537, only four of those bishops remained in office. The newly constituted episcopal bench was staffed with a number of men who had served the King in the matter of his divorce both from the Queen and from Rome, and with many favourers of radical reform, led by Cranmer as Archbishop of Canterbury. It is also notable that the majority of bishops in 1537 were theologians. Only six of the bishops in office in that year had been trained in the law, four of whom had been appointed before the break from Rome. After the resignations and episcopal deaths of 1539 the proportion of theologians declined again slightly. Twelve of the bishops in office at the end of that year are known to have been theologians, while the number trained in the law rose to eight. The conservative reaction centred around the fall of Cromwell and the Act of Six Articles at first sight appears to have led to a preference for bishops from an educational background more typical of the beginning of the King's reign. However, only two of the six bishops appointed between 1537 and 1540 were lawyers. Edmund Bonner had been active in the matter of the King's divorce, and his promotion to the episcopate in 1538 was not unexpected. John Bell's appointment to Worcester after the resignation of Hugh Latimer was also a natural progression, Bell having been vicar general and Chancellor of the diocese since 1518, acting in that capacity during the absentee episcopates of Silvestro de'Gigli, Giulio de'Medici and Geronimo de'Ghinucci, as well as being a chaplain to Henry VIII. The new appointments which resulted from the creation of six new sees between 1540 and 1545 demonstrate a continuing trend towards the appointment of theologians to episcopal office. Four of the six were filled by theologians newly raised to the episcopate, and one by the translation of a theologian, Bird of Bangor, to Chester. Westminster was filled by the appointment of Thomas Thirlby, Doctor of Civil Law and of Canon Law, though it might be argued that a theologian was unnecessary in a

---

[32] Guy, *Tudor England*, p. 73.

diocese created essentially to provide for a bishop whose first duties would be to the Court. The other vacancy created by the formation of these new dioceses was filled by a canon lawyer, Arthur Bulkeley. Further deaths and resignations after 1540 led to a situation at the end of the reign of Henry VIII in which two-thirds of the bishops were theologians. Only eight of the twenty-seven sees were held by lawyers, six of whom had a training in canon law. By the end of the reign of Edward VI, only two lawyers, Thirlby and Sampson, were in full possession of their sees, a third, Tunstall, being in the process of deprivation, the diocese of Durham having been dissolved by Parliament. Nineteen of the other twenty bishops were theologians, including all eight of those raised to episcopal office during the reign.[33] During Mary's reign, eighteen new bishops were appointed and two who had been papally provided while in exile in Rome took possession of their sees. In addition, four bishops-elect were nominated during 1558, but whose appointments were never completed owing to the death of the Queen. Out of the twenty-four, eighteen were theologians (one of whom was also a canon lawyer) and two were civil and canon lawyers. Of the ten bishops who continued in office, or who were restored to their former sees during the reign, half were theologians and half were lawyers. The changing constitution of the bench of bishops in the English Church from 1520 to the eve of the Elizabethan settlement reflected the changing demands of the office on its holders. Just as the state required bishops less to perform a ministry of diplomacy centred around the Court, so the Church perceived a growing need for spiritual leaders well-versed in the things of God. The integration of the two, a particular interpretation of which was expressed by the exercise of the supremacy of the king within the Church, led to the appointment of theologians rather than lawyers to serve in the episcopal state. This was most evident in the choice of bishops of both the Edwardian and Marian regimes. In the face of the usually perceived antithesis between the two, the move towards a theologically competent episcopate was the result in both reigns of a desire for more pastorally active bishops, able to preach the Word of God and inspire others to do the same.

Certain colleges at Oxford and Cambridge seem to have predominated

---

[33] Throughout these analyses it has been impossible to place William Barlow amongst either the theologians or the lawyers. Although he has been claimed for both Oxford and Cambridge, no record survives for him of any degree taken, or of a grace to proceed thereto. His extant writings give no further evidence which might place him conclusively with one group or another, and the attribution to him of a treatise on geography suggests that he had interests beyond either field of study. He must remain a prime example of an individual who, while almost certainly undertaking study at a university, took no formal qualifications as part of that course, a situation which was much more common in his day than in the present.

in the supply of future bishops for the English Church in the period under study.[34] In a number of cases, membership of a college is not recorded, though from graduation records and other sources, attendance at one of the universities may be presumed. Where membership of a college may be conjectured, the individual concerned has been included in these figures. However, one in eight of the bishops in the period under study cannot be placed with any accuracy at a particular college; for a small number, there survives no record of any period of study at university whatever. Cambridge supplied the greater number of martyred bishops, Fisher in 1535, then Cranmer, Latimer and Ridley in 1555–56. Significantly, it was to Oxford that the latter three were taken to stand trial, and where they were executed; Hooper and Ferrar were burned in their own cathedral cities. The reputation of Cambridge as a centre for the propagation of heretical ideas was reflected in the prevalence of future bishops who were Cambridge men and who contributed to the spread of Reformation in England. At the very least, it suggests that the university was a centre where new ideas were taken up with particular vigour. Gonville Hall, for instance, which produced three bishops of distinctly Protestant leanings, was noted in 1530 as a centre for the spread of heresy. On the other hand, a number of Marian bishops were Cambridge men, and overall the balance of those who favoured the Reformation and those who opposed it was more or less even.

Aside from their study in the universities of Oxford and Cambridge, a significant number of bishops undertook periods of study at foreign universities. Table 2 of Appendix III provides a summary of this activity, so far as it is known, for the bishops from 1520 to 1559 (including those elected but unable to take possession of their sees). Most of the bishops included in the table had undertaken their study before 1530; those who became bishops after that date were appointed, or took possession of their sees, during the reign of Queen Mary. This reflects the practice, common before the break with Rome, of sending the most promising scholars and churchmen to study in one of the great European centres of learning. Reginald Pole's study at the University of Padua, for instance, was encouraged by the King, who also provided Pole with financial support. A number of future bishops took advantage of a period of exile from the prevailing religious regime in England to undertake study at a foreign university. Both Richard Pates and Thomas Goldwell, for instance, commenced their academic careers at the University of Oxford, and then went on to study in at least two foreign universities. Pates was appointed ambassador to the Imperial court from 1533 to 1537, and again in 1540; in that year, he fled to Italy. Both Pates and

---

[34] See Appendix III, Table 1.

Goldwell held episcopal office in the English Church under Queen Mary, and each sat in the Council of Trent as bishops of the English Church, Pates as Bishop of Worcester in 1546–47 and again in 1551 (having been papally provided to the see in 1541 though without effect until 1555) and Goldwell as Bishop of St Asaph in 1561–63. Coverdale spent sufficient time at Tübingen in Germany to obtain his doctorate in theology. On the whole, however, the numbers of future bishops (as indeed of other potential students) who studied at foreign universities declined in the years immediately following the Henrician break with Rome.

A number of bishops are known to have travelled overseas for reasons other than study before appointment to episcopal office. Several visited the English Hospice of St Thomas the Martyr at Rome; Richard Nykke is known to have been there in 1483, and in 1496 Robert Sherburne was responsible for rebuilding its chapel. Cuthbert Tunstall was in Rome in 1505. John Clerk was on the personal staff of Cardinal Bainbridge, Archbishop of York, from 1510 to 1514 in Rome where Bainbridge had been sent as ambassador in 1509. Clerk returned to Rome in the spring of 1523 as resident ambassador while elect of Bath and Wells, and was consecrated bishop there in December of the same year. During that time he undertook a thorough reform of the English Hospice, which seems to have been effective though dependent on his presence in Rome.[35] He returned to England in August 1528 with Cardinal Campeggio's legation sent to resolve the matter of the King's divorce. John Stokesley was in Rome in 1523 where he borrowed books from the Vatican Library, and while there met Richard Pace, English ambassador to Venice and familiar of Reginald Pole from his time as a student at the University of Padua. John Bell, while Vicar General of Worcester diocese, was sent to Rome by Henry VIII to attend the Lateran Council (1512–17) where he probably attended Silvestro de'Gigli (then Bishop of Worcester). William Knight was engaged on a number of diplomatic missions throughout his career, including an embassy to the Pope in 1527–28 to promote the King's divorce. Edward Fox, who was much employed on diplomatic missions both before and after his episcopal appointment, often in connection with the royal divorce, was in Paris with Reginald Pole after 1528 to press for the University's opinion on that matter; soon afterwards, in England, Pole had the interview with Henry VIII which ultimately led to his twenty-two year exile. Fox was also sent on an embassy to Rome with Stephen Gardiner in 1529, and was later associated with Nicholas Heath and Robert Barnes in an embassy to the Lutheran princes at Schmalkalden in December 1535 after the matter of the King's divorce had been settled within the realm. Edmund Bonner

---

[35] *The English Hospice in Rome: The Venerabile Sexcentenary Issue*, vol. XXI (May 1962), pp. 164, 171.

was much engaged on foreign embassies both before and after his appointment as bishop, and indeed the latter may have been to some extent a reward for his service in the former, as well as providing him with a higher status when dealing with emperors, kings and popes. After the Henrician break with Rome, there is a definite shift in the underlying reasons for foreign travel, at least amongst those who held, or later attained, episcopal office. While Christendom presented a seamless robe, it was natural that gifted scholars should spend some time at the great centres of learning outside England, and that bishops should find themselves fully integrated with the life of the Church in Rome and elsewhere, forming as they did an integral and organic part of the universal Church. Once the English Church was no longer in full communion with the See of Rome, such opportunities no longer afforded themselves; travel abroad, by senior clergy at least, tended to be confined to diplomatic business (including the King's central concern of the early years of the schism, namely the obtaining of a divorce from Catherine of Aragon), and to maintaining and building political alliances, regardless of whether these were with those of the Reformed or Roman obedience. The few exceptions among the later bishops, such as Cranmer and Hooper, tended towards the development of relationships amongst Reformed churches, some of which were to bear fruit in the reign of Edward VI with the comings and goings of a number of leading Reformers. When English and Welsh students once again began to migrate to the Continent after 1560, it was often with a view to returning in holy orders to serve the clandestine Catholic community, or at the very least to escape the Protestant settlement of religion then established under Queen Elizabeth.

Chapter Four

THE BISHOP AND PREACHING

The subject of preaching, and its practice by the bishops of the fifteenth and early sixteenth centuries, is one which demonstrated a separation of theory and practice. The centrality of the ministry of the Word in the exercise of episcopal functions was frequently acknowledged in theory and more frequently disregarded in practice. Many ecclesiastical Reformers complained of clergy, and bishops in particular, who failed to exercise a preaching ministry. The revival of the study of the sacred languages and a desire to return to the sources of revelation and of secular literature, characteristics of that intellectual movement which advocated what was known as the new learning, only served to make this omission more apparent. When Erasmus published his new edition of the New Testament in Greek and Latin in 1516, his opinion as to the centrality of the preaching of the word was clearly set out in the opening verse of St John's Gospel. His choice of the word *Sermo* to translate the Greek *Logos*, rather than *Verbum*, was most significant. Not only did he choose to use a word which signified something active, the Word as spoken, as preached, he also made this alteration in a verse familiar to any priest from its liturgical usage at the end of the ordinary of the Mass. Marsilius of Padua, the medieval political thinker whose writings were known in England even before the publication of a partial English translation of his *Defensor pacis* in 1535, taught in that work that the preaching of the divine law, and the administration of the sacraments in accordance with it, were of the essence of the priesthood.[1] The gulf between theory and practice may be explained, at least in part, by the fact that the office of the diocesan bishop in the English Church in 1520 had become one which had much to do with the service of the Crown and little to do with the active spreading of the Gospel. The men selected for episcopal office by the King and his father were on the whole those who by training and experience were most suited for this role. The majority of English and Welsh sees in the first twenty years of the reign of Henry VIII were held by men trained in the civil law. A minority of bishops,

[1] *Defensor pacis*, p. 24.

81

among them Blythe, Fisher and Longland, held degrees in theology. In a medieval ethos where the sacramental functions of the bishop were largely delegated to suffragans, and where jurisdiction was exercised by the bishop's vicar general and commissary, preaching was not considered to be the prime concern of the bishop. Only as bishops became less involved with matters of state, and more with matters of religion, did the ministry of the word begin to assume the importance amongst the bishops which a few of their number believed it should. Where the bishops did preach, it was often at court or to learned gatherings of clergy. The bishop who preached to his flock in their native language was not unknown; Fisher, though the most notable, was not the only example. It was with bishops who had been touched by the teachings of Continental reform that the mould itself began to be broken.

John Fisher, Bishop of Rochester, rose to become the foremost preacher in England during the reign of Henry VII. He was also known throughout Christendom as the model of a perfect bishop. Fisher was more inclined towards the new learning than any of his contemporary brother-bishops. His concern with education, demonstrated by his contacts with the University of Cambridge, of which he was Chancellor from 1514 to his death, and particularly in his own foundation of St John's College, was interconnected with his concern for the ministry of preaching. In a sermon preached at St Paul's before a number of abjured Lutheran heretics (including Robert Barnes), he quoted from Romans 10:14, 'how shall the people believe if they hear not?', and asked 'And howe shall they here without it be preached unto them?' Drawing on the parable of the sower, he likened the seed to God's word, the true ministers of that seed being the preachers who cast it onto good and stony soil alike.[2] His practical response to this concern was the attempt to create a preaching clergy, through improved clerical education at institutions like St John's College, and the exercise of a personal ministry of preaching. His ministry included not only the usual Latin sermons *ad clerum*, at court, or at Paul's Cross, but also preaching in the vernacular to ordinary people in their parish churches.[3] Rochester diocese was smaller in area than any other in England or Wales, and only two others had fewer parishes. The accessibility of the diocese made this style of preaching a practical possibility, especially for a bishop who may have been present in his diocese for as much as ninety per cent of the time.[4] Preaching is a fundamental part of the episcopal office, equal in

---

[2] Fisher, J., *A sermon had at Paulis . . . concernynge certayne heretickes* (London, 1526), sig.D.ii,v.

[3] Thompson, S., 'The Bishop in his Diocese', in Bradshaw and Duffy, p. 77.

[4] Bradshaw and Duffy, Appendix II.

importance to supervisory and sacramental duties, according to Fisher's *Sacri sacerdotij defensio* (1525), a defence of the Catholic doctrine of priesthood against Luther's doctrine, written in reply to the latter's *De abroganda missa privata* (1522).

A number of bishops in the period to the break with Rome were concerned to provide for adequate preaching in their dioceses. Collections of homilies had been available to parish clergy since the Middle Ages. *Speculum sacerdotale*, for instance, contained nearly seventy sermons for feasts and saints' days, although a good deal of the material was from sources like the popular *Golden Legend*, which contained their share of flights of fancy. Amongst the Henrician bishops, Fisher and Longland are known to have preached regularly, and both printed large numbers of their sermons; like John Stokesley they authorized the publication of important preaching material for the use of their clergy, encouraged by the Archbishop of Canterbury William Warham who saw the provision of such material as a means for eradicating the new heresy of Luther. It also provided for the lack of preaching ability amongst the parish clergy. Most preaching was undertaken by itinerant friars, not by resident seculars. Indeed, in 1535 Edward Lee, Archbishop of York, declared that he knew of only a dozen secular priests capable of preaching, all of whom were non-resident. Cranmer's provision of books of homilies (the first of which was published in 1547) was part of an established tradition of providing material for clergy unable to compose their own sermons. Susan Wabuda has suggested that this concern of a number of bishops for the maintenance of orthodoxy and the suppression of vice linked late medieval practice with the Reformation. Sermons were printed by bishops so that other clergy could use them in the fight against heresy. Indeed, one of the principal means of restoring Catholic orthodoxy employed by the Marian bishops was to be the publication of books of homilies, though the programme was curtailed by the premature death of the Queen.[5]

Preaching was often given first place in expositions of the nature of the episcopal office. John Longland, in his Good Friday sermon to the King and Court at Greenwich in 1538, had declared that

> The verye offyce of a bushop is *predicare, orare, & sacrificare sive offerre*. To preache, to praye, to doe sacrifyce and to offer.

Longland's style of preaching was derived more from the traditional methods associated with the old learning than with the more literal

---

[5] Strype, *Ecclesiastical Memorials*, vol. I, pp. 291–2; Heath, P., *The English Parish Clergy on the Eve of the Reformation* (London, 1969), pp. 74, 95; Wabuda, S., 'Bishops and the Provision of Homilies, 1520 to 1547', *Sixteenth Century Journal*, 25 (1994), pp. 551–2; Bowker, *The Henrician Reformation*, pp. 11–12.

exegesis associated with the new. The scriptural commentary most acknowledged in his sermons as the source of quotations was the *Glossa Ordinaria*, a work of the twelfth century which had become the standard commentary of the Middle Ages. Despite this, Thomas More declared that Longland, 'a second Colet', used to say that he had gained more light on the New Testament from the writings of Erasmus than from almost all the other commentaries he possessed.[6] Longland certainly considered the failure to see that the Word was preached to be the mark of a bad bishop. One who failed thus in his duty did not even deserve the name:

> Euery bushop of the worlde is not named a bushop by god. For some cometh into that offyce, not by the holy goost, not electe of god (as John sayth) Not entrynge *in ouile ouium per ostium, sed ascendens aliunde* [in the sheepfold by the gate but climbing in by another way] (John 10)

Some became bishops by worldly means, through the influence of their friends, by 'unlawfull laboure', or simony; 'suche are not named bushops by god'. They do not enter by him who said '*Ego sum ostium, Ego sum via, veritas & vita*' [I am the door, I am the way, the truth and the life] (John 10:7, 14:6). They suffer their sheep to perish 'for lacke of bodyly and goostly foode and sustenaunce, for lacke of preachynge, for lacke of good ensample'. They live 'not bushoply nor priestly. For they came in not by god, nor by grace'. The bishop's role should include the studying of Scripture and then explaining it to the people. Longland seemed to be suggesting that bishops who had entered their office by unlawful means were not true bishops. In so far as they failed to carry out genuine episcopal functions, 'to preache, to praye, to doe sacrifyce and to offer', they were illustrating the falsehood of their office.[7] The sermon was directed primarily at the failure of the bishop of Rome to carry out the office of a true bishop, and the nature of Longland's remarks reflected this preoccupation.

The bishops of Henry's reign up to the formal break with Rome seem rarely to have been popular preachers. Those trained in the civil law, in particular, tended to preach in Latin to a learned audience on the few occasions when they exercised that ministry. As the number of bishops inclined towards reform increased in the later 1530s, so the desire to provide an effective preaching ministry increased. William Barlow, soon after his appointment as Bishop of St Davids, wrote to Cromwell that he wished to maintain a household of men learned in divinity and law, and made serious efforts to move his establishment to Carmarthen, in the

---

[6] Blench, *Preaching*, p. 27.
[7] *A Sermonde made before the Kynge*.

centre of his diocese, so that his preachers might better reach the 'unregenerate Welsh'.[8] Cranmer attempted to redirect resources to create a more active, preaching clergy, and sent Reforming preachers into the peculiar jurisdictions of the archbishopric of Canterbury, giving them a foothold in areas where they might otherwise have failed to gain an entry.[9] John Bird, shortly after his appointment to the newly created diocese of Chester, attempted in 1546 to obtain the wardenship of Manchester College in order to finance a centre for a preaching ministry. Of all the appointments to the episcopal bench made by Henry VIII, it was Hugh Latimer who made the most significant personal contribution to the development of a preaching episcopacy.

Latimer's opinions on the episcopal office were publicly aired as early as 1528 in a sermon *ad clerum* in St Mary's University church in Cambridge. In the presence of Nicholas West, Bishop of Ely, he set about contrasting the high calling of a bishop with the character and performance of the bishops of the time. His complaints may not have been entirely fair; John Fisher had dedicated his *Defensio Regiae assertionis* to West on account of his pastoral zeal in residing in his diocese and preaching to his flock.[10] Furthermore, West was known as a patron of the new learning and an associate of notable humanists like Colet, More and Tunstall.[11] Latimer seems to have been summoned before Wolsey as a result of his remarks before West, and was able to explain himself to such a satisfactory degree that he obtained a licence from the Cardinal to preach.[12] Latimer had been concerned to exercise a pastoral ministry from the start of his parochial career. Shortly after his installation to the living of West Kington in Salisbury diocese (January 1531) he preached a sermon in a nearby parish in which he compared nonpreaching prelates to the thief and robber who 'entereth not by the door into the sheepfold, but climbeth up some other way' (John 10:1). His opposition to worldly prelates and false bishops has been said to show a Lollard influence. The same text was used later by Longland to support the view that a bishop who had entered his office by worldly

[8] *LP*, XI, 1428.

[9] Preachers bearing Cranmer's licence were sometimes inhibited by the local ordinary; see Wabuda, S.R., 'The Provision of Preaching during the English Reformation: With Special Reference to Itineration, c.1530–1547', Cambridge PhD, 1992, pp. 117–20.

[10] Felicity Heal tentatively places West in his diocese for eight of the first ten years of his episcopate; 'The Bishops of Ely and their Diocese during the Reformation Period: ca. 1515–1600', Cambridge PhD, 1972, p. 7.

[11] Logan, F.D., 'Doctors' Commons in the Early Sixteenth Century: A Society of Many Talents', *Historical Research*, 61 (1988), p. 157.

[12] The only surviving record of the interview is BL Harleian ms 422, fols.84–6. See *Acts and Monuments*, vol. VII, App.IV; Chester, A.G., *Hugh Latimer: Apostle to the English* (Philadelphia, 1954), p. 30; Gwyn, *The King's Cardinal*, p. 494.

means was not a true bishop. It is unlikely that he was influenced by the same source, suggesting that the concern for preaching prelates was common to all those concerned with the reform of the Church.[13] When Latimer was raised to the office of bishop in August 1535, he seems to have been unable to break free from the ties which bound his new colleagues to Parliament, Convocation and the service of the Crown. Extant records indicate that he did not arrive in his diocese of Worcester until October 1536, a year after his consecration. Two-thirds of his time seems to have been spent in London, as he can be located in his diocese for only fifteen of his forty-five months as bishop.[14] Despite his absence, he was active in encouraging the spread of new ideas. In 1536 he was unsuccessful in an attempt to intercede with the King for the preservation of Great Malvern Priory from dissolution. He seems to have been of the opinion at the time that certain such institutions ought to be retained to maintain bases for itinerant preachers.[15] He probably began to issue licences for preachers soon after his consecration, and seems to have sought men of similar opinions to himself. Furthermore, he refused licences to conservatives, even if they had degrees in theology and were known to be discreet.[16] He also chose men of known Reforming zeal as his chaplains, and set them to preach frequently within the diocese. The men he chose included one Master Garrett or Garrard, who may be

[13] Chester, *Latimer*, pp. 67–8; Longland, *A Sermonde made before the Kyng*; Dunnan, D.S., 'The Preaching of Hugh Latimer: A Reappraisal', Oxford DPhil, 1991, p. 75. Dr Dunnan considers Lollard teaching to have been a predominant influence on Latimer's early preaching along with Lutheranism and Christian humanism, derived principally but not exclusively from Thomas Bilney (pp. 101, 236–7). He further suggests (p. 151) that Latimer's refusal to take up the office of bishop again in 1547 was influenced by Lollardy's lack of a positive model of reformed episcopacy in its ecclesiology. Dr Dunnan also points out that Latimer's later preaching shows less influence of Lollardy than his earlier sermons. Rosemary O'Day, however, suggests that Latimer's theology was primarily Lutheran, and that all his teaching was underpinned by the doctrine of justification by faith alone; the scarcity of references to antiquity or humanist scholarship in Latimer's sermons supports her view that this was a significantly lesser influence. She sees him as modelling himself on prophets like Amos and Hosea, sent to castigate Israel for its sins ('Hugh Latimer: Prophet of the Kingdom', *Historical Research*, 65 [1992], pp. 264–6). An alternative to Dr Dunnan's suggestion regarding Latimer's unwillingness to take up episcopal office again might be that Latimer felt unable to combine the duties he was called upon to perform at Court with the obligations he felt towards personal preaching in his diocese, the same conflict which had troubled him during his four years at Worcester when he was so often prevented from exercising the ministry he believed to be fundamental to his office. This would also accord with his self-image of a prophet calling the whole nation to repentance.

[14] Chester, *Latimer*, p. 106.

[15] Cooper, C.H. and Cooper, T., *Athenae Cantabrigienses* (Cambridge, 1858), vol. I, p. 132.

[16] Wabuda, 'The Provision of Preaching', pp. 104–8.

identified with the Thomas Garrett active in 1528 in disseminating heretical books in London and Oxford. Another, Dr Rowland Taylor, had been active in Cambridge in the early 1520s, where he had been associated with Latimer. Taylor later became domestic chaplain to Cranmer, and was executed as a heretic in Mary's reign. Rodolf Bradford had been implicated in Latimer's troubles with West and Wolsey in 1528 and went on to become a key figure in the network of English and Continental Reformers which developed during the period of Marian Catholic restoration. When Latimer had need of an additional suffragan bishop to work alongside Andrew Whitmay, Bishop of Chrysopolis *in partibus infidelium*, he submitted Bradford's name to the King along with that of Henry Holbeach, the prior of Worcester. Of the two, Holbeach was chosen and consecrated to the newly created suffragan title of Bristol in March 1538, becoming dean of the cathedral chapter when the priory of St Mary, Worcester, was dissolved in 1540. Latimer himself resigned his see in July 1539, weeks after Parliament had passed the Act of Six Articles. His resignation was taken as a protest against the King, and he was imprisoned for several months. On his release under the general pardon of all those imprisoned under the Act, he was forbidden to preach, the order for which was not rescinded until after the death of Henry. Once free to preach again, a main area of attack was the state of the holders of episcopal office at the commencement of the reign of King Edward. One of his earliest renewed attacks against nonpreaching prelates was delivered late in 1547, printed afterwards by John Day, and known as the Sermon on the Ploughers. In the sermon, Latimer referred to

> one that passeth all the other, and is the moste diligent prelate and preacher in al England. And wil ye know who it is? It is the Deuyll. He is the moste dilygent preacher of all other, he is neuer out of his dioces, he is neuer from his cure . . .[17]

The bishops and other worldly prelates are the source of the problem:

> For euer sence the Prelates were made Lordes and nobles, the ploughe standeth, there is no work done, the people sterue. Thei hauke, they hunt, thei card, they dyce, they pastyme in their prelacies with galaunte gentlemen, with theyr daunsyng minyons, and with their freshe companions, so that ploughyng is sette asyde. And by the lordyng and loytryng, preachyng and plough- yng is cleane gone.[18]

---

[17] Latimer, H., *A notable Sermon of the reuerende father Maister Hughe Latemer, whiche he preached in the Shrouds at paules church in London, on the .xviii. daye of January, 1548* (London, 1548), sig.C.iii,r.

[18] *Ibid.*, sig.B.iii,v.

Latimer also believed that even when these bishops were exercising their office, they missed its chief purpose, and should be 'preachers not bell-hallowers'.[19] Like Fisher, he equated an unpreaching ministry with the enemy who sowed darnel in the field of good seed:

> The bishops and prelates, the slothful and careless curates and ministers: they with their negligence give the devil leave to sow his, for they sow not their seed; that is they preach not the word of God; they instruct not the people with wholesome doctrine; and so they give place to the devil to sow his seed.[20]

Latimer was called upon to give the seven Friday sermons to the Court at Westminster during Lent 1549; many of his sharpest attacks were against bishops who failed to preach themselves or make other provision in their dioceses. He alluded to a bishop (Tunstall) who was busier as president of a council (the Council of the North) than in his episcopal duties, and rebuked John Veysey of Exeter for inactivity, going so far as to refer to Coverdale, then preaching in Devon, as Veysey's 'suffragan'.[21] Once again, Latimer may have been less than fair; Tunstall, for example, had been ranked alongside Fisher and Longland as a preacher by Johann Fabri on his visit to England in 1527.[22] Latimer's definition of the episcopal office includes as essential an active preaching ministry both personally and through a highly trained and well educated clergy, for if the shepherd fails to feed his flock with the Word of God, then the sheep will perish.

The compilers of the 1537 Bishops' Book were in no doubt as to the importance of preaching, calling it

> the chief and most principal office, whereunto priests or bishops be called by the authority of the gospel . . . it is their office to oversee, to watch, and to look diligently upon their flock, and to cause that Christ's doctrine and his religion may be truly and sincerely conserved, taught, and set forth among Christian people, according to the mere and pure truth of scripture; and

---

[19] A Sermon preached before King Edward VI, 5 April 1549, *Sermons and Remains*, ed. Corrie, G.E., Parker Society, 2 volumes (Cambridge, 1844–45), vol. I, p. 176.

[20] Fisher, *A sermon had at Paulis*, sig.D.ii,v; Latimer, *Sermons and Remains*, vol. II, p. 189.

[21] The remark seems to have been based on Coverdale's exercise of a preaching ministry in Veysey's diocese, supplying a need created by the Bishop's failure to fulfil the obligations of his office as Latimer understood them. It was natural that, when the aged Veysey was retired in 1550, Coverdale should be appointed to Exeter in his place. There is no suggestion, despite the assertion in Thompson, S., 'The Pastoral Work of the English and Welsh Bishops, c.1500–1558', Oxford DPhil, 1984, p. 7, that Coverdale was performing the sacramental functions of a bishop while possessing the status of some sort of episcopal coadjutor.

[22] Rex, *Fisher*, p. 29.

that all erroneous and corrupt doctrine, and the teachers thereof,
may be rejected and corrected accordingly.[23]

In Bullinger's *De episcoporum*, published the following year and presented to the King, the essence of the bishop's office was to be the
minister of God's word, so much that the terms *episcopus* and *minister
verbi dei* were almost interchangeable.[24] The more conservative King's
Book of 1543, in its parallel passage on the sacrament of order, made
much less of the preaching office of the Church's ministry. The office and
duty of bishops consisted in 'true preaching and teaching the word of
God unto the people', in ministering the sacraments, offering the sacrifice
of the altar, in administering penance and excommunication, and in
praying for the Church and the flock committed to them.[25] The power of
preaching was much reduced; it may be suggested that this resulted from
the dissemination of Reformed doctrine through a particularly active
preaching ministry in certain dioceses. However, this was still clearly
distant from the constant teaching of the Middle Ages, that priests were
ordained primarily to offer the sacrifice of the Mass, not for preaching or
teaching the Word of God.[26]

The failure of bishops to preach, or to delegate the duty to suitable
persons, was a constant complaint of the Reformers in England. Thomas
Becon, whose zeal for reform came from Latimer at Cambridge,
considered a priest or bishop who did not preach as no more genuine
than a 'Nicholas' or boy-bishop, an idol, 'and indeed no better than a
painted bishop on a wall'.[27] John Hooper related an incident in 1546
when he was in a town where the bishop neither preached nor provided a
deputy, though the people seemed to him to be 'apt and ready, by
inspiration of God's Spirit, to hear the truth, if they had a preacher'.
Despite the fact that the town was an episcopal see (Hooper does not
state which), the bishop 'preached neither God, neither the devil, but let
his flock wander as sheep wander without a shepherd'.[28] Hooper's
answer, expressed in *A declaration of Christ and his office* (1547) was to
present Christ as the example of a model bishop, one who executed the
true function of that office in preaching and teaching the people.[29]
Christ's command to Peter and the apostles was clear: they were to
please God in their vocation as ministers of the Church by teaching all

[23] Lloyd, *Formularies*, pp. 109–10.
[24] Bullinger, *De episcoporum*, 'Peroratio ad Regem', fol.179r.
[25] Lloyd, *Formularies*, p. 278.
[26] Marshall, P., 'Attitudes of the English People to Priests and Priesthood, 1500–1553', Oxford DPhil, 1990, p. 161.
[27] *The Catechism of Thomas Becon*, ed. Ayre, J., Parker Society (Cambridge, 1844), p. 320; Marshall, 'Attitudes', p. 119.
[28] 'Answer to the Bishop of Winchester's Book' (1547), *Early Writings*, pp. 142–3.
[29] 'A Declaration of Christ and his Office' (1547), *Ibid.*, p. 19.

that Christ had said to them; 'Ite in universum mundum, et praedicate evangelium omni creaturae' ['Go out into the whole world, and preach the Gospel to all creatures'] (Mark 16:15).[30] After his return from exile, Hooper found the situation in England still to be highly unsatisfactory. Writing to Bullinger from London (25 June 1549), he complained

> Such is the maliciousness and wickedness of the bishops, that the godly and learned men who would willingly labour in the Lord's harvest are hindered by them; and they neither preach them-selves, nor allow the liberty of preaching to others.[31]

A clear statement of his opinions on the episcopal office after his return to England may be found in *A Declaration of the Ten holy command-ments* (1549) in the discussion on the eighth commandment, 'Thou shalt not steal.' Referring to Titus 1:5, he considered that the office of bishop had degenerated from its original as found in the Scripture; 'the primitive church had no such bishops as be now-a-days'.[32] The main reason for this was the growth of riches in the Church, such that 'bishops became princes, and princes were made servants'; as a result, there was a general lack of preaching. Their only concern seems to be their personal comfort;

> when they have the reward of learning, they teach no more, as bishops and ministers of the church; whom the prophet calleth dumb dogs that cannot bark, their mouths be so choked with the bones of bishopricks and benefices.[33]

The bishop should attend to the spiritual welfare of his flock, by directing some of his income to the promotion of an active preaching ministry in the Church. The mixing of civil and ecclesiastical authority which began in the post-Constantinian Church has been the downfall of the episcopal office. Without echoing his language, Hooper was clearly expressing the sentiment of Luther's theory of the *zwei reiche*, the distinction of temporal and ecclesiastical authority which may not safely be confused, a theory with which Hooper the theologian was fully conversant.

In a series of sermons on the prophet Jonas for Lent 1550, Hooper developed a number of themes concerning the nature of episcopal office, still sharply critical of the holders of that office at the time. It was after these sermons, at Easter 1550, that Hooper was offered the see of Gloucester, made vacant by the death of its first bishop, John Wakeman. The right and duty to preach the Word of God was not something that could be taken on by an individual without a definite vocation, which

[30] 'Answer to the Bishop of Winchester's Book' (1547), *ibid.*, pp. 145–6.
[31] *Original Letters*, Vol. I, p. 65.
[32] *Early Writings*, p. 396.
[33] 'Exposition upon Psalm LXXVII' (published 1580), *Later Writings*, p. 357.

may come from the Church or, like that of the prophet Jonas, directly from God; 'no man can or may teach truly the word of God, but he be called ordinarily, or extraordinarily'.[34] The ordinary ministry of God's Word is exercised when the Church is sound; no man ought to appoint himself to preach or minister when there is no corruption of doctrine in the Church, and when the sacraments are rightly ministered, as in the time of Moses, or of the Apostles. The extraordinary call comes from God only in times when the ministry of the Church is corrupt. It is noteworthy to compare the similarity of Hooper's teaching with that of the more conservative Bonner and Aldrich on whether a king or other lay person might preach the word in extraordinary circumstances. Taking St Paul as an example, they admitted the possibility of a preaching ministry set up by direct divine inspiration where the regular ministers of the Church were not available.[35] Christ commanded his Apostles to preach (see Mark 16, Matthew 28, 2 Timothy 4), and preaching is the mark by which bishops and ministers of the Church are known from ministers of the devil, 'not by shaving, clipping, vestments, and outward apparel'.[36] Bishops and priests should be resident in their cures, and not leave their duties; they should be concerned with preaching, and not with empty ceremony. The ministry consists of many

> dumb bishops, unpreaching prelates and such ass-headed minis-
> ters . . . Christ instituted neither singers nor massers, but
> preachers and testimonies of his true doctrine.[37]

The second sermon provided Hooper with an opportunity to castigate the contemporary trend amongst the ministry to encourage superstitious practices rather than preaching, and to warn of the potential harm to the commonweal from a lack of the word. In the context of a discourse on the casting of lots by the sailors to see why they had been troubled by a storm, the lot falling upon Jonas, Hooper complained

> The bishops and priests unquiet the ship of this realm two
> manner ways: one by the neglecting of their true duty, the
> other by a defence of a false and damnable superstition. In the
> primitive and apostolical church, the office of a bishop and priest
> was to teach in the congregation of the faithfuls [sic] the doctrine

---

[34] Sermon 1, 19 February 1550, *Early Writings*, p. 447.

[35] 1540 commission on doctrine, BL Cotton ms Cleopatra E.v. fol.46.

[36] *Early Writings*, p. 449. It would be interesting to find pictorial evidence of the retention of the tonsure in Edward's reign; episcopal habits are certainly known to have been retained, as witnessed by Hooper's own battle against them in respect of his own consecration. The image of Edward VI handing out the bible to his bishops and nobles which forms a frontispiece to Cranmer's 1548 *Cathechismus* seems to show a full set of clerical heads of hair. See Plate IV.

[37] *Early Writings*, p. 451.

of the prophets and apostles, according to the commandment of Christ. Matt. xxviii. Mark xvi. Eph. ii. Now is this integrity turned into false idololatry [sic] and devilish superstition – to sing and say mass in the congregation of God.[38]

This train of thought returned in the third sermon. The office of bishops and priests in the primitive Church was to be preachers of God's Word, and ministers of Christ's sacraments; 'not to sacrifice for dead nor live, not to sing or mass, or any such like'. Those who have not been called to that original ministry are not shepherds, but 'ravening wolves to devour the flock of God'.[39] The true vocation of bishops and priests consists in studying and preaching the Word of God, administering the sacraments 'christianly', and severely using 'discipline and correction of indurate men's faults'. The latter aspect was raised to a full mark of the Church from its strong but subordinate emphasis in Calvin's writings by John Knox, who was active in England at this time.[40] The Edwardian Ordinal reflected this understanding of the office of bishop in its final collect:

> . . . send down upon this thy seruant, thy heauenly blessynge, and so endue hym with thy holy spirite, that he preaching thy worde, may not only be earneste to reproue, beseche, and rebuke with al pacience and doctryne, but also may be to such as beleue, an wholesome example in worde, in conuersacion, in loue, in faith, in chastitie, and puritie . . .[41]

After Hooper finally accepted the office of bishop, and was consecrated to the see of Gloucester in March 1551, he set about putting into practice his theory of episcopacy. He embarked upon a thorough visitation of his diocese and issued a set of injunctions. He also prepared annotations on Romans 13 for the clergy of his diocese in 1551 'for a help unto you, and also unto the people' to follow the commandments. The chapter of St Paul was commended because it 'entreateth of all the second table [of the ten commandments] and duty of a christian man, how he should use himself with and towards all sorts of people'. Furthermore, it is the place where St Paul discusses the place of authority in the Church and the world, and the relationship between secular and spiritual authority. All who serve a cure in the diocese and cannot teach and preach 'to the people the like doctrine' are commanded, every Saturday and Sunday, to 'read unto the people this thirteenth chapter, as I have here set it forth'.[42] His prefatory epistle is

---

[38] Sermon 2, 26 February 1550, *Ibid.*, p. 460.

[39] Sermon 3, 5 March 1550, *Ibid.*, p. 480.

[40] Discipline was never made one of the marks or *notae* of the Church by Calvin (see *Institutes* IV.i.9, p. 1023); it became the third 'mark' in the 1560 Scots Confession.

[41] *The First and Second Prayer-Books*, p. 317.

[42] 'Annotations on Romans XIII' (1551), *Later Writings*, p. 96.

signed 'Yours with all my heart, Brother and fellow-preacher, John Gloucester'.[43]

Hooper's successor at Gloucester was equally concerned with the establishment of an active preaching ministry in his diocese. At the opening of the reign of Queen Mary, James Brooks had complained of the suppression of Catholic teaching and its universal replacement by heretical preaching; 'the mouths of godly preachers are stopped: but every blasphemous tong rouleth at large'.[44] After his appointment as bishop, Brooks was required to act as deputy for the Cardinal Arch-bishop of Canterbury in the 1556 metropolitical visitation of his diocese. Significantly, the first of his injunctions resulting from the visitation required

> that all parsons, vicars, and curates, having the gift and talent of preaching, shall frequently and diligently occupy themselves in the same, according to the decree of the late Synod [of West-minster, 1555–56], in that behalf provided, opening the scriptures accordingly, and not forgetting to declare the right use of the godly ceremonies of the Church, as they come in course from time to time.[45]

Cardinal Pole's Legatine Constitutions of 1556 required all bishops to undertake the duty of preaching personally, referring to ancient canons of the Church and especially to the second decree on preaching of the Council of Trent, and to organize a body of preachers in their dioceses to take over the work which had previously been undertaken by friars, at least until the education of the parish clergy as a body enabled them to undertake this duty.[46] Thomas Goldwell at St Asaph, in similar circum-stances to Brooks, took control of preaching in his diocese. His set of injunctions for 1556 required

> that no parsons, vicars, and curates do admit any preacher to preach in their church, without he be licenced by the ordinary; and that they either preach themselves, or provide that the parishioners have every quarter of the year one sermon at the least.[47]

The revision of the statutes of Durham Cathedral by Cuthbert Tunstall sought to lay additional weight upon the duty of preaching. The dean

---

[43] *Ibid.*, p. 98.
[44] Brooks, *A sermon . . . at Paules crosse*, sig.G.iii.
[45] Brooks' Injunctions for Gloucester Diocese, 1556, *Articles and Injunctions*, vol. II, p. 401.
[46] Bray, G., ed., *The Anglican Canons, 1529–1947*, Church of England Record Society vol. VI (Woodbridge, 1998), p. 103; Hughes, *The Reformation in England*, Vol. 2, p. 234.
[47] Goldwell's Injunctions for St Asaph Diocese, 1556, *Articles and Injunctions*, vol. II, p. 410.

and chapter were charged to 'sow the seed of the Word of God' in the churches of which they were patrons 'lest through lack of knowledge of the law of God the flock of Christ perish'.[48]

Interim measures to deal with the problem of a shortage of able preachers who conformed with the Catholicism of Mary's reign centred around the provision of homilies to be read to the people on Sundays and feasts, in the same way that the Book of Homilies of 1547 sought to make up for the shortage of Reformed preachers. Queen Mary's Articles of 1554 required of each diocesan bishop that the people should be compelled to attend their parish churches to hear divine service 'as of reason they ought', to receive instruction and thereby to be led to unity. For this purpose, the bishops were commanded that a 'uniform order be set forth by homilies, or otherwise, for the good instruction and teaching of the people'.[49] Edmund Bonner, Bishop of London, sought to meet this requirement by means of his treatise *A Profitable and Necessary Doctrine with certain Homilies adjoined thereto*. The treatise not only provided a means for instructing the laity in sound doctrine but was also a link with the later years of the reign of Henry VIII. By retaining the *King's Book* of 1543 as a framework, Bonner and his chaplains provided a degree of continuity with the recent past founded on the book which had been a focus for traditionalists during the reign of Edward VI.[50] Bonner's visitation of London diocese, from September 1554 to October 1555 (the Articles for which were adopted by other bishops for their own visitations, including Pole's metropolitical visitation of 1556) resulted in a set of Injunctions for his diocese. In them he required all parsons, vicars and curates of every parish and other priests having cure of souls within the diocese and jurisdiction of London to study his treatise, and to read a chapter weekly to their congregations. The same book was enjoined upon other dioceses later in the reign as an interim measure.[51] The definitive book of homilies promised by the 1556 synod never materialized, though the seventeenth-century historian Gilbert Burnet recorded that he had seen a scheme of them in Matthew Parker's papers at Corpus Christi College, Cambridge.[52] For the longer term, Brooks expected his clergy to study Scripture and to give him an annual account of their progress, in the meantime ensuring that a quarterly sermon was given in their churches by themselves or some other competent person.[53] Finally, to

---

[48] Loach, J., 'The Marian Establishment and the Printing Press', *English Historical Review*, 101 (1986), p. 139.
[49] *Articles and Injunctions*, p. 328.
[50] Duffy, *The Stripping of the Altars*, p. 534.
[51] *Articles and Injunctions*, pp. 360–1, 401.
[52] Hughes, *Rome and the Counter-Reformation*, p. 79.
[53] *Articles and Injunctions*, pp. 402–3.

ensure that Bonner's book would be available to those required to study and use it, the book was included in a list of items which each parish church was to own.[54]

Thomas Watson's *Holsome and Catholyke doctryne concerninge the seuen Sacramentes of Chrystes Church, expedient to be knowen of all men, set forth in maner of shorte Sermons to bee made to the people* (published in 1558) had the same purpose as Bonner's treatise, being intended for use in his diocese of Lincoln. The work is in the form of a series of thirty sermons on the seven sacraments. The first sermon explains the number of the sacraments and outlines their effects. The remaining sermons treat each sacrament in turn, in the order in which they might be expected to be received (baptism, confirmation, eucharist, penance, order, matrimony and extreme unction). The sacraments of baptism and holy order warrant two sermons each, while those of confirmation and matrimony three each. Those sacraments which had been subject to most debate in the sixteenth century are discussed in the central series of eighteen sermons; the sacrament of the altar is discussed in seven sermons, followed by eleven on the sacrament of penance. The work concludes with a sermon on the last sacrament, extreme unction. The centrality of the sacrament of the altar is as would be expected in a work of this nature; indeed, Watson refers to it as the highest sacrament.[55] However, the importance given to the sacrament of penance would suggest that it, with its requirement of at least annual recourse to auricular confession to a priest, was seen to be one of the principal means of restoring Catholicism amongst the ordinary people.

While the Reformation had been taking root in England, the Council of Trent had begun its deliberations under three legates, the chief of whom was Reginald Pole. In an early pronouncement, on the episcopal office, the Council affirmed that the chief duty of the bishop is to preach the gospel; indeed, there had been (unsuccessful) pressure at the Council to impose on the diocesan bishop the obligation to preach every Sunday and holy day. If the bishop himself were lawfully hindered, he might appoint other competent persons to discharge this office.[56] On the return of Catholicism and the restoration of papal authority in England, Queen Mary's 1554 Injunctions ordered the bishop of each diocese to see that 'a uniform doctrine be set forth by homilies, or otherwise, for the good

---

[54] *Ibid.*, p. 408.

[55] Watson, *Holsome and Catholyke doctryne*, fol.clvi v.

[56] Fifth Session, Reform, 17 June 1546: *Conciliorum oecumenicorum decreta*, pp. 667–70; *Canons and Decrees of the Council of Trent*, pp. 26–8. Jedin, *History*, vol. II, pp. 103–7. Pole achieved release from his legatine duties on the grounds of ill health in October 1546; the decrees on episcopal preaching, therefore, were finalized under his presidency.

instruction and teaching of the people'.[57] Sermons at Paul's Cross in support of the new regime were organized early in the reign, and in August 1553 Gardiner as Chancellor was empowered to license preachers under the Great Seal for the whole realm, while in 1555/6 the Synod of Westminster reminded bishops of their personal duty to preach, and that to delegate this duty to others was an abuse.[58] Mary's Archbishop of Canterbury, Reginald Pole, as well as presiding at the sessions of the Council of Trent which dealt with preaching, had also been active on the Continent during the 1540s in encouraging its practice, calling upon Peter Martyr and Bernardino Ochino to preach in Viterbo, from whence (unfortunately for Pole) they finally fled to Protestantism. Pole's concern with the study of theology as the crown of knowledge and the necessary completion of a classical education began to appear from 1532 in his correspondence with Jacopo Sadoleto, humanist Bishop of Carpentras.[59] Settled in Padua but paying frequent visits to Venice, his household at the time included Thomas Goldwell, later Bishop of St Asaph. Over the next four years, his growing interest in sacred literature was sustained and developed by his association with members of the Oratory of Divine Love and their supporters, most particularly Gasparo Contarini with whom he had formed 'the closest bonds of friendship' by October 1534; during the same period, he came into contact with new biblical scholarship, attending lectures on Isaiah by the Hebrew scholar Jan van Kempen.[60] After the collapse of the Regensburg talks, the task of combating heresy in the Italian towns fell to the spirituals influenced by Valdes and his circle, a group supported by Pole and Contarini. To aid this, both Pole and Contarini wrote manuals of instruction for preaching; Pole's treatise, no longer extant, was *De modo concionandi*, completed about Christmas 1541.[61]

Throughout the period under study, the practice of preaching by the bishop or one authorized by him grew in importance. Other than in a few notable cases, the Henrician bishop was a minister of the state more than a minister of the word. The most important public pulpit in the land, at Paul's Cross in the churchyard of the cathedral church of the diocese of London, saw perhaps twenty episcopal sermons between 1534 and 1547,

---

[57] Blench, *Preaching*, p. 285.
[58] Pogson, R.H., 'Reginald Pole and the Priorities of Government in Mary Tudor's Church', *Historical Journal*, 18 (1975), p. 17; Pogson, R.H., 'Cardinal Pole – Papal Legate to England in Mary Tudor's Reign', Cambridge PhD, 1972, pp. 267, 271; Hughes, *Rome and the Counter-Reformation*, p. 79; Bray, *The Anglican Canons, 1529–1947*, pp. 100–7.
[59] Fenlon, *Heresy and Obedience*, p. 28.
[60] *Ibid.*, p. 30.
[61] Quirini's edition of Pole's *Epistolae* mistakenly attributes to him Contarini's work of the same name. Fenlon, *op. cit.*, p. 62.

given by eleven bishops. In the six years of the reign of Edward VI, thirty-six episcopal sermons were given, while in Mary's reign forty-seven were preached in just five years.[62] This reflects the growing importance of popular preaching by the bishop in person throughout the period under study. Henrician bishops trained in theology were in a minority, at least in the earlier part of the reign, and few exercised an active, popular pastoral ministry amongst their flock. The bishops who are known to have performed an active preaching ministry in the period were amongst those who were theologians by training. More sermons by John Longland and John Fisher, both bishops who were also doctors in theology, have survived than from any other early sixteenth-century clergyman.[63] This is most likely due to the importance and popularity of their printed sermons, both Longland and Fisher having had a significant corpus published in their lifetimes. The development of preaching by the bishop himself as a fundamental element in the episcopal office belonged more to the reigns of Edward and Mary. Popular preaching by the Edwardian bishop resulted from a conviction that the Church was only present where the Word was preached and the sacraments administered according to Christ's original ordinance. The provision of an educated ministry, of popular preachers able to spread the gospel among the people, was of prime concern to bishops who otherwise might have been considered doctrinally very divergent. Fisher, with his concern for the University of Cambridge, and Barlow, eager to reorder his diocese so as to make it geographically more conducive to evangelization, along with Latimer's personal ministry, provide a variety of examples from the earlier part of the period. The provision of books of homilies, both on a national scale as in 1547, and on a diocesan scale as encouraged by the 1554 Injunctions and envisaged by the Synod of Westminster, set about supplying a temporary want while an able and well-trained clergy was in preparation. The suggestion that episcopal revenues ought to be diverted to pay for this programme was made on a number of occasions, though after the redistribution of ecclesiastical wealth from the dissolutions of the monasteries and chantries, and from the surrender and exchange of episcopal properties with the King, any large-scale transfer of wealth into clerical education was dependent on the monarch's good will and freedom from financial restraint as well as on the new major lay landowners who had benefitted from the redistribution. The influence of Continental developments, both Catholic and Reformed, contributed to the growth of a more pastoral, preaching episcopate during the reigns

---

[62] Thompson, S., 'The Pastoral Work of the English and Welsh Bishops', pp. 169, 172.
[63] Rex, *Fisher*, p. 31. A number of Fisher's published sermons contain a woodcut image purporting to be of the Bishop preaching; see Plate V.

of both Edward and Mary.[64] For some, the fact of holding episcopal office required them to carry out an active preaching ministry; Nicholas Ridley told Princess Mary that he felt bound to preach because of his office and calling.[65] It is interesting to note that the influence of the teachings of Continental Protestantism upon extreme Reformers such as John Hooper led them to a position on the preaching office of bishops which was substantially the same as that expressed by the Council of Trent. The same understanding was common amongst the Marian bishops, particularly those appointed to episcopal office by the Queen, and despite personal doubts of his ability, Pole preached all over his diocese.[66] Although some bishops continued in office whose commitment to a personal ministry of preaching was slight, they were removed from office along with those who made that ministry a priority after the accession of Queen Elizabeth. The way was then cleared for the establishment of a new episcopate where the role of bishop as preacher could take its place as the prime function of the holder of that office.

---

[64] The contribution of the bishops to education, both lay and clerical, in the period in question, is discussed in the next chapter.
[65] Thompson, 'The Pastoral Work of the English and Welsh Bishops', p. 171.
[66] Pogson, 'Cardinal Pole – Papal Legate', p. 272.

Chapter Five

BISHOPS AND THE PROVISION OF EDUCATION

If the bishops were to be the prime movers in the preaching of the Word in their dioceses, they needed to be supported by a learned and educated body of clergy equipped fully for the task. The educational shortcomings of the clergy were a source of almost universal concern amongst the early reformers, in England as much as on the Continent. In 1528 William Tyndale complained of the English clergy that

> they wot no more what the New or Old Testament meaneth, than
> do the Turks: neither know they of any more than that they read
> at mass, matins, and evensong, which yet they understand not: . . .
> a great part of them do understand no Latin at all, but sing, and
> say, and patter all day, with the lips only, that which the heart
> understandeth not.[1]

The bishops were not unaware of the failings of their clergy in this matter. A concern for education as an essential component of the episcopal office was derived from the idea of the bishop as the first and foremost preacher in his diocese. Many bishops sought to improve clerical education for the express purpose of raising the standard of preaching in the Church, there was no conception of an integrated training programme for priesthood as a whole at the end of the Middle Ages. Until the idea of the seminary was first proposed by Cardinal Pole, the main (and only formal) school of ministerial training was the university; Oxford and Cambridge received a number of endowments in the years preceding 1520 to the end that they might perform this task more effectively. The extent of Pole's own concern with this problem, at an early stage in his career and before his relationship with his kinsman the King was severed, may be found in the dialogue composed by Thomas Starkey, probably between 1529 and 1532, just after he had left the future Cardinal's household. In it, Pole was made to state

---

[1] Tyndale, *Obedience*, pp. 54–5 (prologue to the Reader). A copy of this work seems to have come into the possession of the King, perhaps through the agency of Anne Boleyn.

ther ys a nother grete faute wych ys the ground of al other almost, & that ys concernyng the educatyon of them wych appoynt themselfe to be men of the church, they are not brought up in vertue & lernyng as they schold be nor wel approvyd therin before they be admyttyd to such hye dygnyte, hyt ys not convenyent men wythout lernyng to occupy the place of them wych schold prech the word of god & tech the pepul the lawys of relygyon, of the wych commynly they are most ignorant them-selfe, for commynly you schal fynd that they can no thyng dow but pattur up theyr matyne & mas, mumblyng up a certayn nombur of wordys no thyng understonde[2]

A return to the literal meaning of the Scriptures, associated with the study of the biblical languages of Hebrew and Greek, was an important element in the widespread movement of reform which was often known as the new learning. The movement was an important element in the development of Protestant Reformation, and was commonly associated with the spread of heretical ideas. While containing within itself potential for division and error, it was also recognized as a powerful tool for promoting and reforming the Catholic faith. A number of bishops of the period gave their support to the new learning, particularly in its emphasis on Scripture and the biblical languages, through supporting the study of it in the universities. In September 1517 Edward Lee, later Archbishop of York, was at Louvain to study Greek and Hebrew, and took part in a dispute with Erasmus over the latter's *Novum instrumentum*.[3] Stokesley and Fisher probably both learned Hebrew at the same time, certainly by the end of 1517.[4] Fisher considered that his pastoral obligations prevented him from devoting as much time as he would have wished to the study of the sacred languages, and felt aware of his limitations in them.[5] In 1535, as a result of the break with Rome, Royal Injunctions to Oxford and Cambridge stopped the study of canon law and replaced the study of the *Sentences* of Peter Lombard and the medieval commentators with that of Scripture 'according to the true sense thereof'. Regius Professorships of Greek and Hebrew were founded at Cambridge in 1540, and at Oxford in 1546.[6] One of the most influential biblical translators of the period, rewarded in the reign of Edward VI with the see of Exeter, was Miles Coverdale. Owing much to William Tyndale, whose own work had been proscribed, Coverdale produced the first complete version of both Testaments in English in 1535, printed on the

---

[2] Starkey, T., *A Dialogue between Pole and Lupset*, ed. Mayer, T.F., Camden Fourth series, vol. XXXVII (London, 1989), pp. 87–8.

[3] Rex, *Fisher*, p. 52.

[4] *Ibid.*, p. 58.

[5] *Ibid.*, p. 61, from Lambeth Palace ms 2342, fol.29v.

[6] Blench, *Preaching*, p. 31.

Continent but intended for use in England. A second edition appeared under royal licence in 1537. In 1538, Coverdale produced a fresh version of the New Testament with an accompanying Vulgate text which went through five editions. The 1539 Great Bible, issued by royal authority, was also Coverdale's work, and remained the official version for the rest of the reign. Of the bishops appointed in Mary's reign, Ralph Baynes, Bishop of Coventry and Lichfield from 1554, had won great distinction for himself abroad as a Hebrew scholar, having been Professor of Hebrew at the University of Paris from after 1550 to 1553. He was one of the pioneers of Hebrew learning in England, publishing *Prima rudamenta in linguam Hebraicam* in Paris in 1550. John Christopherson, one of the original Fellows of Trinity College by its foundation charter in 1546, had fled to Louvain on the accession of Edward VI, where he produced translations into Latin of Greek Church historians. The College supported his exile, and in return received the dedication of his translation into Latin of Philo Judaeus.[7] As Master of Trinity College, Cambridge, from 1553, and Bishop of Chichester from 1557, he was one of the leaders in the revival of Greek learning at Cambridge along with Thomas Watson of Lincoln, as well as one of Cardinal Pole's commissioners for visitation of the University in 1556/7.[8]

Not all the bishops were in favour of the new learning. As Bishop of London, Richard Fitzjames caused trouble for his humanist Dean, John Colet. Colet's foundation of St Paul's School had attempted to bring the educational reforms of Italy to England, where he sought to produce an educated laity trained in Latin and Greek.[9] Fitzjames seems to have based his charges against Colet around the use of certain vernacular translations of the creed and other prayers, though his preaching against those who could only give 'bosom sermons', reading from a script, was taken personally by Fitzjames (as intended). It seems most likely that it was views expressed in Colet's sermons that formed the core of the accusation, in particular, that images should not be worshipped. His case may have been prejudiced by heretical interpretations placed on his words reported to the Bishop. However, both the King and the Archbishop of Canterbury, William Warham, came to Colet's support and rescued him from this embarrassing situation.[10] Erasmus had a low opinion of Fitzjames, referring to him as a superstitious and irredeemable Scotist in his firm adherence to scholastic philosophy.[11] Fitzjames was not the only bishop to disapprove of the new learning. Henry

---

[7] McConica, J., *English Humanists and Reformation Politics under Henry VIII and Edward VI* (Oxford, 1965), p. 269.
[8] Hughes, *Rome and the Counter-Reformation*, pp. 92–3.
[9] McConica, *op. cit.*, p. 48.
[10] Brigden, *London*, p. 70; McConica, p. 72.
[11] Emden, *Biographical Register, Oxford to AD1500*, vol. II, p. 692.

Standish, Bishop of St Asaph, objected strongly to Erasmus' New Testament, and preached at Paul's Cross against the translation of the opening verse of St John's Gospel, 'In principio erat sermo,' and was even reputed to have begged the King to save England from the new translation.[12] John Longland, on the other hand, was linked with the humanists not because of his learning but as a result of his practical reforms, particularly through preaching, a course of action approved of in its early years by Warham.[13] Despite Thomas More's description of Longland as 'a second Colet' who claimed to have gained more light on the New Testament from the writings of Erasmus than from almost any other commentary in his possession, he belongs to the old learning in the Scriptural interpretation of his sermons.[14]

Educational foundations and endowments were of great importance among the bishops of the sixteenth century compared with other forms of charity such as hospitality towards the poor.[15] Richard Fox was probably the principal episcopal supporter of the growth of education in the early Tudor period. In 1507, under papal authority, he made new statutes for Balliol College, Oxford. However, his most significant foundation was Corpus Christi College, Oxford, an institution which was intended to give a special place to the study of the humanities, public lectureships in Greek and Latin being founded as well as one in theology (though his original plans were for a monastic house of studies of a type already familiar in Oxford).[16] The statutes for the College were issued in 1517, with supplementary statutes signed by the founder in February 1528, the year of his death. His intention was to promote reform in the Church through the new learning, by eradicating heresy and error and promoting the orthodox faith. The foundation was an English adaptation of the type of trilingual college which was flourishing at Alcala in Spain. In the same year as the foundation of Corpus Christi College, another trilingual college was founded at Louvain. Only the omission of Hebrew from the curriculum prevented Fox's establishment from meeting the strict trilingual standard.[17] In his will he bequeathed over a hundred books to the College.[18] Several other bishops supported the spread of education in various ways, many by benefactions to their former places of study. Edmund Audley, Bishop of Salisbury, supported Lincoln College, Oxford, in this way, as did John Bell, Bishop of

[12] Scarisbrick, 'The Conservative Episcopate', p. 347.

[13] Bowker, *The Henrician Reformation*, p. 11.

[14] Blench, *Preaching*, p. 27.

[15] Heal, *Of Prelates and Princes*, p. 96.

[16] Marett-Crosby, A., 'Robert Joseph and his Letter Book', in *Benedictines in Oxford*, ed. Wansbrough, H., and Marett-Crosby, A. (London, 1997), p. 143.

[17] McConica, *English Humanists*, pp. 82–3.

[18] The books are listed in Emden, *Biographical Register, Oxford to AD1500*.

Worcester, for Balliol College, Oxford, and the University of Cambridge. David Pole, Marian Bishop of Peterborough, bequeathed his large library of books on law and theology to All Souls' College, Oxford. George Day, Master of St John's College, Cambridge from 1537 to his appointment as Bishop of Chichester in 1543 and one-time chaplain to Fisher left the College a copy of the Complutensian Polyglot Bible. The bequest reflects the importance not only of the study of the sacred languages at St John's, but also the importance of humanistic developments on the Continent at Alcala and elsewhere as influences upon the development of learning in England during the first half of the sixteenth century. Thomas Thirlby was a benefactor to Jesus College and Trinity Hall, Cambridge, as well as to his see of Ely. Trinity Hall also benefited from the establishment of three fellowships in law, two for canonists and one for a civilian, as well as one scholarship, by another of its former members, Richard Nykke, Bishop of Norwich. In the manner of their medieval predecessors, many bishops were keen to promote the education of those aspiring to university by the founding of grammar schools, often in the locality from which they originated. Robert Sherburne, Bishop of Chichester, founded a grammar school at Rolleston in Staffordshire around 1520. John Veysey, Bishop of Exeter, was a great benefactor to his native Sutton Coldfield, founding there a grammar school which has survived to the present century. In 1546, the second year of his archiepiscopate, Robert Holgate founded grammar schools in York by letters patent, at Old Malton (where he had been prior of the Gilbertine House) and at his birthplace of Hemsworth. For all these establishments he drew up statutes in accordance with contemporary developments in the new learning.[19] Many Marian bishops continued to promote and support the more general field of education apart from that aimed solely at providing an active preaching clergy. Maurice Griffith, Bishop of Rochester, was appointed trustee of Dr Geoffrey Glynn for the foundation of a grammar school at Bangor.[20] In March 1558, Owen Oglethorpe founded and endowed a grammar school and hospital at Tadcaster in Yorkshire. Provision for education was a noteworthy feature of both royal and episcopal visitation articles and injunctions. Injunctions for the religious houses in 1535 ordered a daily lesson of one hour's length in Scripture. Visitors to the University of Oxford established new lectureships to replace the scholastic teaching which they had abolished. Theological lectures were also instituted for

---

[19] Dickens, *The English Reformation*, p. 273; Dickens, *The Marian Reaction in the Diocese of York*, Part 2, *The Laity*, p. 26.
[20] Emden, A.B., *A Biographical Register of the University of Oxford, 1501–1540* (Oxford, 1974), 'Maurice Griffith'. Glynn was the brother of William, Bishop of Bangor.

cathedral bodies, the first being those in the Royal Injunctions for Salisbury of 1535–36.[21]

Cardinal Wolsey was one of the main promoters of education in the first half of the sixteenth century, receiving praise even from Erasmus, who wrote to him in 1519:

> The study of the humanities, hitherto somewhat fallen, is rebuilt; the liberal arts, still struggling with the champions of ancient ignorance, are supported by your encouragement, protected by your power, gilded in your reflected glory, and nourished by your magnificence, as you offer princely salaries to attract outstanding scholars to come and teach. In the getting-together of libraries richly furnished with good authors of every kind, you rival Ptolemy Philadelphus himself, who owes his fame to this even more than to his crown. The three ancient tongues, without which all learning is handicapped, are revived among us by you, for I regard the generous benefactions now offered to the famous university of Oxford a blessing to the whole of Britain.[22]

Wolsey's activity extended both to the support of existing institutions and the foundation of two establishments, a grammar school in his native town of Ipswich and a college at Oxford. Cardinal College at Ipswich was founded in 1528 on the model of Winchester College, funded by the impropriation of a number of parsonages and monasteries.[23] Cardinal College at Oxford was complementary to the foundation of Richard Fox, in a substantially enlarged form. This had the effect of increasing the concentration of talent at Oxford and providing an impetus to increased humanist activity.[24] In 1525, Robert Sherburne sent Wolsey books for his new college at Oxford. Amongst those recruited by Wolsey was the Italian Franciscan Nicholas de Burgo, who was still drawing a stipend as professor of theology at Cardinal College after Wolsey's fall, and who assisted Edward Fox in the compilation of the *collectanea satis copiosa*.[25] Wolsey's foundation at Oxford made exten-

---

[21] *Articles and Injunctions*, vol. I, pp. 125–6. This was a logical extension of existing canon law. A decree of the Third Lateran Council (1179) had required a benefice to be provided in each cathedral church for a master who would instruct clerics and poor scholars. This was extended at the Fourth Lateran Council (1215) to all churches with sufficient resources, with metropolitan churches required to provide a master competent to teach theology. Tierney, B., *Medieval Poor Law* (Berkeley and Los Angeles, 1959), pp. 19–20.

[22] Erasmus to Wolsey, from Antwerp, 18 May [1519], *The Correspondence of Erasmus*, vol. VI, *1518–19*, ed. and trans. Bietenholz, P.G., Mynors, R.A.B., and Thompson, D.F.S. (Toronto, 1982), pp. 366–7.

[23] Strype, *Ecclesiastical Memorials*, vol. I, part 1, pp. 130–2.

[24] McConica, *English Humanists*, p. 83.

[25] Greenslade, S.L., 'The Faculty of Theology', in *The History of the University of Oxford. Volume III: The Collegiate University*, ed. McConica, J. (Oxford 1986), pp. 304, 341–2.

sive provision for the training of able preachers. Four public sermons were to be given each year in the College chapel to which the people of Oxford were to be summoned by the ringing of a bell. Further, the College's five doctors of theology were to preach seven times a year for ten years after receiving their doctorates. Any member of College who left without obtaining a doctorate but intending to return to take it at a later date was to give at least one public sermon each year in the interim.[26]

Wolsey's fall in 1530 put his educational foundations at risk. In order to try to save them, he wrote to his former servants Stephen Gardiner (then Secretary of State) and Thomas Cromwell. Gardiner had been appointed one of Wolsey's commissioners for the revision of the statutes of his two colleges. Although his foundation at Ipswich was completely lost, the revenues falling into the King's hands, Gardiner and Cromwell were able to obtain the King's support for the college at Oxford by advising him to refound it in his own name, 'so he might have the glory of being called its Founder'. Wolsey's intentions in founding the school at Ipswich have been seen as being for the good of his home town, according to Strype 'to stand an eternal testimonial of his piety and love thereunto'.[27]

Another foundation which seems to have benefited from the concentration of humanist studies in Oxford is the Benedictine house of studies, Gloucester College. The letters of Robert Joseph, a Benedictine of Evesham, give an impression of Oxford in the 1520s as a place where Erasmian humanism was flourishing. The letters were compiled between 1530 and 1533, and many date from the period of his first residence at Gloucester College, from 1521 to 1530. The works of Erasmus are quoted directly in the letters on eighty-nine occasions.[28] At least one later bishop, Anthony Kitchin, may be placed with some certainty at the College during that decade; another, Robert Warton, probably also studied there. Both men were able to hold episcopal office through changes of monarch without loss of position, Kitchin being the only diocesan bishop to take the oath of Supremacy of Elizabeth I. To suggest that their compliance was a result of their Erasmian background may be to speculate beyond the evidence.

John Fisher's zeal for a preaching ministry within the Church included not only his personal active practice but also the creation of an educated preaching clergy, an idea which was central in his concern with the University of Cambridge.[29] He was elected Chancellor of the University

---

[26] Gwyn, *The King's Cardinal*, p. 350.
[27] Strype, *Ecclesiastical Memorials*, vol. I, part 1, p. 181.
[28] *Benedictines in Oxford*, pp. 134, 141, 145; McConica, *English Humanists*, p. 94.
[29] Bradshaw, B., 'Bishop John Fisher, 1469–1535: The Man and his Work', in Bradshaw and Duffy, p. 4.

in 1504, and then re-elected annually until 1514 when he was elected for life. He encouraged the study of Greek and Hebrew, and a readership in Greek was established in 1519. His own college, Michaelhouse, had been founded to train a small number of priest-fellows in theology, and to maintain masses for its founder.[30] Fisher's statutes for St John's College reflect a concern that the students should not waste their time on abstract theological disputation, but should learn to argue and preach on matters of practical benefit to Christians, a concern which was possibly unique among medieval and early Tudor academic statutes and almost certainly derived from the Bishop's own experience as a practical administrator and pastor who knew the problems and difficulties involved in preaching the Word.[31] This combined powerfully with Fisher's own commitment to the new ideas of Christian humanism; the influence of neoplatonism, an important element in the new learning, is evident in a published sermon of Fisher's dating from 1525/6. Preaching before a number of abjured Lutheran heretics, including Robert Barnes, he applied the favourite metaphor of the circle to the Scriptures; 'every part of scripture is lyke a roundel: for it hath no corners'.[32] He applied an even more striking metaphor to his exposition of the necessary unity of the Word of God and the teaching of the Church:

> It is lyke of it & of a songe, where be many syngers, that diversely descant upon the playne songe: but for as moche as they all agre withouten any gerryng, withouten any mystunynge, they make al but one songe, & one armony. In lyke maner it is of the scriptures of god, and of the doctryne of the churche:[33]

The Welsh dioceses in the latter half of the reign of Henry VIII were the centre for a considerable amount of episcopal activity in the matter of general educational provision. In a letter to Cromwell dated 31 March 1538, William Barlow sought to make provision for the education of his diocese by moving his episcopal seat to Carmarthen, geographically central to his diocese of St Davids and the most frequented place therein. He sought a grant of the Grey Friars house in that town, where the King's grandfather, Edmund Tudor, first earl of Richmond, was buried, in order to use the revenues to maintain a free grammar school and a daily lecture of Holy Scripture. Despite his arguments that this would tend to abolish superstition, and annoy but four or five persons only, he was unsuccessful and his seat remained in its traditional location to the

---

[30] Underwood, M. 'John Fisher and the Promotion of Learning', in Bradshaw and Duffy, pp. 25–6.

[31] Rex, *Fisher*, p. 191. Dowling, M., 'John Fisher and the Preaching Ministry', *Archiv für Reformationsgeschichte*, 82 (1991), p. 289.

[32] *A sermon had at Paulis . . .*, sig.E.ij,r.

[33] *Ibid.*, sig.D.iii,v.

furthest west of the diocese.[34] Cromwell, however, was far from averse to the provision of schools of learned preachers. In 1539 he was working with Cranmer on the project of the foundation of new bishoprics; they were concerned that the dioceses should have deaneries and colleges of prebends containing students who could be prepared for later ecclesiastical promotion, so that every bishop would have close at hand a college of learned clergy.[35] Ultimately, however, in 1541 Barlow was successful in setting up a grammar school in Brecon. His contemporary at St Asaph, Robert Warton, had similar plans in 1539 when he too wrote to Cromwell expressing a wish to move his cathedral either to Wrexham or to Denbigh, and to found a grammar school for the education of his clergy. It seems that his concern for his diocese was expressed at a distance, as he seems seldom to have dwelt at St Asaph but parcelled out lands belonging to his see at long leases.[36] Another approach to the education of the Welsh was attempted by Arthur Bulkeley. In 1542, soon after his appointment as Bishop of Bangor, he instructed his clergy, as well as schoolmasters and the heads of households in his diocese, to give religious instruction in the Welsh language to their charges.[37] Warton and Bulkeley were the first in a long series of bishops to show a concern for St Asaph and Bangor; up to the dissolution of those dioceses at the Commonwealth, all the bishops had long-standing Welsh connections. The other Welsh sees of St Davids and Llandaff, however, had the privilege of sympathetic bishops only until the latter years of Queen Elizabeth's reign; despite this, however, this increased interest by the diocesan bishop from the early years of the Henrician schism was a significant improvement of the lot of the Church in Wales.[38]

Not all bishops were equally diligent in applying the resources of their bishoprics to good use. The use made of the temporal wealth of many of the sees, and the reluctance of civil authority to intervene in the application of episcopal revenues, was a complaint of many reformers. John Hooper blamed the degeneracy of the episcopal office on the abuse of the riches of the bishoprics and the blindness of the magistrates who suffered the abuse to continue. This reflected his understanding of the civil power as the source of the bishop's authority, and directly responsible for the right exercise of the episcopal office. Although he accepted

---

[34] *LP*, XIII, part 1, 634.
[35] McConica, *English Humanists*, pp. 213–14; Strype, J., *Memorials of the Most Reverend Father in God Thomas Cranmer* (Oxford, 1840), Book I, Chapter xix, p. 107.
[36] Williams, G., *Recovery, Reorientation and Reformation: Wales c.1415–1642* (Oxford, 1987), p. 294; Griffiths, G.M., 'A St Asaph "Register" of Episcopal Acts, 1506–1571', *Journal of the Historical Society of the Church in Wales*, 6 (1956), pp. 34–5.
[37] Williams, *op. cit.*, p. 295.
[38] Fincham, *Prelate as Pastor*, p. 26.

that bishops should be reasonably provided for, any surplus should be put to some other godly use.[39] He wished to divert the resources of his bishopric to the education of his clergy. In a letter to Bullinger, shortly after his consecration in 1550, he wrote:

> As primitive antiquity employed the revenues arising from this office to the edification of the church and the education of the young, I could wish each of these objects to be restored by me, which can in no way be effected unless I shall be aided by the assistance of pious and learned men.[40]

His desire for assistance in the task of preaching to his diocese was drawn from his view that bishops and pastors, like the prophet Jonah, should not only reside in their cures but should 'walk abroad, and cry out the commandment of the Lord.'[41] Hooper recognized that his own diocese of Gloucester suffered from a severe shortage of learned and able preachers. One way in which he sought to address this problem in the short term was to provide a set of annotations on Romans 13, to be read each week by the clergy to their people that they 'may learn to know, love, and fear the better the king's majesty, and other such magistrates as be by him appointed over the people'.[42] The emphasis on using episcopal revenues to train ministers on a diocesan basis, specifically for ministry in the Church, and without reference to the universities, was a characteristic of the idea of a seminary held in Catholic Reformed circles, though the seminary was not exclusively a Catholic invention. In 1551 Martin Bucer had appealed to Edward VI to convert colleges of the universities to training schools for the provision of sufficient Reformed ministers for the needs of the Church.[43]

The legatine synod summoned in 1555 by Cardinal Pole made the first formal attempt to resolve this common concern, which became the most significant development of the Marian Reformation never to come to fruition in England in the lifetime of any of those involved. The requirement that each diocese should undertake the education of a number of individuals 'tamquam ex seminario' pre-empted the decrees of the Council of Trent.[44] Pole's seminary legislation was indebted to the work of Giberti of Verona.[45] The synod also ordered the resumption of the study of canon law in both universities; until the establishment of

---

[39] 'A Declaration of the Ten holy commandments' (1549), *Early Writings*, p. 398.
[40] Hooper to Bullinger, London, 29 June 1550, *Original Letters*, vol. I, p. 90.
[41] 'Fifth Sermon upon Jonas' (March 1550), *Early Writings*, p. 511.
[42] 'Annotations on Romans XIII' (1551), *Later Writings*, p. 96.
[43] In De Regno Christi; O'Day, R., *The English Clergy: The Emergence and Consolidation of a Profession, 1558–1642* (Leicester, 1979), p. 27.
[44] *Ibid.*, pp. 82–3.
[45] Fenlon, *Heresy and Obedience*, pp. 251, 256.

seminaries, they would be the only institutions for the training of clergy. As Legate he appointed a commission to carry out a visitation of the University of Oxford around July 1556; one of the commissioners was James Brooks, Master of Balliol College up to his appointment to the see of Gloucester in 1555. Pole became Chancellor of Oxford University in October, and promulgated a set of statutes in November. He had been Chancellor of the University of Cambridge since March, and carried out a visitation in 1557, delegating his authority to a commission which included three bishops. Cuthbert Scott, Bishop of Chester, was the chief of the commissioners, the other two bishops being John Christopherson, also Master of Trinity College, and Thomas Watson, Master of St John's College. All three bishops were Cambridge men, and all held degrees in theology. The success or failure of the restoration of Catholicism rested upon the successful establishment of an educated, preaching clergy, able to teach not only by word but by example. The fundamental principle behind the establishment of the seminary was the development of habits of prayer and of study. This principle served the Continental Catholic Reformation well in practice, and was to train Catholic priests who would return to England in later years to work, as they understood it, as missionaries. The accession of Queen Elizabeth only three years after the synod passed its seminary legislation, and the change of course which the English Church again underwent, prevented the establishment of Catholic seminaries in England, though a number of colleges were later established at the Universities with the same intention. The ideal of seminary education, that colleges should be set up in every diocese for the training of clergy, was never realised, despite the attempts not only of Pole and the Catholic Reformers but also of a number of the chief advocates of thoroughgoing Protestant Reform.

Plate I. The arms of Reginald Cardinal Pole, Archbishop of Canterbury (from Pole's register; Lambeth Palace Library)

Plate II. The modern arms of the See of Canterbury (Lambeth Palace Library)

Plate III. Henry VIII delivers the Great Bible to his bishops and ministers (title page, Great Bible of 1541; Lambeth Palace Library E165)

Plate IV. Edward VI delivers the Bible to his bishops (Cranmer, *Cathechismus*, 1548; Lambeth Palace Library 1548.04)

Chere after foloweth a mornynge remembraū
ce had at the moneth mynde of the noble prynce
Margarete counteſſe of Rychemonde ⁊ Darby
moder vnto kynge Henry the. vii. ⁊ grandame t
oure ſouerayne lorde that nowe is/ vppon whoſ
ſoule almyghty god haue mercy.

Plate V. John Fisher preaching (title page, Fisher, J., *Hereafter foloweth a mornynge remembraunce*, London 1509, BL G1202; reproduced by permission of the British Library)

Plate VI. The burning of Nicholas Ridley and Hugh Latimer (from Foxe, J., *Acts and Monuments*, Lambeth Palace Library H5067.A5)

Plate VII. The burning of Thomas Cranmer (from Foxe, J., *Acts and Monuments*, Lambeth Palace Library H5067.A5)

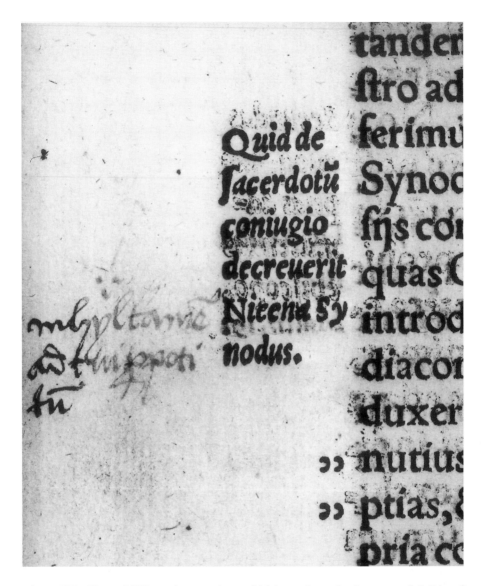

Plate VIII. Henry VIII on the marriage of bishops (marginal note on fol. 94v of Bullinger's *De episcoporum . . . institutione et functione*, BL 1010.c.3; reproduced by permission of the British Library)

Chapter Six

PRAYER AND SACRIFICE: THE LIFE OF
THE BISHOP

By the end of the Middle Ages it was generally accepted that the holding of episcopal office included the obligation to exercise hospitality. Three scriptural texts, 1 Timothy 3:5, Romans 12:13 and Hebrews 13:2, informed much late medieval thinking on this requirement. Paul's first letter to Timothy was used in the sixteenth century on both sides of the Reformation divide to support conflicting models of episcopal office, the specific verse mentioned being applied to the debate over clerical celibacy. If a bishop could not demonstrate his ability to govern his household, how could he be able to govern the Church? Those who sought to allow the clergy to marry argued from this text that marriage, rather than celibacy, was required of the clergy. The transition from a celibate (if not always chaste) clergy to a married one had implications for both the financial and the social status of the bishop. At the same time, traditional episcopal revenues were coming under considerable pressure from a Crown anxious both to reward loyal service and to exercise the control afforded by the newly defined Royal Supremacy over the Church.

The keeping of hospitality was doubly incumbent upon the late medieval bishop. As one of the Lords Spiritual, the temporal baronetcy annexed to his see carried with it the same obligations as to household and retinue as those demanded of the Lords Temporal. Furthermore, as successor to the Apostles and (in his diocese) chief pastor, the bishop had a spiritual duty to care for the needs of his flock, especially the most vulnerable among them. The early Middle Ages saw the growth in the size of dioceses and the rise in importance of the parish as a unit of the local Church and a centre for pastoral organization in the local community. As a result, the obligation to exercise appropriate steward-ship of the goods of the Church in the service of the poor was extended and devolved to the parochial pastoral clergy. The parish became a separate economic unit within the diocese, with the parish priest responsible for administering the revenues of his own church. The sources of the canon law on hospitality, dating from the fourth to the sixth centuries, assumed a simple division of the revenues of the diocese by the bishop. By the late Middle Ages they no longer came into his hands to be divided.[1]

The early Fathers often referred to the property of the Church as 'the patrimony of the poor', a phrase which occurs several times in the twelfth-century collection of canon law sources, the *Decretum* of Gratian. Several texts in that document support the view that the goods of the Church are meant for use in the service of the needy. Augustine, for instance, asserted that 'the things of which we have charge do not belong to us but to the poor', while from Ambrose came the text 'The Church has gold, not to hoard away, but to share out and to help those in need.' Jerome was more specific in placing the responsibility with those holding pastoral office; 'whatever the clergy have belongs to the poor, and their houses ought to be common to all'. From Ambrose came also the image of the practice of hospitality forming a series of concentric circles. A man's first duty was to his close family, and so the innermost circle consisted of the household; extending outwards, it took in spiritual and other kin, neighbours, friends and finally strangers.[2] The 'hierarchy of care' advocated by Ambrose required the Church to address itself both to the level of need and to the worthiness of recipients; John Chrysostom, on the other hand, insisted that the exercise of hospitality should take no regard of persons.[3] The model suggested by Ambrose seems to have taken precedence by the early sixteenth century. Hugh Latimer's yeoman father differentiated the hospitality offered to his poor neighbours from the alms he gave to the needy.[4]

Later commentaries on the canon law supported the view that the clergy had some right to Church property, even if only to provide for their own support, and in a sense the texts could be understood to be as much pious exhortations as formal legal definitions.[5] A later amplification of the law interpreted 'whatever the clergy have' as meaning whatever they administer, and that the sense in which this 'belongs to the poor' is as a source for providing sustenance. The poor were to be supported from the goods of the Church, according to the medieval canonists who most commonly used the term *tenere hospitalitatis* to describe this obligation. Indeed, the most common use of the term 'hospitality' in the later Middle Ages was to describe the relief of the

[1] Tierney, *Medieval Poor Law*, p. 70.
[2] Heal, *Hospitality*, p. 19. Dr Heal's important, thorough and ground-breaking work has formed the basis of much of the discussion of hospitality in the present chapter.
[3] *Decretum, distinctio* 82, *ante* c.1. Heal, *op. cit.*, p. 224.
[4] Latimer, *Sermons*, p. 101; Heal, *op. cit.*, p. 16.
[5] *Decretum* C[ausa] 12 q[uaestio] 1 c[anon] 28, C.12 q.2 c.70, C.16 q.1 c.68; Tierney *op. cit.*, p. 40.

poor by the clergy.[6] The role of the bishop was central to the provision of clerical hospitality, according to several passages in the *Decretum*. A number of passages in the *Decretum* make clear the centrality of the office of bishop in the obligation of the clergy to provide hospitality. In one text, Gratian suggests that the law forbade the consecration of a bishop if he were found to be lacking in hospitality. The bishop was not only to supervise the care of the poor but also to divide the total revenue of his diocese to ensure that a due portion was distributed among them.[7] The classical division of the revenues of the Church, set out in several texts of the *Decretum* dating back to the fifth century, was fourfold: one part was to be retained by the bishop for himself, one was to be distributed amongst the clergy, one part was to be assigned to the building and repair of churches, and one part to the relief of the poor. Later, the tithe was generally adopted as a form of compulsory ecclesiastical taxation, and a similar fourfold division (sometimes threefold: for the clergy, church buildings and the poor) was applied to it. By the fifteenth century the obligation of hospitality which canon law imposed upon the episcopal office had passed to the holders of parochial benefices with the rise in importance of the parish as the prime unit of the local church. Felicity Heal has suggested that the canonists considered the parochial clergy to have assumed the obligations of ordinaries within their own territories.[8] The assumption that the obligation of hospitality lay primarily with all those having cure of souls is found in William Lyndwood's 1443 collection of, and comprehensive commentary upon, the canons of the English provincial synods. The constitutions of John Pecham, Archbishop of Canterbury, were the principal text which required parochial clergy to provide for the poor, which Lyndwood applied equally to bishops.[9] Using texts from the *Decretum* in his commentary, Lyndwood stated that the text spoke particularly of bishops.[10] Though the bishop had no direct control over the application of revenues from benefices, he held broad powers of jurisdiction by which he was enabled to check abuses in the administration of those revenues and to ensure that they were used for the purposes prescribed by canon law, including poor relief. The requirement of hospitality at the end of the Middle Ages was incumbent upon the whole body of the clergy, and especially those exercising the cure of souls. While the bishop continued to hold the power to exercise oversight in the right application of

[6] Hostiensis, *Commentaria ad X*, 2.12.4, fol.42, and 3.34.8, fol.128; Tierney *op. cit.*, p. 42; Heal, *op. cit.*, p. 14.
[7] Gratian quotes a decree of the Council of Antioch empowering the bishop to dispense the property of the churches to the needy; C.12 q.1 c.23.
[8] *Decretum*, *distinctio* 85 *ante* C.1. Heal, *op. cit.*, p. 224.
[9] Lyndwood, *Provinciale*, Lib.III, Tit.4, Cap.3 (pp. 132–3).
[10] *Dist.* 89, c.12 q.1; C.16 q.1; Lyndwood, p. 132.

119

ecclesiastical revenues, less emphasis was placed upon his role as the prime example and chief provider of hospitality, though *liberalitas* or generosity was one of the qualities essential in a bishop which by the sixteenth century was expected also of the true lord or gentleman.[11]

All the bishops in office in the middle of the sixteenth century would have been familiar with the canon law relating to the clerical obligation of hospitality. Many had studied civil and canon law at university, and a number had attained the degree of doctor in one or both disciplines. In any case, each bishop had available to him in his diocese expert canonists, thus ensuring that he was fully aware of both his rights and his duties. Further, much of the medieval canon law on hospitality found its way into the secular poor laws enacted by the later Tudors. The 1552 Act 'for the provision and relief of the poor' required alms for the poor to be collected in each parish church. This had indeed formed an important part of the 1549 Communion Service, where the congregation were instructed to move at the Offertory to place their alms in the 'poore menne's box' which had been set up by Royal Injunction in the previous year.[12] Any who refused to give were to be reported to the bishop.[13] While the medieval canonists would have expected the bishop to exercise his ordinary jurisdiction and command the offender, it was not until the legislation of 1563 that a compulsory contribution could be levied should the bishop's exhortations be unsuccessful.[14]

The actual practice of hospitality in early modern England, however, 'remains extraordinarily elusive'.[15] John Fisher praised the practice in commending the 'godly hospitality and charitable dealing with her neighbours' of Lady Margaret Beaufort in a context which makes the two synonymous.[16] The dedication of his defence of Henry VIII's *Assertio* to Nicholas West portrays the Bishop of Ely as a man genuinely concerned for the welfare of his diocese, an image supported by the tradition that West was exceptionally generous in his hospitality.[17] Fisher's fellow theologian, John Longland, described the ideal bishop as one who fed his flock not only with the spiritual food of preaching but also with bodily food, through exercising proper hospitality.[18] Perhaps the chief example of the exercise of temporal

---

[11] *Ibid., dist.* 86. Heal, F., 'The Archbishops of Canterbury and the Practice of Hospitality', *Journal of Ecclesiastical History*, 33 (1982), p. 548.

[12] An action which may have been the basis of the charge in the Western Rising of 1549 that the new service was like a 'Christmas game'.

[13] Tierney, p. 127.

[14] *Ibid.*, p. 131.

[15] Heal, *Hospitality*, p. 287.

[16] Funeral sermon of Lady Margaret Beaufort; Heal, *Hospitality*, p. 15.

[17] Heal, 'The Bishops of Ely', p. 9.

[18] *A Sermonde made before the Kynge.*

and spiritual lordship in the members of the episcopal bench during the period under study may be found in the person of Thomas Wolsey. His retinue was intended to display both his temporal status as Chancellor and his spiritual status as Archbishop and Papal Legate. Though he had not been known for any particular generosity before his fall, an early biographer noted that soon afterwards he was keeping at Southwell

> a noble house and plenty both of meat and drink for all comers, both rich and poor, and much alms given at his gate. He used much charity and pity among his poor tenants . . .[19]

Wolsey was by no means unique in the lavish exercise of hospitality. William Warham was noted as a good host, consuming most of the annual revenue of his see of Canterbury on hospitality, and he was expected to give an extravagant feast for his enthronement celebration in 1504.[20] Erasmus described him as delighting in the company of the learned, warm and generous in his reception of them at his board, always provisioned for the care of strangers; not delighting in magnificence, the consumption of wine or heavy eating he often sat at the board solely to converse with others.[21] This model of the ascetic godly churchman, of which Wolsey was so often cited as the antithesis, owed much to a traditional portrayal of such clerics, and not necessarily to a true depiction of reality. On this occasion the description rings true when considering the close relationship between Warham and his friend and fellow bishop, John Fisher. The tradition of lavish entertainment in the archiepiscopal household was inherited by Cranmer, who carried to the office certain reforming ideals which conflicted with traditional extravagance in the practice of hospitality. He sought to develop a model of godly superintendence in the archiepiscopal household which replaced secular rituals of temporal lordship with a generous concern for the poor and needy. The traditional image of the worldly ascetic which had been applied to Warham and his predecessors was translated to Cranmer; he was often said to have sat at table with his gloves on his hands as an indication to his servants that he would eat nothing. There is a close identification between Erasmus's description of Warham and the picture of Cranmer drawn by his early biographer Morice and used later by John

---

[19] Cavendish, G., *Life of Wolsey*, ed. Sylvester, R.S., and Harding, D.P. (New Haven, CT, 1962), p. 142.

[20] Heal, 'The Archbishops', pp. 544–63. The four richest English sees, Winchester, Canterbury (income over £3,000 each per annum), Durham and Ely (over £2,000 each), all drew heavily on their resources to pay for hospitality and the costs of diplomatic missions.

[21] Erasmus, *Ecclesiasticae sive De Ratione Concionandi* (Antwerp, 1535), p. 71; Heal, 'The Archbishops', pp. 552–3.

Foxe.[22] However, as the senior churchman in the realm under a Supreme Head who demanded continuity with the past, not innovation, Cranmer was unable to make significant changes in a reformist direction to the structure of his own household. Henry VIII held firmly to a traditional model of prelatical ceremoniousness and grandeur in the operation of episcopal households, rather than the Reformers' concern for the needs of the poor. Such traditional Henrician notions of episcopal hospitality were reflected in the 1540 draft statutes for the cathedrals of the new foundation, made by Nicholas Heath, George Day and Richard Cox.[23] Cranmer was, however, able to make some demands on the clergy by a set of regulations reflecting his concern in particular for the relief of the poor. The regulations were issued in 1541, and were based upon an ordinance of the time of Edward II. While sumptuary legislation with regard to clothing was not uncommon at the time, it was rarely concerned with the regulation of household expenditure on food. The clergy were to be limited in the range and type of dishes served at their tables; for archbishops, six kinds of meat were allowed, for bishops, five, for archdeacons, four, and so on down the hierarchy.[24] The income saved was to be applied 'in plain meats for the relief of poor people'. The nourishment of idle serving-men at lavish episcopal and prelatical tables had long been a concern of those with reforming tendencies, and Cranmer's attitude may be linked with his belief, derived from the teaching of Luther, in the efficacy of good works as the necessary fruits of faith (though not in themselves contributory to salvation).[25] This change in the understanding of the relationship between good works and salvation contributed to a fundamental redefinition of charitable giving in England after the break with Rome.

The practice of hospitality in various forms was commended by others of reforming tendencies. Hugh Latimer, in recognition of the importance of Christmas as a season of special conviviality and generous exercise of hospitality, wrote in 1531 to Sir Edward Baynton that he intended to visit his West Kington parishioners to make merry with them at that season (being ordinarily non-resident) 'lest perchance I never return to them'.[26] In his injunctions for the Cathedral priory at Worcester after the

[22] Heal, 'The Archbishops', p. 555; see also *Acts and Monuments*, vol. VIII, pp. 13, 20–2.

[23] Thompson, A.H., ed., *The Statutes of the Cathedral Church of Durham*, Surtees Society, vol. CXLIII (1929); Heal. *Hospitality*, pp. 262–3.

[24] Pole's legislation at the 1555 synod of Westminster also limited the size and style of episcopal households, as well as the number of dishes permitted at their tables.

[25] Corpus Christi College, Cambridge, ms 106 no 348, printed in Wilkins, *Concilia*, iii, p. 862, Starkey, *Dialogue*; Cranmer, *Remains*, ii, pp. 164–8; Heal, *Hospitality*, pp. 267–8; Heal, 'The Archbishops', pp. 554–5.

[26] *LP*, V, 607.

1537 visitation he required the monks to distribute surplus food to the poor each day, and to ensure that distributions were carried out in each parish where the priory held patronage.[27] At the dissolution of the monasteries, Latimer sought to redirect their wealth towards works of charity and education.[28] In 1538 he wrote to Thomas Cromwell requesting that the priory of Great Malvern should not be suppressed, but that the prior be permitted to turn the house to good purpose,

> not in 'monkrye', but for teaching, preaching, study etc., with good housekeeping, for he has always been much given to hospitality, for which he is much commended in these parts.[29]

The Royal Injunctions issued by Cromwell in 1536 and 1538 obliged non-resident parochial clergy able to spend more than £20 annually to give at least the fortieth part of their revenue publicly to the poor.[30] The enquiry into the giving of the fortieth part was the only reference to hospitality amongst the episcopal visitation articles and injunctions of the Edwardian period, and though the 1548 Royal Injunctions for Lincoln Cathedral are concerned with the charitable implications of the obligations of the residentiaries, the general Royal Injunctions of 1547 themselves made no specific mention of hospitality.[31] However, Cranmer's articles for the visitation of his diocese in the same year enquired of incumbents whether they resided in their cures and kept hospitality, 'and if they be absent, or keep no hospitality, whether they do make due distributions among the poor parishioners or not', though its place towards the end of the articles may suggest the subject to have been of less importance (or in less need of enquiry because less frequently a problem) than many of the other areas of enquiry. There is a danger in drawing conclusions from arguments *ex silencio* in visitation records, as Dr Heal has pointed out; the absence of complaints may mean that no questions were asked, reflecting the indifference of the visitors rather than the adequacy of those subject to the visitation.[32] The same matter was followed up by Hooper in his articles for Worcester diocese in 1550.[33] In a sermon given after his appointment but before his consecration, Hooper had asserted that the bishop's household should be

---

[27] *Articles and Injunctions*, pp. 13–14.
[28] Dunnan, D.S., 'The Preaching of Hugh Latimer: A Reappraisal', p. 149.
[29] *LP*, XIII, 2, 1036 (13 December 1538).
[30] *Articles and Injunctions*, p. 10; Heal, *Hospitality*, p. 262.
[31] Heal, *Hospitality*, p. 263.
[32] *Concilia*, iv, 24; Heal, *Hospitality*, pp. 244–5, 264–5. The same point is made by A.H. Thompson in *Visitations in the Diocese of Lincoln, 1517–31*, Lincoln Record Society vols. XXXIII, XXXV, XXXVII (1940–47).
[33] *Articles and Injunctions*, vol. II, p. 305.

the school or treasure-house of good ministers, to serve the word of God, and ministration of the sacraments . . . . If the fourth part of the bishopric remained unto the bishop, it were sufficient; the third part to such as should teach the good learning; the second part to the poor of the dioceses; and the other to maintain men of war for the safeguard of the commonwealth.[34]

In a work written in answer to the book of the Bishop of Winchester (Gardiner) on the sacrament of the altar, he quoted the virtues commended by St Paul in a true bishop: 'Maritus unus uxoris, vigilantia, sobrietas, modestia, temperantia, hospitalitas, &c.'[35] His exposition of the Ten Commandments developed the theme of episcopal hospitality and compared the ideal with the reality of the bishops of the day. Bishops should apply their goods to the poor; however,

> our bishops . . . apply the best part of their bishoprics to a prodigal use in their own houses, or in large fees and gifts, hospitality, and other benevolence upon the rich.

He could find nothing in the New Testament nor any bishop of the early Church who provided an example of the use of 'the goods of the Holy Ghost, the riches of the poor, the possessions given for the preservation of godly doctrine and the ministry of the church, as they do'.[36] The apostles, and their successors for 400 years, set an example for good bishops. The degeneracy of the contemporary episcopate could only be reversed by a return to scriptural models, particularly those found in the pastoral epistles: 'that bishop doth most honour unto the realm, that keepeth his household, and disposeth the same according to the form and rule of the word of God'.[37] Hooper applied this model at Gloucester, where he formed a modest episcopal household devoted to charity and the care and support of the poor, dividing the revenues of his diocese according to the traditional pattern set out in canon law. It became known as a centre for evangelism and for poor relief, though the needy that were fed at his table were expected to accept instruction in the Lord's Prayer, the creed and the commandments along with their food. The ascetic nature of his household may have been influenced by his upbringing in the strict environment of a Cistercian monastery.[38]

Among the foreign divines invited to England by Cranmer to support

---

[34] 'Fifth Sermon upon Jonas' (March 1550), *Early Writings*, p. 396.
[35] 1 Timothy 3:2: 'Married only once, watchful, sober, modest, temperate, hospitable'); 'Answer to the Bishop of Winchester's Book' (1547), *Early Writings*, p. 245.
[36] 'A Declaration of the Ten holy commandments' (1549), *Early Writings*, p. 397.
[37] *Ibid.*, p. 398.
[38] *Acts and Monuments*, vol. VI, p. 644; Heal, *Hospitality*, pp. 266–7; Heal, 'The Archbishops', p. 553; Heal, *Of Prelates and Princes*, p. 166.

the Reformation, Martin Bucer was notable for the household which he had kept at Strassburg while supervisor of the Reformed Church there. Peter Martyr had direct experience of Bucer's hospitality while fleeing from Italy and the consequences of his apostasy in 1542. His establishment seemed to Martyr to be

> a house of hospitality – such usual entertainment giveth he towards strangers, who are constrained to travel for the Gospel and for Christ's cause.

The spirit and body were together refreshed in an atmosphere of sobriety and moderation which contrasted sharply with many contemporary episcopal households. He seemed to take seriously the teaching of the canonists that wealth was custodial, and should be employed for the poor and needy. Martyr was led to the conclusion that Bucer represented the very image and model of a bishop, of the sort found in the primitive Church.[39]

The tradition of spending most of the revenues of the see of Canterbury on hospitality continued after the appointment of Reginald Pole, though descriptions of his practice conform with the model of asceticism applied to both his predecessors. In Pole's case, however, the description may have been a more accurate depiction of reality rather than the result of rhetorical conventions. Pole sought to encourage virtuous living in his clergy as equally important to preaching as a form of witness, and desired households to be sober, pious and charitable. He wished prelates to abstain from luxury, rather keeping an honest household, distributing as much as possible to the poor. In this, he was probably influenced by his close friend and associate Contarini whose 1517 treatise on the episcopal office had advocated the avoidance of gluttony and the exercise of hospitality to the needy as important features of the organization of the bishop's household.[40] Among the canons of the national synod held under Pole's presidency at Westminster in 1555–56 were certain proposals regarding the episcopal household, many of which were drawn directly from the practice of Gian Matteo Giberti, Bishop of Verona. The fifth decree of the synod made example of life a type of preaching. As such, bishops were to live strict and exemplary lives, be modest in dress (silk, for instance, was proscribed) and in the size and style of their

---

[39] Gorham, G.C., ed., *Gleanings of a Few Scattered Ears during the Reformation* (London, 1857), pp. 21–2. Calvin studied under Bucer from 1538 to 1541; his master's influence may be detected in his later writings on church government. Calvin in his turn exercised an influence over English ecclesiastical organization through his correspondence with Edward VI and Protector Somerset. Hooper, too, was in Strassburg during Bucer's superintendence. Bucer's influence upon the English Church had begun well before his arrival in Cambridge in 1549.

[40] Contarini, *De officio episcopi*, in Olin, *The Catholic Reformation*, p. 94.

households. They were required to be 'content with just so many attendants as are needed for the management of the cure entrusted to them, the government of their households, and the daily uses of life'. They should not serve more than three or four dishes at their tables, and should have Scripture or other edifying works read at mealtimes, following the monastic model, so as to avoid idle chatter. Surplus revenues were to be spent on the poor and on supporting young scholars.[41] In his Legatine decrees Pole did not directly address the question of hospitality, though he treated non-residence and lack of hospitality as a serious issue in his 1555 Canterbury visitation, and returns from the parishes show that sixteen complaints were made that hospitality was not kept.[42] There is some evidence that other Marian bishops sought to ensure that the practices of residence and of hospitality were being kept. Bonner's articles for the 1554 visitation of the diocese of London are a clear example. Hospitality and residence appear high on his list of enquiries, and are seen as complementary. Rather than enquiring about the division of parochial revenues, they seek to establish a threefold model for the relief of the poor, by example, by teaching and by alms.[43]

The practice of hospitality by the holders of episcopal office, as of any pastoral cure, was to a great extent taken for granted as an essential feature of the office. The scarcity of reference to it by the bishops, whether advocating its practice or investigating its absence, may signify either a general lack of importance associated with hospitality or, more likely, an acceptance of its practice as normal and necessary as a part of the pastoral office. The theory upon which the exercise of hospitality was based remained constant throughout the period despite the closure of the canon law faculties at Oxford and Cambridge.[44] The principal change which affected the way in which hospitality could be exercised by the bishops came with the removal of clerical celibacy in the early years of the reign of Edward VI.

The 1549 *Act to take away all positive Laws against Marriage of Priests* (2 and 3 Edward VI, c.21, repealed by 1 Mary, Stat.2, c.2) authorized a practice which had been advocated by many Reformers (and practised

---

[41] Bray, ed., *The Anglican Canons, 1529–1947*, pp. 106–9; Hughes, *The Reformation in England*, vol. II, p. 234; Hughes, *Rome and the Counter-Reformation*, pp. 76–80.
[42] Heal, *Hospitality*, pp. 268–9, 287, citing Lambeth Palace Library ms VG4/2.
[43] Wilkins, *Concilia*, iv, p. 105; Heal, *Hospitality*, p. 268.
[44] The closures seem to have had little impact in practice; as a result of the interconnectedness of civil and canon law, knowledge of one in the sixteenth century led almost inevitably to study of the other. Indeed, it is by no means certain that the study of canon law ceased at Oxford and Cambridge with the formal closure of the faculties, and manuscript evidence suggests that some academic study of canon law may well have continued into the seventeenth century. Helmholz, R.H., *Roman Canon Law in Reformation England* (Cambridge, 1990), pp. 151–3.

by a number) for some years. Robert Ferrar defended clerical marriage with such frequency in his sermons to his flock at St Davids (even though many of his clergy had previously been in *de facto* 'marriages' before the passing of the Act) that his hearers complained that they 'wearied with hearing one tale'.[45] The marriage of the higher clergy of the English Church was a source of particular controversy throughout the period. The majority of Marian deprivations were for marriage, not for invalid ordination under the new Ordinal or for other associations with reforming activity; it has been suggested that many would have remained in their benefices and conformed with the theology and ceremonial of the day had the authorities not been so strict to prosecute married clergy.[46] On the other hand, the penalties imposed upon married priests were less severe than for other crimes, suggesting perhaps that incontinence was not considered to pose a direct political or religious threat, and many deprived Marian clergy were given other livings after separating from their wives, in accordance with Queen Mary's instructions to her bishops.[47] In Wales, the number of deprivations for marriage was unexpectly high. In the 1530s the clergy of the diocese of Bangor had argued that their 'hearth companions' were necessary for the provision of the hospitality which their parishioners expected of them, and no doubt many took the opportunity to regularize their long-standing relationships. It seems that the reimposition of compulsory celibacy caused more upheaval among the Welsh clergy than any other change during the sixteenth century.[48]

Fisher had condemned the Reformed doctrine on the freedom of the clergy to marry as early as 1526. In a sermon preached before a number of abjured Lutheran heretics he expounded the teaching that there are three manners or states of life: the lowest being the married state, the middle state, widowhood, and the highest, virginity. The three states correspond to the promise of an increase in fruit of thirtyfold, sixtyfold and the hundredfold for those who follow Christ. Examples of the highest state include our Saviour himself, Mary his mother, and St John the Evangelist. The Lutherans turned this order upside down; those

---

[45] Williams, *Wales, c.1415–1642*, p. 297.

[46] Dickens, *The Marian Reaction in the Diocese of York*, Part 1, p. 16; the suggestion is made by M.L. Zell, in 'The Personnel of the Clergy in Kent, in the Reformation Period', *English Historical Review*, 89 (1974), pp. 513–33; evidence from other parts of the country (for instance, Dickens, 'Robert Parkyn's Narrative of the Reformation', *English Historical Review*, 62 [1947], pp. 58–83) suggests that this observation is probably valid for much or all of the English Church.

[47] *Articles and Injunctions*, vol. II, p. 327; Grieve, H.E.P., 'The Deprived Married Clergy in Essex, 1553–61', *Transactions of the Royal Historical Society* (1940), pp. 142–5; O'Day, *The English Clergy*, p. 29.

[48] Sheils, W.J., *The English Reformation 1530–1570* (Harlow, 1989), p. 5; Williams, *Wales, c.1415–1642*, p. 302.

consecrated to celibacy or virginity forsook their religion and their vows. Luther himself was one of the worst examples, having broken his own vows to marry a nun.[49] After Fisher's death and the break from Rome, the discipline of clerical celibacy continued to be enforced in the English Church under Henry VIII. A number of Reformers, both in England and on the Continent, sought to change the King's mind on the matter. Support came from Heinrich Bullinger, who proposed clerical (and especially episcopal) marriage in his 1538 treatise *De episcoporum institutione et functione*, which he had addressed to King Henry VIII:

> The office of bishop is a holy way of life from God. Now marriage is also a holy estate instituted by God. What then prevents the use of this holy estate to one who is in that holy office?[50]

He continued with an argument from the account of the Council of Nicea by the fifth-century Church historian Sozomen, that the Council did not require married bishops, priests, deacons and subdeacons to separate from their wives before ordination, on the grounds that the Apostles did not separate from their wives. However, the King remained a constant opponent of clerical marriage, much to the inconvenience and discomfort of episcopal spouses. His displeasure was expressed in the margin of the presentation copy of Bullinger's work, against the irrelevance of the above argument that both marriage and the episcopate were instituted by God.[51] His opposition, which Professor Scarisbrick attributes as much to a fear that clerical marriage would exacerbate the nepotism which existed even with a celibate clergy, found expression in the preamble to the Act of Six Articles, where the requirement was raised in status from what was generally considered a matter of discipline to that of divine ordinance.[52] It was not until the reign of his son that bishops and priests were permitted to marry. It seems that, with the notable exception of Wolsey, in the early sixteenth century the bishops of

---

[49] *A sermon had at Paulis*, sig.G–Giiij.

[50] Bullinger, *De episcoporum*, fol.94v.

[51] The presentation copy of Bullinger's *De episcoporum* in the British Library has the shelf mark 1010.c.3; the title page is inscribed 'POTENTISS. REGI ANGLIAE DOMINO SUO CLEMENTISS. H. BULLINGERUS. D.D.' The King's annotation is in the margin of fol.94v, and is the only manuscript marginal note in the copy. See Plate VIII.

[52] During the passage of the Act through Parliament, opposition to the view that celibacy was a matter of divine ordinance came from Cranmer, Shaxton, Latimer, Barlow, Hilsey and the abbots of Gloucester and Westminster. Goodrich was undecided, while the rest of the Lords Spiritual (except Rowland Lee, who was absent) believed that the marriage of priests was contrary to divine law. *LP* XIV (i), 1065; Redworth, G., 'A Study in the Formulation of Policy: The Genesis and Evolution of the Act of Six Articles', *Journal of Ecclesiastical History*, 37 (1986), pp. 59–60; Scarisbrick, *Henry VIII* (London, 1968), pp. 540–2.

the English Church had a high regard for their own chastity.[53] As the ideas of Continental reformers began to permeate the realm, and certain senior churchmen had direct experience of married priests while carrying out diplomatic missions, so the earlier solid observance began to waver. Cranmer (who had been married before, while still in minor orders, his first wife dying in childbirth) married the niece of the Lutheran Osiander in 1532 while on an embassy to the court of Charles V. At the time he was in priest's orders, and therefore subject to the law of celibacy. It has been suggested that he may have felt able to set aside the law on the basis of 'an untidy *cuius regio eius religio* justification', as the laws of the province where he was at the time permitted the marriage of priests.[54] It seems that the King had no knowledge of Cranmer's marriage when he appointed him Archbishop of Canterbury, though by 1543 Cranmer had confessed, and with Henry's tacet approval recalled his wife from her family in Germany where he had sent her for safety four years earlier.[55] William Barlow's son (also William) was born while his father was Bishop of St Davids; he later became Archdeacon of Salisbury. Barlow also left five daughters, all of whom were married to bishops. Another bishop who seems to have married during the latter years of the reign of Henry VIII was Robert Ferrar, one-time chaplain to Cranmer, who succeeded his patron Barlow as Bishop of St Davids.

Marriage was often considered a proof of sincere commitment to the Reformed cause in those who had renounced monastic vows. The marriage of Luther, the former monk, has been noted. Peter Martyr, formerly a member of the Canons Regular of the Lateran, like Cranmer married twice (his first wife died in 1553); he spent most of his married life in Oxford, where on his installation as a Canon of Christ Church took up residence with his wife; she and the wife of Richard Cox, the Dean, became the first women ever to reside in any hall or college in Oxford.[56] Another married former religious, John Hooper, wrote from Strassburg early in King Edward's reign supporting the practice of episcopal marriage. Writing in 1547, the year in which he had entered marriage himself, he supported the view from 1 Timothy (3:2) that amongst the virtues commended in a true bishop should be included that he be 'maritus unus uxoris'.[57] Towards the end of the reign of

---

[53] Wolsey is the only bishop in the period covered by this study who is known to have fathered a child (Thomas Winter) outside wedlock. Marshall, 'Attitudes', p. 205.

[54] MacCulloch, D., 'Two Dons in Politics: Thomas Cranmer and Stephen Gardiner, 1503–1533', *The Historical Journal*, 37, 1 (1994), p. 21.

[55] Guy, *Tudor England*, p. 181; Ridley, J., *Thomas Cranmer* (Oxford, 1962), pp. 131–53

[56] McNair, *Peter Martyr in Italy*, pp. 285–6. Martyr's wife was noted by Foxe for her generosity toward the poor; *Acts and Monuments*, vol. VIII, pp. 296–7.

[57] Literally 'the husband of one wife'; 'Answer to the Bishop of Winchester's Book' (1547), *Early Writings*, p. 245.

Edward VI John Ponet wrote a book on the lawfulness of priests' marriage, recognizing perhaps a certain popular reluctance to accept the innovation. Ponet himself was the subject of an unfortunate matrimonial incident when in July 1551 he was noted as having divorced the wife of a Nottingham butcher whom he had married illegally.[58] The Archbishop of York, Robert Holgate, later claimed to have been compelled into matrimony in order to demonstrate his commitment to the Reformed cause.[59] Neither of Henry's daughters was in favour of clerical marriage, and while Elizabeth was able only to express distaste for the practice (or unwilling to go further), Mary was able to enforce its proscription. In this she had the firm support of conservatives like James Brooks, who preached against clerical marriage at Paul's Cross in 1553, and who was rewarded with the see of Gloucester the following year. The influence of the 1536 commission of cardinals (which had included Pole and Contarini) only began to be felt in England after the accession of Mary and the restoration of communion with the see of Rome. Their report to Pope Paul III stated that the bishop or parish priest should reside 'as a shepherd with his flock', and not be absent except for some grave reason 'because they are the bridegrooms of the church entrusted to their care'.[60] The model of the bishop wedded to his see was one held by many exemplary bishops, including John Fisher. The episcopal ring, placed on the hand at consecration, was a symbol of the wedding of the bishop to his particular church, and reflected the image of Christ wedded to the Church. The model ceased to be appropriate when episcopal wives were taken, contradicting the image of the bishop wedded exclusively to his see, and perhaps even suggesting a type of bigamy on the part of the married bishop. Later, however, in the reign of Edward VI, clerical marriage was permitted and even encouraged. As a result, when the former discipline was restored under Mary, the marital status of the bishops who had taken advantage of the change in law became a serious impediment to the exercise of episcopal office. The bishops knew well that St Paul's description of an ideal bishop in his first letter to Timothy saw him as 'maritus unus uxoris'. While supporters of clerical marriage took this as a proof text that celibacy was contrary to the scripture, opponents of the practice had the traditional model of the bishop wedded to his see which also found support in Scripture in the depiction of the Church as the bride of Christ. By identifying the relationship of Christ and the universal Church with the bishop's relationship to the particular church in his charge, the ideal from 1 Timothy could be upheld.

---

[58] Strype, *Ecclesiastical Memorials*, vol. II, part 2, p. 54. For an example of popular discontent, see Dickens, 'Robert Parkyn's Narrative of the Reformation', pp. 58–83.
[59] Dickens, *The English Reformation*, p. 274.
[60] Consilium . . . de emendanda ecclesia, in Olin, *The Catholic Reformation*, p. 189.

A number of bishops in office at the accession of Queen Mary lost their office as a result of their married state. The case of the Archbishop of York has been noted. John Harley, Bishop of Hereford, was deprived on account of marriage in 1554. Paul Bush, Bishop of Oxford, was also required to resign his bishopric on account of his marriage; proceedings against him commenced in March 1554, even though his wife had died in October 1553. However, it should be noted that deprivation from episcopal office on account of marriage was not considered to invalidate the order. John Bird, deprived from Chester for marriage, was permitted to act as suffragan to Bonner in the diocese of London along with John Hodgkin (Bishop of the suffragan see of Bedford), who was restored to his former office after he had separated from his wife and done penance. John Scory, deprived of Chichester for marriage, was also permitted to exercise his ministry within Bonner's diocese, though in 1554 he fled the realm, becoming superintendent of the English congregation of exiles at Emden.[61] After the accession of Queen Elizabeth, laws permitting the marriage of priests were once again enacted, even though the Queen's own preference (at least for her bishops) might well have been for a celibate ministry. The character of the episcopal household had altered through a greater emphasis on the place of the bishop in his diocese, and by the addition of dependent spouses and children. The changes of the previous forty years led to a decrease in the value of bishoprics, though the wholesale depredation suffered by the monasteries was never extended to them. The office of bishop still carried with it the opportunity and obligation of hospitality. The addition of a wife and family to episcopal households had a subtle effect upon the way hospitality was exercised. Episcopal dependents were naturally considered before the wider circle of friends, benefactors, servants and the poor at the gate. This did not prevent married bishops from exercising due oversight of poor relief, though the demands made upon shrinking resources by growing families left them less able to distribute relief with the degree of largesse available to their celibate predecessors. Nonetheless, despite some quite fundamental changes in the composition of their households, a number of Reforming bishops were able to exemplify the potential for effective pastoral action which still subsisted in the episcopate in its newly reformed guise.

[61] Frere, W.H, *The Marian Reaction* (London, 1896), p. 78.

Chapter Seven

EPISCOPAL ACTIVITY I: THE ERADICATION OF HERESY

The role of the bishop as the guarantor of the faith, the focus of unity, and the guardian against heresy and schism, is one which has a long history. As early as the third century, Cyprian, Bishop of Carthage, wrote to Cornelius, Bishop of Rome, that

> heresies arise and schisms come to birth only because God's bishop is not obeyed, and people overlook the fact that in a church there is only one who, here and now, is deputizing for Christ as priest and judge.[1]

In his tract *De ecclesiae catholicae unitate*, he understood the bishops to be the glue which holds together the universal church. The believer knows he is part of the church because his bishop is part of the unity which forms the whole.[2] By the Middle Ages, perhaps as a result of painful experience, it had come to be accepted in many quarters that the holding episcopal office was by itself no guarantee of orthodoxy. Marsilius of Padua taught that the pope or bishops might possibly be heretics, though he did not state that there had ever been an instance of a heretical pope.[3] The writings of Augustine were prominent amongst the works of the Fathers which were consulted by those who actively sought the reform of the Church. To bishops presented with the presence of heresy in their charges, Augustine was important as a model for the resident bishop who countered heretics by force as well as by argument. The active prosecution and elimination of heresy was a function primarily of the juridical power of the Church. Heretics were seen as a danger to the stable order of society and a threat to secular authority, and the condemned heretic was handed over to the secular power for execution of sentence. Heresy trials could only be conducted by those with ordinary jurisdiction, namely bishops and inquisitors. In England

---

[1] Cyprian to Cornelius, *De ecclesiae catholicae unitate*, ed. and trans. Bévenot, M. (Oxford, 1971), p. 113.
[2] Hall, S.G., *Doctrine and Practice in the Early Church* (London, 1991), pp. 89–90.
[3] *Defensor pacis*, p. 142.

from the 1490s onwards heresy was included in the jurisdiction of those diocesan officials who could be regarded as ordinaries by virtue of holding their commission 'generaliter', covering the whole diocese.[4] The means by which episcopal control was ordinarily effected was the visitation, an organized tour of inspection of the diocese, and which had for centuries been an important feature of ecclesiastical organization. During such visitations all lesser jurisdictions were inhibited, and the bishop exercised power in person or through specially appointed individuals.[5]

In the ordinary visitation of a parish church the visitor was primarily concerned with the fabric and with matters of discipline (clerical and lay). An inventory was taken (often prepared beforehand) of the ornaments, vestments and books, an inspection made of the fabric of the church, the baptistery and the cemetary, and inquiries made of parochial lands and sources of income for the clergy. The visitor would also seek to establish that the discipline of the Church was being upheld. As part of the formal liturgical functions associated with the visitation, the visitor (if a bishop) would administer confirmation. The whole process of parochial visitation had become such a matter of routine that most of the documents of the period follow a standard formal legal pattern. This is less the case with the visitation of cathedral chapters and especially of monasteries, where the latter institutions provide the larger part of such records in the later Middle Ages, usually relating to specific defects in the conduct of the house where a formal document of correction was issued. The visitation of monastic houses continued throughout the period of Reformation up to the point where royal visitation took over, and effectively was used as the formal process whereby the monasteries were ultimately dissolved in the later 1530s. Indeed, the bishops of Henry VIII seem to have been assiduous in carrying out this duty, and Cranmer noted that the dioceses in his province were being duly visited by their ordinaries.[6] The coming of the royal supremacy and the advent of the royal visitation from 1535 led to a radical change in the use to which visitations were put, becoming a tool for the establishment of the new orthodoxy which replaced the former dependence on custom and the canon law of the Roman Church. This coincided with a period of general uncertainty as to the extent to which the bishop's authority derived from the office itself, or from a higher authority (formerly the pope, now apparently the king). As a result, visitation records after 1535 become more varied, and move away from the use of common forms and

---

[4] Davis, J.F., *Heresy and Reformation in the South-East of England, 1520–1559*, Royal Historical Society Studies in History Series vol. XXXIV (London, 1983), p. 6.
[5] Churchill, *Canterbury Administration*, vol. I, p. 131.
[6] *Articles and Injunctions*, vol. I, pp. 117–18.

standard records, thus becoming more useful for the process of determining the specific concerns of the visitors themselves, for promoting their particular doctrinal positions.

The spread of Lutheran teaching in England in the 1520s provoked a significant response from many of the bishops, while at the same time proving itself to be a source of inspiration for many future bishops. The meetings of reform-minded individuals said to have taken place in the White Horse Tavern in Cambridge included Elizabeth's first archbishop, Matthew Parker, while several future diocesans appointed under Henry, Edward and Elizabeth (amongst them, Latimer, Ridley and Coverdale) were also in Cambridge at the time of the meetings. It is possible that Cranmer may not, as is often thought, have taken part in the meetings. The basis of knowledge about the meetings is a single reference in Foxe, who is also quite specific about which colleges the regular members came from, and Jesus College is not one of these. Equally, attendance at the meetings did not necessarily lead to commitment to the cause of Reformation; Stephen Gardiner, one of the most conservative of Henry VIII's bishops, admitted in 1545 that he had been present at the meetings, perceiving them at that time to be without malice, discussions between men of some learning of a sort with which Gardiner was familiar at Cambridge. It is interesting to note that of the two, Gardiner rather than Cranmer was the one who showed more interest in reform thought during his university years, while there is no evidence to suggest that either man held unorthodox theological views, at least before 1532.[7]

The episcopal response to the new heresy was led by Wolsey. In 1521, by virtue of his legatine authority, he sent instructions to all the English bishops that any books or manuscripts which contained Luther's teaching should be delivered up to the bishop of the diocese, who should send them to Wolsey, reminding them of the forty-two Lutheran errors which had been condemned a year earlier by Pope Leo X. In May 1521 he presided over a public burning of heretical books at Paul's Cross in London, at which John Fisher preached.[8] Henry Standish, Bishop of St Asaph, was one of Wolsey's examiners of heretics in 1525, and took part in the trials of Thomas Bilney and others in 1527 and 1531. Cuthbert Tunstall, though not by nature a persecutor of heretics, issued warnings in 1524 and 1525 to a gathering of London booksellers about distributing heretical literature. In 1527 he commenced a visitation of London diocese with his Vicar General, with the particular purpose of

[7] MacCulloch, 'Two Dons in Politics', pp. 7–8, 17–18; Haigh, *English Reformations*, p. 58.
[8] Strype, *Ecclesiastical Memorials*, vol. I, part 1, pp. 55–6; Haigh, *English Reformations*, p. 57.

detecting heretics and heretical books, though he tended to be as lenient as he could with heretics themselves.[9] He also commissioned Thomas More in 1528 to reply in English to Protestant pamphlets, intending by this to counter heretical writings by orthodox books. As the only bishop on the bench at the time to have had first-hand experience of the Reformation in Germany (he had been present at Worms in 1520–21), he laid particular stress on the dangers of Lutheranism, a concern which he shared with William Warham.[10] Episcopal approval for newly imported books was required from the autumn of 1524, which could be obtained only from Wolsey, the Archbishop of Canterbury (Warham), and the Bishops of London (Tunstall) and Rochester (Fisher).[11] On 24 May 1530 a list of proscribed books and heresies was published under the auspices of the Archbishop of Canterbury. After the conservative reaction of the later Henrician period symbolized by the Act of Six Articles, the prohibition of writings deemed heretical was again an important part of the process of eradicating the unorthodox. Bonner's 1542 list of prohibited books included all the works of Luther and Calvin. The same concern was exhibited in the Marian Church, where the decrees of the 1556 synod required all books to be published under the bishop's *imprimatur*, a method of control decreed in the Fourth Session of the Council of Trent (8 April 1546).[12]

Foxe considered John Longland to be 'incited with his own fierceness' in the prosecution of heretics after studying the Bishop's early registers.[13] It is known that he personally examined some 350 heretics in 1521 and 1522, as a result of which four burnings took place. His intention appears to have been to make a strong impression on his diocese from the beginning, at just the time when Lutheran ideas were beginning to spread widely. He seems to have exercised a high degree of control over the spread of heresy, by control of preaching and swift reaction to any threat to his authority or to the faith of the Church. The diocese of Lincoln was large and unwieldy, though the ports of Lincolnshire were not a notable channel of heretical book smuggling. For much of Longland's episco-

---

[9] As, for instance, at the trial of Bilney. It has recently been argued by Glyn Redworth that Tunstall was the main driving force behind the Act of Six Articles, which supports the view that his leniency derived from his humanist background rather than from any covert leanings towards unorthodox doctrines. Redworth, 'A Study in the Formulation of Policy', p. 45; Walker, G., 'Saint or Schemer? The 1527 Heresy Trial of Thomas Bilney Reconsidered', *Journal of Ecclesiastical History*, 40 (1989), pp. 221, 228; McConica, *English Humanists*, p. 73; Chester, *Latimer*, p. 30.
[10] Thompson, 'The Pastoral Work of the English and Welsh Bishops', pp. 126–7, 129.
[11] McConica, *English Humanists*, p. 73.
[12] Hughes, *Rome and the Counter-Reformation*, p. 77; *Conciliorum oecumenicorum decreta*, pp. 664–5; *Canons and Decrees of the Council of Trent*, p. 19.
[13] *Acts and Monuments*, vol. IV, p. 242.

pate, before the reorganization of dioceses between 1540 and 1545, it included the University of Oxford, while the Archdeaconry of Hunting-don lay in close proximity to the city of Cambridge in the diocese of Ely. The more conservative reputation of Oxford may be accounted for in part by his long connections with the University, as chancellor, and visitor of many colleges.[14] Warham praised Longland for his 'fervent zeal for the reformation to be made as well of heretycall doctrynes as of mysbehavior in manners', and asked that he print more of his sermons.[15] The prominence of Longland and Tunstall amongst the bishops con-cerned with the elimination of heresy in the 1520s and early 1530s should be seen in the context provided by a remark of Thomas More, writing in 1533. In his opinion, if anyone were to survey the English dioceses it would be hard to find four persons punished for heresy in five years in any diocese, except for Lincoln and London, the dioceses of those two bishops.[16]

John Fisher, Bishop of Rochester, like Longland a theologian by training, tended to emphasize the role of the bishop as shepherd rather than as ruler or judge.[17] In the dedication to the Reader from the *Assertionis Lutheranae confutatio* he considered that his duty as a bishop and shepherd was to help weaker souls where their faith was in doubt. The blood of God's flock would be on his hands if he failed to protect it from the ravening wolves ('lupina rabie') by his negligence.[18] Fisher considered the bishop to have a central role in the elimination of heresy, and that one of the principal reasons that the episcopal office was established was that its holder should be for his diocese the guarantor of orthodoxy, an opinion strongly reminiscent of Cyprian. Indeed, the proximity of the Kent ports to his diocese meant that Fisher was required to spend more of his time searching out heresy than many bishops, particularly those with sees in the more conservative north of the country.[19] Heresy cases almost always attracted Fisher's personal attention, and he placed considerable emphasis on the visitation of his diocese. Unlike many of his fellow bishops, he was personally involved in most of the visitations.[20] Fisher himself was to suffer execution, on 22 June 1535, for his opposition to the King's marriage and the royal supremacy, one of the first victims of the new Henrician orthodoxy. Although Fisher was the only diocesan bishop to pay with his life for

[14] Bowker, *The Henrician Reformation*, pp. 181–2.
[15] Thompson, 'The Pastoral Work of the English and Welsh Bishops', pp. 126, 129; LAO Episcopal Register XXVI, fol.205.
[16] Haigh, *English Reformations*, pp. 52–3.
[17] Thompson, 'The Bishop in his Diocese', in Bradshaw and Duffy, p. 68.
[18] *Assertionis*, fol.2r.
[19] Thompson, 'The Bishop in his Diocese', p. 69.
[20] *Ibid.*, p. 74.

opposition to the Henrician supremacy, he was not alone amongst his brother bishops in considering that the King's actions amounted to heresy; John Stokesley later regretted his own lack of courage, wishing that he had been strong enough to stand with Fisher in the face of advancing heresy.[21]

Opinions differ as to the extent to which the University of Cambridge was a hotbed of heretical ideas in the 1520s and 1530s. Certainly, in 1555, it was to Oxford that the three celebrated former bishops and Cambridge men were taken for trial, suggesting that this perception of Cambridge had currency even then. The University was situated in the diocese of Ely where the bishop up to the break with Rome was Nicholas West, a civil lawyer, statesman and diplomat. He was not at first a hunter of heretics; the role had been forced upon him by developments in his diocese, largely but not exclusively emanating from Cambridge. In June 1528 at a synod held at Barnwell in the diocese of Ely, West, though a supporter of humanists and the new learning, attacked 'biblia secundum novam interpretationem', probably because of his concern at the spread of Reformed ideas in his diocese through the medium of the printed word.[22]

The political and religious changes of the 1530s led also to changes in the procedure for heresy cases. From 1533, heresy trials could only be conducted after an indictment in common law or on the evidence of two witnesses.[23] However, the procedure was hedged round by royal writs; the imperial ambassador speculated that the imprisonment for praemunire of Richard Nykke, Bishop of Norwich, resulted from his burning of Thomas Bilney without the King's writ.[24] The more usual manner of procedure was by commission or statute. Cranmer's register contains five commissions, issued under Cromwell's signature, aimed principally against Anabaptists and sacramentarians.[25] During the period in question, the definition of what was heretical and what was not underwent a series of drastic changes. Cranmer suggested in a paper to Henry VIII that many truths formerly considered heresies had been brought to light through the diversity of opinion which had come to exist. Specifically, he referred to the change in understanding of the authority of the bishop of Rome, and raised other questions on free will, purgatory, the invocation of the saints and other contentious matters, though leaving them unanswered.[26] Despite his plea for openness in theological discussion,

---

[21] Duffy, *The Stripping of the Altars*, p. 592.
[22] Chester, *Latimer*, pp. 23–5. The interview with Wolsey is recorded in BL Harleian ms 422, fols.84–6, which once belonged to John Foxe.
[23] 25 Henry VIII c.14; Davis, *Heresy*, p. 12.
[24] *LP*, VII, 171.
[25] Davis, *Heresy*, p. 14.
[26] BL Cotton ms Cleopatra E.v. fol.51r.

in 1538 'An acte abolishing diversity in Opynions' was passed, which summarized orthodoxy in six articles, any deviation from which led to trial before royal commissioners by way of accusation by two honest witnesses or indictment before twelve jurors. By the Act, which came into force in 1539, conservative doctrine was reimposed upon the English Church. The guarantor and focus of the Church's unity was to be found in the supreme Headship of the King, by whose authority the Articles were enforced. In this way, the Supremacy took on a role which had formerly been exercised only by the holders of episcopal office or their delegates. As a result of the Act, a number of reform-minded individuals sought exile on the Continent. Among them was John Hooper, who left England in 1539, and lived for a time in Strassburg where he married in 1547. He spent the next two years with Heinrich Bullinger in Zürich, then returned in 1549 to the more favourable conditions which prevailed under Edward VI. Casualties of the Act were to be found even amongst the bishops; Latimer and Shaxton were forced to resign from their sees by Cromwell.[27] Shaxton had earlier come under the eye of Richard Nykke; he is mentioned in a letter of the Bishop (16 June 1531) as one of the book agents in his diocese, and as having been accused by the Vice-Chancellor of the University of Cambridge of preaching heresy in a sermon *ad clerum* on Ash Wednesday.[28] In a letter written in 1530, Nykke had claimed that the two major sources of heretical ideas were books which had infected people living near the sea, and Gonville Hall in Cambridge.[29] Shaxton was a member of Gonville Hall, as was William Repps, Nykke's successor at Norwich. Furthermore, soon after he became Bishop of Salisbury, Shaxton had been in conflict with Cromwell over a controversy between the Bishop and city of Salisbury. Shaxton had mentioned a grant of Edward IV to the bishop of Salisbury which stated that the mayor there was the bishop's mayor, and the citizens the bishop's citizens. Cromwell reproved him for this, stating that all the power he had depended on the confirmation of the present king. Shaxton was forced to acknowledge this, and further, to admit that he relied very little upon such grants for his power.[30] In Latimer's case, his resignation in 1539 was taken as a protest against the will of the King; he was imprisoned for several months and prevented from preaching for the remainder of the reign.[31] The Act was modified in 1543 by 35 Henry VIII

[27] Chester, *Latimer*, p. 149.
[28] *LP*, V, 297.
[29] Elsewhere he said 'I hear no clerk that hath comen lately out of that college but savoureth of the frying pan, though he speak never so holily.' Venn, J., *Caius College* (London, 1901), p. 34; Houlbrooke, R.A., *Church Courts and the People during the English Reformation, 1520–1570* (Oxford, 1979), p. 226.
[30] Strype, *Ecclesiastical Memorials*, vol. I, part 1, p. 335.
[31] *Ibid.*, p. 151.

c.5 to prevent malicious accusations by requiring all future trials to take place by indictment.[32]

The Bishops' Book of 1537 made a distinction between *potestas ordinis* and *potestas iurisdictionis*. Episcopal jurisdiction was divided into three parts, the first of which related to the bishop's duty 'to rebuke and reprehend sin, and to excommunicate the manifest and obstinate sinners'. The separation of those who persevere in their sin from the sacramental life of the Church was not only 'a medicine to the offenders themselves, but also an example and satisfaction unto those persons which were before with their said manifest sins offended'. The authority of the episcopal office to correct sin was qualified in two ways. It extended to the use of the word only, violent force or physical means being expressly excluded. Further, it was noted that bishops were not bound to exercise their jurisdictional power by any commandment of God in a mechanistic way, but that they should moderate the execution of their right to excommunicate if they thought that the contrary would be unhelpful to the offender or disturb the peace of the Church.[33] The medieval coercive *potestas iurisdictionis* was to be interpreted in the light of the gospel.

The members of the 1540 Commission on matters of doctrine held divergent views on the matter of excommunication. Cranmer believed that bishops and priests were neither commanded nor forbidden by Scripture to excommunicate, but where the laws of a region give them authority to excommunicate, there they ought to use it 'insuche crymes as the lawes haue suche authoritie in'. On the other hand, where the laws of the region forbid them, they have no authority at all; in addition, the law may allow even laymen ('thei that be no priestes') to excommunicate.[34] This is fully in accord with Cranmer's understanding at the time of the civil magistracy as the source of episcopal power and authority. The other commissioners are reported to have disagreed over the ability of laymen to excommunicate. Some considered that the authority to excommunicate had been given only to the apostles and their successors, while others believed that laymen might excommunicate 'yf thei be appoynted by the high ruler', in some cases wth the qualification that the power of excommunication 'was giuen vnto the churche, and vnto suche as the churche shall institute', locating the authority in the hands

---

[32] Davis, *Heresy*, p. 16. The trial of Anne Askew in 1546 is an example of the use of heresy proceedings to pursue political ends; it was the desire of the laymen Wriothesley and Rich to implicate Queen Katharine Parr in Askew's heresy that led them to rack her, with their own hands, in the Tower, even though the ecclesiastical investigations into her heresy had been concluded. An account of the trial is in *Acts and Monuments*, vol. V, pp. 537–51.

[33] Lloyd, *Formularies*, pp. 108–9.

[34] BL Cotton ms Cleopatra E.v. fol.59v.

of the Church while allowing it to delegate that authority to lay persons. Ironically, the three bishops on the commission who admitted the right of excommunication to duly authorized laity were deprived of ecclesiastical office on the accession of a lay person, Queen Elizabeth, some twenty years later.

With the 1547 repeal legislation, heresy proceedings as formerly understood largely disappeared, with only a few cases remaining, some for minor infringements of discipline and others, more serious, against Anabaptists. The preaching of the more extreme Reformers attracted attention from radicals whose opinions included the rejection of the incarnation, the promotion of antinomianism, and even the denial of Christ's saving work. Large numbers of Anabaptists attended Hooper's daily lectures in 1549, much to his great disquiet expressed in a letter to Bullinger of June that year.[35] It was perhaps ironic, given Hooper's fear of the consequences of Anabaptist teaching, that in the controversy over the use of episcopal vestments at his consecration, he was himself accused of Anabaptism by Ridley.[36] The elimination of the Pope's religion during the reign of King Edward often took on the characteristics and borrowed the language of earlier persecutions of Lollard and Protestant heresy. Cranmer's articles for the 1548 visitation of Canterbury diocese enquired whether the parish clergy who had encouraged pilgrimages, the veneration of images, or other 'such superstition, have not openly recanted and reproved the same'.[37] Clerks who could not subscribe to the Forty-Two Articles were to be considered 'unhable and recusant' if they failed to respond to instruction in the new orthodoxy, the establishment of which was the work of the Reforming bishops and their courts.[38] Many popish practices, especially the use of primers, beads, images or relics, were treated as heresies. John Hooper's 1551 Visitation Injunctions for the diocese of Gloucester ordered them to be put away and avoided in churches and private homes; anyone discovered to be using them was to be admonished to put them away and destroy them. If the clergy were unable to make their parishioners conform to this injunction, they were to be reported to Hooper: 'advertise me of their obstinacy and contempt of God's laws and the king's majesty's, by the which they [images etc.] are condemned and abolished most justly'.[39] The offence was against the laws of God and king, which were here identified with one another. However, Hooper considered that it was part of the true vocation of bishops and priests that they should 'severely use discipline and correction of indurate men's

[35] *Original Letters*, vol. I, pp. 65–6; Brigden, *London*, p. 443; Davis, *Heresy*, p. 19.
[36] Brigden, *London*, p. 466.
[37] *Articles and Injunctions*, p. 179.
[38] Davis, *Heresy*, p. 99.
[39] Hooper, *Later Writings*, pp. 135–6.

faults'.[40] The necessity for handing over the offender to the secular arm for punishment is unnecessary where the source of the Church's authority is its royal head. Hooper later made a clearer distinction between the Church's power to excommunicate and the responsibility of the secular authority after the accession of Queen Mary. In his Apology (compiled against reports that he had cursed the Queen) he stated:

> It is both against God's laws and man's, that the bishops and clergy should be judges over any subject within this realm; for it is no part of their office. They can do no more but preach God's word, and minister God's Sacraments, and excommunicate such as God's laws do pronounce worthy to be excommunicated.[41]

The role of the diocesan bishop was, for Hooper, to be found in the name itself; they are called *dioecesani*, from *dioeces* signifying 'to govern and to defend'. Bishops are called to 'govern the churches committed unto their charges, and defend them from false doctrine'.[42] Should they fail in this duty, they would be held responsible; 'as many souls as perish by their negligence or contempt of God's word, shall be required at their hands'.[43] All newly appointed bishops were required to subscribe to a number of articles in the course of their consecration according to the Ordinals of 1550 and 1552. The consecrating Archbishop was to ask the bishop-elect

> Be you ready with al faithful diligence, to banishe and driue away al erronious and straunge doctryne, contrary to god's worde, and both priuately and openly to call upon, and encourage other to the same?

and later,

> Wil you maintain and set forward (as muche as shal lie in you) quietnesse, peace, and loue, emonge al men? And suche as be unquiete, disobedyente, and criminous within your Diocesse, correcte and punishe, accordyng to suche aucthoritie, as ye haue by gods worde, and as to you shalbe committed, by the ordinaunce of thys realme?[44]

The authority of the bishop to eliminate heresy and error, and to correct wrongdoing, although derived from the Word of God, was committed to him by the laws of the realm.

During the reign of Edward VI, a number of diocesan bishops were

---

[40] Fifth Sermon upon Jonas, March 1550, Hooper, *Early Writings*, p. 504.
[41] Hooper, *Later Writings*, p. 559.
[42] 'Answer to the Bishop of Winchester's Book' (1547), *Early Writings*, p. 143.
[43] 'A godly Confession and protestacion of the christian faith' (1550), *Later Writings*, p. 91.
[44] *The First and Second Prayer-Books*, pp. 316–17.

removed from their sees as a result of their failure to conform with the new Protestant orthodoxy and to co-operate with the Crown in its establishment and furtherance. The first to be deprived was Edmund Bonner, on 1 October 1549; among his examiners was John Hooper, who was himself to suffer trial and execution for opposing the prevailing orthodoxy five years later. Bonner's deprivation was widely expected to be the first of many, as witnessed by a remark made in a letter written soon afterwards, that 'it is openly spoken that there shalbe more quondam Busshoppes yn England shortlye'.[45] Bonner was followed by Day, Gardiner and Heath, deprived of their sees in 1551, and by Tunstall whose see was dissolved by Parliament in 1552. In addition, the active practice of popery, particularly in sensitive circles, was sought out and punished. For instance, on 29 April 1551, Francis Mallet, chaplain and confessor to Princess Mary (later nominated to the vacant bishopric of Salisbury), was committed to the Tower by order of the Privy Council for celebrating Mass for the princess's household.

Popery was not the only heresy to be condemned in the reign of King Edward. In 1550 Ridley had been sufficently concerned to enquire after the teaching of radical doctrines during his visitation of London diocese.[46] In January 1551 a commission was set up, consisting of thirty-one bishops and divines including the Archbishop of Canterbury and the Bishops of Ely, London, Lincoln, Norwich and Rochester, against Anabaptists and sectaries. In a letter to his friend John Bradford, Ridley spoke of typical heresies assailing his ears:

> as some to deny the blessed Trinity, some the divinity of our Saviour Christ, some the divinity of the Holy Ghost, some the baptism of infants, some original sin, and to be infected with the errors of the Pelagians, and to re-baptize those that have been baptized with Christ's baptism already.[47]

During his last examination before the heresy commissioners on 30 June 1555, he referred to the 'detestable errors of the Anabaptists' which he and the other bishops had encountered.[48] Latimer considered that the sectarians detracted from the true presence of Christ in the eucharist, with its sacramental or spiritual nature, by seeing in the eucharist 'a bare

---

[45] Letter of Richard Scudamore to Sir Philip Hoby, 23 February 1550, *Camden Miscellany XXX*, Camden Fourth Series, Volume XXXIX (London, 1990), p. 122.
[46] *Articles and Injunctions*, p. 233: '13. Whether any do preach or affirm all things to be common, or that we ought to have no magistrates? 14. Whether any do preach or say that it is not lawful for a Christian man to swear before a judge . . .? 15. Whether any teacheth and sayeth that Christ took no Flesh and Blood of the Blessed Virgin Mary?'; all of these are characteristic doctrines held by Anabaptists of the period.
[47] *The Works of Nicholas Ridley*, ed. Christmas, H., Parker Society (Cambridge, 1843), p. 367.
[48] Ridley, *Works*, p. 265.

and naked sign'. He also objected to the pacifism found in the movement, and the denial of the magistrate's right to punish the evil-doer.[49] The five major heresy trials of Edward's reign were all of radical sectarians. The heretical views represented ranged from the anti-Trinitarian rationalism of Michael Servetus which was later to be associated with the teaching of Faustus Sozzini (Socinianism) to the libertine antinomianism of certain varieties of Anabaptism. Into the latter category came Joan Bocher, *alias* Joan of Kent, who was burned in 1549 as an abjured Lollard who had relapsed. Cranmer himself headed the commission which tried and condemned her.[50] Indeed, Cranmer seems to have been much preoccupied throughout the reign of Edward VI with the suppression and eradication of radicalism. In the final year of the reign a heresy commission (directed chiefly at Kent) was headed by him and occupied his full attention from October 1552 to February 1553.[51] Concern at Anabaptist doctrine continued into Mary's reign, where the doctrines and practices of Anabaptism appeared twice in Bonner's visitation articles for London diocese.[52]

The restoration of Catholicism and the return of the nation to full allegiance to the pope was placed by Queen Mary in the hands of her bishops. Central to this was the role of Reginald Pole, who as Archbishop of Canterbury was to be the spearhead of this process. The bishops in office in November 1554 (the month of Pole's arrival in England) had all been appointed originally during the reign of Henry VIII. Most had in the meantime been removed from their sees by deprivation or retirement under Edward VI, then restored or recalled by Mary. While loyal and able enough, there were no outstanding characters amongst them who might have the charisma to set an outstanding example of zealous and Catholic episcopacy. Furthermore, they had all been involved to some extent with support of the Henrician schism, and were required to seek personal absolution from Pole to rid them of this taint. Pole's background set him apart from his new brother-bishops of the English Church.[53] From 1513 to 1521 he had been a member of Magdalen College, Oxford, where his principal tutor had been William Latimer, friend of Colet and enthusiastic supporter of the new learning. In 1521 the King sent him to the University of Padua to complete his studies, and where he became familiar with Thomas Lupset, a classical scholar who had been educated as a boy in Colet's household, and who had assisted Erasmus in the preparation of his New Testament and edition of the letters of St Jerome. He was also acquainted with the

---

[49] Davis, *Heresy*, p. 37
[50] *Ibid.*, pp. 104–5.
[51] MacCullough, *Thomas Cranmer*, pp. 530–1.
[52] *Articles and Injunctions*, Vol. II, pp. 338, 349.
[53] Loades, *The Reign of Mary Tudor*, p. 292.

English ambassador to Venice, Richard Pace. Venice at this time was a centre for humanist endeavour, and Pole was part of a circle which included the poet Marcantonio Flaminio, and Alvise Priuli who later was to become Pole's devoted follower. Another member of the circle was Peter Martyr Vermigli who was converted to the cause of the Protestant Reformation at the time of his close association with Pole and his circle. This taint of association with a professed heretic later came to be a source of difficulty for Pole, and was to plague him to his deathbed. On his return home to England in 1526, he was pressed into service on the matter of the King's divorce and by 1530 in company with Edward Fox elicited a favourable response from the theology faculty of the University of Paris. After the death of Wolsey in November 1530 he was offered the archbishopric of York by the Duke of Norfolk acting on the King's behalf, subject only to the condition that he declare his opinion on the divorce. Pole refused, and after a difficult interview with the King at which the latter was greatly offended, he sought permission to leave the country again, which was only granted in January 1532, seven or eight months after his original request. He spent some time at Avignon where he called occasionally on the humanist Bishop of Carpentras, Jacopo Sadoleto. Settling in Padua by the end of 1532, Pole carried out a sporadic correspondence with Sadoleto as a result of his newly found concern with the study of theology. In his frequent visits to Venice, he became associated with members of the Oratory of Divine Love which had reassembled there after the sack of Rome, and was first introduced to its founder, Gian Pietro Carafa, by the Bishop of Verona, Gian Matteo Giberti. It was also during this period, between 1532 and 1535, that he developed a close association with Gasparo Contarini, under whose auspices the Oratory of Divine Love had reassembled in Venice. During this period also, his interest in sacred literature grew, and he came into contact with the renaissance of Biblical scholarship . In response to a letter from Thomas Starkey, whom the King had commissioned to elicit Pole's support for the royal supremacy, he produced in 1536 the treatise *Pro ecclesiasticae unitatis defensione*. The work is a defence of the supremacy of the pope, and is a personal attack on the King, seeking to induce him to repent and return to the unity of the Catholic Church. The appearance of the work led to the Act of Attainder against him for high treason in the Parliament of April/May 1538.[54] The following year Pole was summoned to Rome to serve on the papal commission which produced the *Consilium . . . de emendanda ecclesia*, and in December that year was created cardinal.[55]

---

[54] Fenlon, *Heresy and Obedience*, pp. 38–9; Schenk, W., *Reginald Pole, Cardinal of England* (London, 1950), pp. 71–2, 84.

[55] Gleason, *Reform Thought*, pp. 81–100; Fenlon, *Heresy and Obedience*, p. 42; Schenk, *Reginald Pole*, pp. 60–1.

Pole was a member of the commission of Cardinals summoned in 1544 to prepare for the forthcoming Council which had been summoned by Pope Paul III to assemble at Trent in March 1545, and in February 1545 was appointed as one of the three Cardinals appointed to preside over it. The opening was delayed until December 1545, and during the interim nine months Pole produced a treatise on the nature and scope of the Council, *De concilio liber*. The purpose of the Council was to clarify dogma, to reform Christendom, and to restore peace. The recovery of unity with the Lutherans and the reform of the Church had been his main preoccupations since his days at Padua.[56] The final session over which he presided, on 17 June 1546, produced decrees requiring the establishment of lectureships in Scripture and the liberal arts in each diocese, and reimposing the duty of preaching upon bishops and parish priests; preaching was defined as the chief duty of the bishops. However, Pole's health was failing, and after his final speech to the Council on 21 June he was permitted to leave Trent to recover his physical and mental health.[57] In August 1553 he was appointed papal legate to England, though for political reasons was unable to enter the country until November 1554, after the Act of Attainder against him had been lifted. His first public act was to reconcile the realm to the Catholic Church, by a process which took several days in the month of his arrival. A year later, he summoned a national synod, over which he presided, to carry into effect the reform of the English Church. Bishops were to leave aside all secular business. Despite this, Nicholas Heath, Archbishop of York, became Lord Chancellor after the death of Gardiner.[58]

The two main approaches towards heresy of the Catholic reformers, tolerance on the one hand and strict, even harsh, treatment on the other, influenced the relationship between Pole and Carafa and led an initial warmth to grow into coldness and distrust, which resulted eventually in an intense conflict between the two men. The divisions began to appear from about 1532, but came to a head in 1541 with the Ratisbon Colloquy and the dispersal of the circle of Italian *spirituali* which had formed around the Spanish reformer, Juan de Valdés. Contarini had led the Catholic representatives to the discussions with the group of Lutherans who had assembled in the presence of the Emperor Charles V at Ratisbon in April 1541. The parties to the colloquy made progress in the question of justification by faith, adopting a formula acceptable to both parties which included the idea of a twofold justification, whereby

---

[56] Fenlon, *Heresy and Obedience*, pp. 101–4.
[57] *Conciliorum oecumenicorum decreta*, pp. 667–70; *Canons and Decrees of the Council of Trent* (Fifth Session, 17 June 1546), pp. 24–8; Fenlon, *Heresy and Obedience*, pp. 123–34.
[58] Hembry, *The Bishops of Bath and Wells*, p. 128; Hughes, *The Reformation in England*, vol. II, p. 234, Hughes, *Rome and the Counter-Reformation*, pp. 76–80.

the forgiveness of sins was accomplished by the imputed justice (*iustitia imputata*) of Christ, but with positive sanctification acquired by an inherent righteousness (*iustitia inhaerens*) in the soul. The doctrine was propounded vigorously by its adherents at the Council of Trent, but was not adopted, a more comprehensive formula being defined. There was less agreement at Ratisbon, however; violent dissent over the eucharist, discipline, the place of the saints, celibacy, and monasticism as well as questions over the Council and papal supremacy, led to its dissolution scarcely a month later.[59] Contarini's methods, accompanied by the failure of the colloquy, aroused intense suspicion on the part of men like Carafa. In August 1541 Pole was appointed governor of the *Patrimonium Petri*, the largest of the papal states, with Viterbo as its seat of government. It was to Viterbo that the *spirituali* gravitated after the death of Valdés, among them two men under suspicion of heresy, Pietro Carnesecchi (executed for heresy in 1567 at Rome) and Marcantonio Flaminio, the Latin poet. After the collapse of the talks at Ratisbon, the *spirituali* led the campaign against heresy in the Italian cities. Their aim was to use persuasion and discourse, avoiding coercion; to this end, they used preachers of outstanding eloquence and spirituality. They also compiled manuals on preaching; Pole's *De modo concionandi* (1541) is now lost, but a work of the same title by Contarini survives. Ironically, as it turned out, Pole was able to obtain the services of two of the most highly sought *spirituali*, Bernardino Ochino and Peter Martyr Vermigli in his campaign against heresy. Advocates of the other, harsh approach were encouraged in July 1542 when the Roman Inquisition was re-established under the supervision of Cardinal Carafa. Carafa represented the school of thought which had a characteristic attachment to scholastic theology, and a distrust of any association with heresy or heretics.[60] They were highly disapproving of any moves towards reunion with the Lutherans and other heretics which involved anything less than their total and unquestioning submission to the Roman obedience. In the same month Ochino was recalled to Rome to take in hand the reform of the Capuchin Franciscans, of which he was General; instead, in August 1542, he and Peter Martyr fled to Switzerland and the Protestant Reformation. The grief of the Viterbo circle at their loss was compounded by the sudden death of Contarini on 24 August 1542. Pole and Carafa had by this point moved irreconcilably apart. Pole's work on preaching was condemned by the Inquisition for its aversion to scholastic theology, its attachment to faith as the sole means of salvation, and its emphasis on the pure gospel as the basis of preaching.[61] Carafa's

---

[59] Ott, *Fundamentals*, p. 252; Schenk, *Reginald Pole*, p. 102.

[60] Fenlon, *Heresy and Obedience*, p. 43.

[61] Corviersi, C., 'Compendium di processi del Santo Uffizio', *Archivio della Società Romana di Storia Patria*, III (1880), p. 284, from Fenlon, *Heresy and Obedience*, p. 67.

enthusiasm for the hunting of heresy may be shown by the fact that he fitted out a house in Rome at his own expense where the Inquisition could hold its sessions without waiting for a financial grant to arrive from the Camera Apostolica. The rift between the two men first became public with Carafa's attack on Pole during the conclave of 1549–50 which elected Julius III; Pole refuted his charges, treating Carafa as if he were a madman. The charges against Pole included not only his alleged personal heresy, but also his over-indulgence to heretics while at Viterbo; there was also a rumour (which proved to be false) that he had a daughter. The new Pope set up three commissions of cardinals to oversee the workings of the Inquisition, to reform the datary, and to supervise the workings of the Council shortly to be re-convened at Trent, Pole's name appearing on each. Carafa, not surprisingly, sat on the commission for the Inquisition; after February 1551, Pole's name no longer appeared on the list of cardinals sitting on it. By that same year, the Inquisition had begun to move against the former associates of Valdés and Pole.[62] In August 1553 Pole was appointed papal Legate to England, and arrived in the realm in November 1554.[63] The following May, Carafa was elected Pope. The outbreak of war between Spain and the papacy in September 1556 led to the recall of all papal agents in the territory of Philip II; Pole was mentioned specifically by name in the consistory of 9 April 1557 in which all legations and ministries were revoked. Furthermore, even the status of the Archbishop of Canterbury as *legatus natus* was to be revoked, an action which would have called into question the relationship between the Provinces of Canterbury and York. Robert Holgate, deprived after Mary's accession, had been appointed to York after the schism, and his successor, Nicholas Heath, may never have formally claimed the title.[64] On 21 May, Mary, on behalf of herself and Philip, wrote to the Pope to plead that England should not be left without a Legate; a further letter in the same vein followed from Pole on 25 May. Despite this, Pole was recalled to Rome (though the Queen kept from him the letter which ordered this), and the Pope appointed William Peto as Cardinal and Legate for England, though he declined the honour on

---

[62] Fenlon, *Heresy and Obedience*, pp. 230–6.

[63] Unfortunately for Pole, this was after initial enthusiasm for Mary had begun to wane, and the persecution of heretics had commenced in earnest; as Pogson aptly puts it, 'just in time to be associated with Mary as villain rather than heroine' ('Cardinal Pole – Papal Legate', p. 6).

[64] Thus Loades, *The Reign of Mary Tudor*, p. 363 note 7. It was, however, in his capacity as Archbishop of York and by that fact *legatus natus* that he consecrated Reginald Pole as Archbishop of Canterbury in March 1556. It may be that the title was never expressly claimed; the right of the Archbishop of York as Legate to consecrate the elect of the Province of Canterbury, however, seems clearly to have been exercised.

account of his great age and infirmity.[65] When Mary died in November 1558, England was without a Legate with a valid canonical mission, and possessed an Archbishop of Canterbury who was under suspicion of heresy. Had Pole survived his Queen for more than just a few hours, it is impossible to predict what the outcome might have been.

The first shot in the Marian heresy campaign was fired by James Brooks, a leading Catholic divine soon to be promoted to the episcopate, in his apology for the restoration of Catholicism preached at Paul's Cross in November 1553 and published almost immediately. In it he stressed the separation between Church and State in matters of religion as a prime source of error. The Catholic Church, he asserted, has the true sense of the Word of God, and 'hath likewise aucthoritie to iudge, and decide al matiers of controuersy in religion'.[66] Drawing on a series of images of the Church taken from Scripture, he referred to it as the mother of all the faithful who 'abhoreth al bastardes, borne of heresie and infidelitie'.[67] The image of the Church as mother was developed through the theme of the essential unity of the Church, referring to Cyprian's maxim that one cannot have God for his Father who does not have the Church for his mother. England has turned against her mother; the Church of England, 'as touching the life of liuely vnitie', is deceased and dead, both 'for lacke of the life of faith, and good belief', and 'as touchinge the life of charitie and good lyuinge'.[68] In Bonner's 1555 work, *A profitable and necessary doctrine*, the same emphasis was placed on the absolute necessity of unity. He explained the position of the Church of England before the restoration of Catholicism by quoting a passage from a sermon of Augustine, in which the Bishop of Hippo was himself quoting from Cyprian:

[65] Peto was an octogenarian Franciscan Observant of the restored house at Greenwich who had been papally provided to the see of Salisbury in 1542 after the death of Cardinal Contarini *in curia Romana*, though unable to claim the temporalities until he was again provided in 1557. The Observants were known to be sympathetic to the new learning, and supportive of Catherine of Aragon in the matter of her divorce. Cromwell had a list of fifteen Observant friars who had voluntarily entered into exile by 1538 as a consequence of the changes in religion, and at least three other exiles are known who do not feature on the list. Peto himself had been confessor to Queen Catherine and to the young Princess Mary, and had been imprisoned in 1532 for his opposition to the King's divorce, being placed in the custody of the Conventual Franciscan Henry Standish, then Bishop of St Asaph. From confinement he went into exile, where from 1544 to his return to England in 1553 he was Warden of the English Hospice in Rome. During his exile Princess Mary seems to have corresponded with him regularly. Brown, K.D., 'The Franciscan Observants in England 1482–1559', Oxford DPhil, 1986, pp. 93, 138–41, 223; Fenlon, *Heresy and Obedience*, pp. 270–1; Loades, *The Reign of Mary Tudor*, pp. 363–4, 366.

[66] Brooks, *Sermon*, sig.B.iiii,v.

[67] *Ibid.*, sig.C.iiii.

[68] *Ibid.*, sig.C.v–D.i.

> Take away saith he (meanynge S.Cypryan) the beame of the
> sonne from the body of the sonne, the vnitie of the lyght, can not
> suffer no diuision: breake a boughe from the tree, the bough so
> broken, can floryshe and budde no more: cut of the riuer from
> the spring, the ryuer so cut of, dryeth vp.[69]

Brooks, who in 1554 was made Bishop of Gloucester, as papal sub-
delegate and head of the commission for the trial of Thomas Cranmer,
made an exhortation to him after his trial and conviction as a heretic, the
purpose being ostensibly to encourage the former archbishop to repent
of his crimes.[70] Brooks reminded Cranmer that according to the tradition
of the Church, heretics could not be martyrs; 'he can not, it is not
possible, for him to be a martur: who is not in the Churche, or to come to
the kingdome'. It seems from the form of his exhortation that Brooks
understood a natural progression in the various stages, each leading to
the next, first breaking from the unity of the Catholic Church, then on to
the ultimate crime, Cranmer's final act of bad faith, open treason against
the lawful sovereign:

> You haue fallen from the vnitie of your mother the holie
> Catholicke Churche, and that by open schiscme. You haue
> fallen from the true and receyued faithe of the same Catholicke
> Churche, and that by open heresie. You haue fallen from your
> fidelitie and promisse towarde God in breaking your order and
> vowe of chastitie, and that by open apostasie. You haue fallen
> from your fidelitie and promisse towardes Goddes vicar generall
> the pope, in breaking your othe made to his holiness at your
> consecracion, and that by open periurie. You haue fallen ffrom
> your fidelitie and allegennce towardes goddes magistrate your
> prince and Sovereign Ladie the Quenes highnes, and that by open
> treason.[71]

Cranmer was the last of five bishops executed in the reign of Queen
Mary, and despite accusations of treason in some of the cases, were all
burned, the traditional method of execution for heretics. It is noteworthy
that, in this reign particularly, the crime of treason was so visibly linked
with that of heresy.

Marian bishops tended to be hesitant in applying the *ex officio*
procedures against heresy when the 1533 Act was restored on the
accession of Queen Mary. They were more prepared to act when the

---

[69] Bonner, E., *A Profitable and necessarye doctryne* (London, 1555), sig.J.iv,r, from
the exposition of the ninth article of the creed, and quoting from Augustine's sermon
clxxxi *de tempore* on the same article of the creed.
[70] BL Cotton ms Vespasian A.xxv fols.13–37. R.H. Pogson suggests that Brooks was
summing up a number of Pole's attitudes in his oration ('Cardinal Pole – Papal
Legate', p. 89).
[71] *Ibid.*, fol.14.

medieval heresy legislation was restored by 1 and 2 Philip and Mary, c.6 (1554):

> For the eschewing and avoiding of errors and heresies, which of late have risen, grown, and much increased within this realm, for that the ordinaries have wanted authority to proceed against those that were infected therewith:[72]

The restoration of three Lancastrian statutes, concerning the arrest and apprehension of heretical preachers (5 Richard II, Stat.2, c.5), the repression of heresy and punishment of heretics (2 Henry IV, c.15), and the suppression of heresy and Lollardy (2 Henry V, Stat.1, c.7), led to a series of prosecutions and executions. A public disputation was held at Oxford in 1554 with Cranmer, Latimer and Ridley, opposed by a number of divines which included several Marian bishops, amongst them Gilbert Bourne, William Glynn, Owen Oglethorpe, Cuthbert Scott and Thomas Watson. The first Protestant to be executed, John Rogers, was burned on 4 February 1555; five days later, John Hooper became the first of the five bishops executed for heresy during the reign, soon followed by the Bishop of St Davids, Robert Ferrar, on 30 March in Carmarthen. On 16 October that year, Ridley and Latimer died together at the stake in Oxford. Finally, on 21 March 1556, Cranmer was consigned to the flames, ending a series of episcopal executions all of which had their origins in the refusal of the bishops to accept the orthodoxy of the state combined with an inability or an unwillingness to submit to exile. The case against Cranmer had been submitted to the Pope by the King and Queen in 1555, and was referred to the Inquisitor General who delegated the investigation of the charges to Brooks. Shortly after the completion of the examination of Cranmer, he was named in a fresh commission with White of Lincoln and Holyman of Bristol to examine and judge Latimer and Ridley.[73] At Cranmer's execution, the Provost of Eton, Dr Cole, included in his sermon the statement that Cranmer's death, along with those of Ridley, Hooper and Ferrar, made a just compensation for the sacrifice of John Fisher.[74]

A number of bishops chose voluntary exile on the Continent rather than remain in the realm under a Catholic regime, amongst them John Ponet, formerly Bishop of Winchester. His view of the Marian heresy executions reflects the opinion current from the earliest persecutions of Christianity, that it is through martyrdom that the Church is watered and grows. In a letter from Strassburg to John Bale, his former chaplain, at Frankfort, he wrote

---

[72] 1 and 2 Philip and Mary, c.6; *Statutes of the Realm*, iv. 244.

[73] Loades, *The Oxford Martyrs*, pp. 192–3.

[74] *Acts and Monuments*, vol. VIII, p. 85. The images used by Foxe to illustrate the burnings of Cranmer, Latimer and Ridley are reproduced at Plates VI and VII.

> The sone brusteth out wher the clouds of popery be thykest, the
> more they quench the cole the more it burneth, blow therfor
> boldly the trumpet of gods treuth, and play the bushop amonge
> your companions ther, as thoughe ye wer amonge your flok in
> yerland.[75]

The role of the bishop as guarantor and defender of the faith, in this case
in the face of persecution, was central to Ponet's thinking. Before his
exile, Ponet had translated a work by Bernardino Ochino against the
primacy of the Bishop of Rome. Ochino argued that the pope was no
longer to be obeyed having lost his authority through falling into heresy,
though formal deposition could only come through a general council.
However, if the pope is above a council, then the only lawful council able
to condemn him would also have to be convoked by him.[76] The
publication of this work may well have been intended to argue for the
futility of the Council of Trent, which had been convoked four years
previously, by demonstrating that the doctrine of conciliarism (whereby
the pope is understood as being subject to a general council of the
Church) held no sway in the Roman Church.

Queen Mary's Articles, sent to all the bishops in March 1554, expressly
charged them with the task of eradicating heresy in their dioceses.[77] False
doctrine was to be purged by sound teaching, set out in approved
homilies, which were to be read to the people when they came to divine
service; the bishop and his officers were to 'compel the parishioners to
come to their several churches' to ensure that this teaching was heard.[78]
Some bishops gained a reputation for harshness in their prosecution of
heresy. The majority of burnings took place in four dioceses, London,
Canterbury, Norwich and Chichester. Out of 282 burnings recorded in
episcopal registers throughout the Marian period, 232 took place in these
four, each of which had major ports through which heretical literature
was able to enter the country; about half the executed heretics in these
dioceses were examined personally by the diocesan bishop. Although the
most famous burnings took place in Oxford, neither there nor in the
diocese of Ely in which Cambridge was situated were there significant
numbers of executions for heresy. Half the burnings carried out in the
four main dioceses took place in Bonner's diocese of London.[79] Certainly
the influence of the Protestant Reformation had been felt very deeply in

---

[75] BL Additional ms 29546, fol.25. The letter is dated to 6 July 1555 by E.J.
Baskerville in 'John Ponet in Exile: A Ponet Letter to John Bale', *Journal of
Ecclesiastical History*, 37 (1986), pp. 442–7. Bale was Bishop of Ossory in Ireland
('yerland').

[76] Ochino, *A tragoedie or Dialoge*, sig.F.iv.

[77] *Articles and Injunctions*, p. 326.

[78] *Ibid.*, p. 328.

[79] Thompson, 'The Pastoral Work of the English and Welsh Bishops', p. 139.

London. Bonner's predecessor was a notable and enthusiastic reformer who had often proceeded with reform in advance of its sanction by Parliament. The diocese also had a long history of Lollardy, particularly in parts of Essex, and the capital, simply by virtue of its importance in the realm, tended to draw to itself those most active in whatever new ideas were being put forward, in religion as in anything else. It was in London that the main congregations of foreign Protestants were to be found, and in London that Court and Parliament had the focus of their activity. It was therefore not surprising that new ideas had taken root there more securely than in much of the rest of the realm. On the other hand, it was also the place where the continuing presence of heresy was most obvious to those in civil government who were concerned with the restoration of Catholic orthodoxy, and where the failure to prosecute heresy adequately was most clearly perceived. Bonner was initially reluctant to proceed with too much vigour; in 1555 he was warned by the Council not to be slack in prosecuting heretics, two months having passed without any convictions. His image as bloody persecutor of the godly derived from his later actions, after his earlier misgivings had been overcome by pressure from government and the goading of obstinate heretics.[80] Other bishops, such as Bonner's former chaplain, Gilbert Bourne, Bishop of Bath and Wells, had a reputation for being humane. Even so, it is generally accepted that nine clergy were burned for heresy in the diocese during Bourne's episcopate, and he was a member of the commission for the trial of John Hooper. Indeed, he had preached a sermon at Paul's Cross in August 1553 justifying Bonner's actions in eradicating heresy.[81] In Exeter diocese, the lead was taken by local magistrates rather than the 'gentle and courteous' Turberville.[82] John Hopton, Bishop of Norwich, had a reputation as an active persecutor of Protestants in his diocese, where according to Foxe forty-six were burned at the stake.[83] He was, however, presented by Foxe as a reluctant persecutor, saying in one case that he was forced to observe the laws of the land even 'if the king were an infidel'.[84] The main source of heretical ideas in the diocese of Norwich had always been the ports. Hopton's predecessor, the conservative Thomas Thirlby, had been translated to Norwich as a place where he

---

[80] *Acts and Monuments*, vol. VIII, p. 86; Hughes, *Rome and the Counter-Reformation*, p. 103; Brigden, *London*, pp. 613–14.
[81] Hembry, *The Bishops of Bath and Wells*, pp. 89, 98.
[82] Vage, J.A., 'The Diocese of Exeter, 1519–1641: A Study of Church Government in the Age of the Reformation', Cambridge PhD, 1991, p. 105.
[83] Emden, *Biographical Register, Oxford 1501–1540*; Dr Thompson's research ('The Pastoral Work of the English and Welsh Bishops') suggests that Foxe exaggerated; his study of the registers of the period suggests that only thirty-four burnings took place in the diocese of Norwich during the Marian period.
[84] *Acts and Monuments*, vol. VII, p. 382.

was unlikely to have any serious effect on the Reformation which already had a firm hold in the diocese. In 1530 its bishop, Richard Nykke, reported that heresy had not greatly infected the gentry or the common people of his diocese; it was then a problem only amongst merchants and those who dwelt close to the ports through which heretical material was entering the realm.[85] Thirlby himself, having been translated from Norwich to Ely in 1554, seems to have taken little interest in heresy; in his diocese during Mary's reign there were three executions of which he sanctioned one. Ralph Baynes, Bishop of Lichfield and Coventry, was reputed for his active persecution of Protestants. He had been a notable public opponent of Hugh Latimer while University preacher at Cambridge, and had assisted at the trial of John Hooper. The reputation of Stephen Gardiner as a vigorous prosecutor of heretics rests chiefly on the evidence of John Foxe, who seems to have had an excessive dislike of the bishop, and little corroborative evidence exists in contemporary sources.[86] It was probably more the case that he took a major part in the examination of prominent heretics rather than an active prosecution of heresy in his diocese. Gardiner seems to have preferred to frighten off heretics than to bring them to book, though he believed that the inspirers of heresy had to be dealt with for the sake of others. As a result, he had a prominent role in early heresy trials at the church of St Mary Overy in Southwark; seeing that the burnings had failed to have the desired effect, he took no further part in the prosecutions.[87] In the diocese of York, where the Reformation seems to have taken a less firm hold than in many other parts of the realm, little attempt to eradicate unorthodoxy amongst the clergy of the diocese was made before April 1554 apart from the arrest and imprisonment of the archbishop, Robert Holgate, in October 1553. Even then, there is little evidence that Holgate's successor, Nicholas Heath, had much influence upon the actual process of heresy prosecution. His reputedly mild and tolerant nature seems to have produced little effect on the local situation.[88] Pole's apparent reluctance or inability to temper the intensity of the English heresy proceedings may well reflect the

---

[85] Haigh, *English Reformations*, p. 55.
[86] Foxe's account of the trial of Anne Askew, for instance, has Gardiner playing an aggressive part in the proceedings, making Bonner's approach seem mild by comparison. Most authorities agree that Gardiner played no leading role in Askew's interrogation, even though he might have had a legitimate interest in the civil aspects of a heresy trial which came close to implicating Queen Katharine Parr in the matter. *Acts and Monuments*, vol. V, pp. 537–51. See also Hamilton, D.L., 'The Household of Queen Katharine Parr', Oxford DPhil, 1992, chapter 5, and Redworth, *Gardiner*, p. 235.
[87] Redworth, *Gardiner*, pp. 330–1; see also Thompson, 'The Pastoral Work of the English and Welsh Bishops', p. 140.
[88] Dickens, *The Marian Reaction in the Diocese of York*, Part 1, pp. 5–8.

fact that he was himself under suspicion.[89] Despite having been named a member of a 1551 commission to revivify the Roman Inquisition, it began in that year to move against his former associates at Viterbo, and Pole's name does not appear in subsequent lists of cardinals sitting on the commission. The election of Carafa as Pope in May 1555, after Pole had begun his work in England, confirmed the position of the persecutors in the highest office of the Roman Church. On the other hand, it is important to bear in mind that Pole, in common with the general spirit of his age, both Catholic and reformed, believed that the first duty of a Christian pastor was to protect the faithful from corrupting influence, by force if necessary.[90] To this end, in December 1554, he commissioned the suffragan Bishop of Dover, Richard Thornden, to hear and try heresy cases in the diocese of Canterbury. Thornden worked alongside Nicholas Harpsfield, Archdeacon of Canterbury, in the examination of heretics; Pole himself took no part in the process.[91] The Marian episcopate sought to establish a godly unity by means which were harsh, but in keeping with the times. It was considered both a right and a duty for the bishop to use whatever means were necessary to seek out and remove heresy. Thomas Watson, Mary's Bishop of Lincoln, addressed this towards the end of the reign by alluding to the model of the Church as the mystical body of Christ. The bishops were the physicians and surgeons who applied 'the sweete medycines of Gods words and his holye Sacramentes' to the diseased soul; as good surgeons, they would also be prepared to cut out uncurable wounds where this became necessary.[92] Susan Brigden has concluded that every martyrdom was a defeat for the persecutors, who did not want the gospellers to die but to be reconciled.[93] While this certainly seems to be true in the majority of cases, where every attempt was made to encourage the condemned to recant and be reconciled, it was ultimately the case that the death of an obstinate heretic which eradicated a source of danger to the immortal souls of others could be seen in its own terms not to have been a complete defeat. It was also true that some persecutors sought the death of certain heretics, and even when as prominent an individual as Cranmer recanted, his life was not spared

---

[89] Pogson also suggests that Pole's experience of heresy in Italy did not prepare him for English heresy ('Cardinal Pole – Papal Legate', p. 10); indeed, the institutionalization of heresy which resulted from the great body of Reformation legislation in England made it very different in character from anything Pole had experienced before.

[90] Fenlon, *Heresy and Obedience*, p. 252.

[91] Loades, *The Oxford Martyrs*, p. 139; *Acts and Monuments*, vol. VII, p. 297; Pole's Legatine Register fol.17; Thompson, 'The Pastoral Work of the English and Welsh Bishops', p. 139.

[92] Watson, *Holsome and Catholyke doctryne*, fols.clviii, clxiii, v.

[93] Brigden, *London*, p. 607.

as a result. With hindsight, the policy of eradication by burning was not a success, and only created martyrs for the cause. The analysis seems generally valid only in retrospect, given the unexpectedly early end to the reign; it might well have been the case, under other circumstances, that the policy of removing key figures would have been seen as a success, even though by the standards of the present day the methods employed were unacceptable. The extent to which heresy was hated and feared at the time must not be forgotten. Foxe relates that Hopton, Bishop of Norwich, said to a woman brought to his heresy court that she would have been better to commit adultery with twenty men than to commit heresy, while Pole, despite his gentleness towards all but the most obstinate, is recorded as having preached that 'there are no theves, no murtherers, no advouterers, nor no kynde of treason to be compared' with heresy.[94] Pole was especially hard toward those in positions of authority whom he saw as having led others into error. He wrote to Cranmer, while the latter was in prison in Oxford, in the harshest tones, likening his actions in leading the realm away from the true Church to those of Satan in causing the expulsion of mankind from paradise.[95]

Throughout the period in question, the maintenance of Christian orthodoxy against error was perceived as a central function of the episcopal office. Despite radical changes of content in the approved deposit of faith, the bishops were at the centre of ensuring its maintenance. Indeed, many bishops were instrumental in the definition and development of that central deposit. While the guarantor of orthodoxy alternated between Crown and Tiara, there was at no time a suggestion from the holders of episcopal office that the means and ordinary focus of unity should be anyone but the bishop. The inability of individual bishops to conform with the official orthodoxy imposed on the English Church led to the removal from office of those individuals, and ultimately in the most extreme cases, to their execution. Finally, the imposition of what became the Elizabethan orthodoxy by means of the Supremacy oath led to the deprivation of almost the entire bench of bishops within the space of a year.

---

[94] *Acts and Monuments*, vol. VIII, p. 224; Strype, *Ecclesiastical Memorials*, vol. III part 2, p. 487 (one of Pole's English sermons).
[95] Lambeth Palace Library ms 2007, fols.245v–246r.

Chapter Eight

EPISCOPAL ACTIVITY II: THE PROPAGATION OF THE MINISTRY

From the earliest times, bishops in the Church have set apart others to share in their ministry of oversight and pastoral care. In the consecration of new bishops they ensured the continuation of their office, while the ordination of suitable candidates to the priesthood, diaconate and other ministries in the Church ensured that sacramental functions and pastoral care were available to the laity at large. Such ordinations were carried out by the diocesan bishop, or by another bishop acting with his authority and by his permission. The ordination of candidates to the minor orders, and on occasions to the subdiaconate, could be delegated to a priest not in episcopal orders, often the abbot or prior to whom the candidates, members of religious orders, were subject. Towards the end of the Middle Ages the holding of ordinations was more usually delegated by the diocesan to other bishops. Other specifically episcopal actions, such as holding confirmations, dedicating and consecrating churches, chapels and churchyards, and the reconsecration of ecclesiastical property following its desecration through bloodshed or pollution, were very frequently carried out by others than the diocesan.[1] The consecration of bishops, on the other hand, was almost invariably carried out by the metropolitan of the province (in the English Church the archbishops of Canterbury and York), with at least two co-consecrators in accordance with the ancient tradition that at least three bishops should share in this action. Ordination to the major orders, and especially the presbyterate, was the sole prerogative of the bishop, and the English Church, even at its most reformed, always took the official position that the diaconate and presbyterate may only be conferred by a duly appointed bishop. Although a small number of its bishops seems to have held the opinion that, in extraordinary circumstances, all the functions of those offices may be validly carried out by laymen, it would seem that such circumstances were never perceived to have been in existence during the period under study. The conferral of

[1] Churchill, *Canterbury Administration*, vol. I, pp. 128–9.

the orders of deacon and priest by the diocesan bishop in person, rather than by his authorized delegate, may be taken as an indicator of the availability and willingness of the diocesan to exercise such a function in his own diocese and the importance attached to that personal celebration. Although the ordination of suitable candidates to the ministry was an important function of the bishop, it had become the general rule by the end of the Middle Ages that ordination services were not conducted by the diocesan bishop but by one of his suffragans.[2] However, in the period under study the key role of the diocesan bishop in the propagation of the ordained ministry was reaffirmed on all sides. Their responsibility rested not only in carrying out the formal act of conferring holy orders, but also in ensuring that ordinands were fit for the office they were to receive. Cardinal Pole's reforming synod of 1555/6 made the point in a way that held true for all shades of opinion within the episcopate: 'besides preaching the Word of God, there is nothing greater enjoined on a bishop than diligent and careful attention to the laying on of hands'.[3]

In essence, then, the one specifically episcopal act for which substantial records survive for the English Church in the period under study is the holding of ordinations. In the period from 1520 to 1559 records survive of over a thousand occasions on which holy orders were conferred. The great majority are to be found in episcopal registers, with a small number recorded in other sources where the registers are missing or incomplete. The practice of recording ordinations in a separate section of a bishop's register was widespread in the period. Some registers, therefore, while being complete in many other respects, contain no record of ordinations, the pages which would have been bound with the main register at the end of a bishop's episcopate having been lost or destroyed. This may account for the total lack of information on ordinations in the diocese of Canterbury for the period. No ordinations for Canterbury diocese are listed in William Warham's register after 1513, nor are any to be found in Cranmer's or Pole's archiepiscopal registers. Warham appears to have celebrated no ordinations personally, all those appearing in his register having been conducted by suffragan bishops acting on his commission.[4] Likewise, none are listed in the records of the Cathedral Priory of Christ

---

[2] There were a few notable exceptions. The three bishops of Bath and Wells whose episcopates spanned the years 1406 to 1465 conducted ordination services personally on 123 occasions out of 242, though their successors Robert Stillington (1466–91), Richard Fox (1492–94), Oliver King (1496–1503) and Adrian de Castello (1504–18) never personally celebrated the sacrament of order. More typical in the fifteenth century was John Kempe, Archbishop of York from 1426 to 1452, who celebrated personally on eight out of 154 occasions. Thompson, A.H., *The English Clergy and their Organization in the Later Middle Ages* (Oxford, 1947), pp. 203–4.

[3] Bray, ed., *The Anglican Canons, 1529–1947*, p. 113.

[4] Churchill, *Canterbury Administration*, p. 103.

Church, Canterbury. The only ordinations to be found in the archiepiscopal registers after 1513 are those which relate to the *sede vacante* administration of vacant dioceses by the see of Canterbury. These have been disregarded for the purposes of the present study, as they fail to shed any light on the practice of personal celebration of ordination by diocesan bishops rather than by suffragans acting on their behalf.[5]

For most of the period under study, the majority of ordinations recorded were conducted by suffragan bishops. The only point at which this was not so was in the period of Queen Mary's reign, where around sixty per cent of celebrations were conducted by diocesan bishops. Henry VIII's bishops were required to perform specific functions at Court, in London, which would suggest that they would thereby be prevented from exercising their function of ministers of the sacrament of holy order. This is certainly supported by the number of occasions on which they conducted ordinations before 1530, and in the period between 1540 and the King's death. However, the uncertainty over their position in the decade during which the break with Rome was effected led to an increase in the number of occasions when the bishops took over the duty of ordaining from their suffragans. While the proportion of diocesan bishops undertaking this duty rose during the reign of Edward VI, the overall number of occasions on which orders were conferred fell, reflecting the significant reduction in the number of candidates presenting themselves for ordination. The excision of the minor orders, the subdiaconate, and the conferring of first tonsure from the Edwardian Ordinals, seems to have made little difference to the overall number of occasions on which orders were conferred. Before the 1550 Ordinal, minor orders were rarely conferred by bishops, diocesan or suffragan, without at least some candidates for major orders being ordained on the same occasion. In 1516 Wolsey had obtained a decree from Leo X that clerical status was to be denied to those who failed to take all the minor orders and the subdiaconate on a single occasion unless they had obtained a benefice. This was complemented by Clement VII in 1528, who permitted Wolsey to degrade criminous clerks with less formality than before. These actions sought to address the problem of clerks in minor orders obtaining benefit of clergy in criminal actions, while safeguarding clerical immunity from secular jurisdiction. As a result, the practice of conferring all the minor orders on a single occasion seems to have been almost universally observed throughout the period to 1550. After the restoration of the Catholic Ordinal and the reinstatement of minor orders, a number of additional ordinations were conducted,

---

[5] A detailed analysis of ordination registers for the period 1520 to 1559, from which the following discussion is drawn, may be found in Appendix III of Carleton, K.W.T., 'Episcopal Office in the English Church, 1520–1559', London PhD, 1995.

principally in the diocese of London, in which candidates admitted to Reformed orders received those orders which had been omitted. The custom of conferring all minor orders on a single occasion seems to have continued throughout the reign of Mary. However, the ordination lists themselves demonstrate a significant decline in the number of men offering themselves for the ministry, probably due in part to the uncertainty of the situation after a few years of rapid change in the constitution of the English Church. Equally, the low number could be a result of many bishops' desire for an adequately educated ministry; candidates who failed to meet their high standards may well have been refused ordination until they could meet their bishop's requirements.

In the years from 1520 to 1529, only two diocesan bishops, John Fisher of Rochester and Charles Booth of Hereford, are known to have celebrated the sacrament of order personally on a regular basis. Fisher had conducted thirty-nine of the forty-two ordination ceremonies in his diocese of Rochester carried out between 1505 and 1535, including all but one from the period under study. This may reflect the influence of his former tutor, William de Melton, whose sermon on the importance of ordination, *Sermo exhortatorius Cancellari Eboracensis . . . (Sermo ad iuvenes)* had been published in 1510. A number of factors facilitated the personal practice of this aspect of the episcopal office for the Bishop. The diocese of Rochester was relatively small, and the duty less burdensome than in larger dioceses; over the period from 1520 to 1529 more than seven times the number of celebrations took place in Lincoln as in Rochester, and throughout the whole of Fisher's episcopate only forty-four priests were ordained.[6] Furthermore, the proximity of Rochester to London made attendance at Court less costly in terms of time away from the diocese. Hereford diocese was also small, with only 254 parishes, so despite the greater distance of his see from the Court in London, at least annual celebrations of ordination were held, and Booth was able to conduct all but four ceremonies personally in the decade of the 1520s. In all other dioceses for which records survive in that period, only isolated instances occur of diocesan bishops conducting their own ordinations. The general rule seems to be that the bishop carried out this ministry personally where his diocese was of a manageable size.

During the five years approximating to the period between the start of the Reformation Parliament and the final break with Rome, there was a doubling in the proportion of ordinations conducted by suffragan bishops. The period was one of some change in the constitution of the episcopal bench, and this had its influence on the practice of personal celebration. Nonetheless, less than one celebration in three was conducted by a diocesan bishop. Tunstall's translation to Durham, where

---

[6] Thompson, 'The Bishop in his Diocese', in Bradshaw and Duffy, p. 76.

he conducted all sixteen ordinations of the period, left a vacancy in London. This was filled by John Stokesley, whose own practice of celebrating ordinations personally on most occasions made up, with Tunstall, the majority of those celebrated in that period. Elsewhere, the practice of delegation to suffragans continued. On two occasions ordinations were conducted in London diocese by other diocesan bishops. Other than on a single occasion in September 1524, John Longland seems to have conducted ordination services personally in his diocese of Lincoln only after 1534. This was almost certainly a reaction to the threat to his episcopal authority from the ambiguous situation which had arisen from Thomas Cromwell's vicarious exercise of the supremacy.[7] In a letter to Cromwell responding to the inhibition of his jurisdiction during the 1536 royal visitation, Longland stated that the power of ordination and confirmation at least would have to be returned to him by virtue of his episcopal orders. He also requested that non-sacramental rights which also pertained to his office (proving wills, correcting sin, and so forth) should be returned to him.[8] Throughout the same period, Fisher and Booth continued to conduct ordinations in their own dioceses in person.

The proportion of ordinations conducted by diocesan bishops in the five years of doubt and uncertainty from 1535 to 1539 was the same as in the five-year period previously. The appointment of a reform-minded bishop, Nicholas Shaxton, to the see of Salisbury, led to a three-year period there in which twelve ordination services were conducted by the Bishop in his diocese. This contrasted significantly with the situation which had existed previously. John Pinnock, Bishop of Syene *in partibus infidelium*, had conducted all ordinations in the diocese for more than fifteen years. For the last ten, this had been on behalf of an absentee Italian, Cardinal Campeggio, who seems at no time to have visited his diocese. After the appointment of Shaxton, the situation changed drastically. He had been educated at Cambridge and was one of the increasing number of theologians being appointed to the episcopal bench. After his resignation in 1539, no ordinations are recorded as having been celebrated by the diocesan bishop in Salisbury until after the accession of Queen Elizabeth. After Fisher's death in 1535, the Rochester episcopal registers contain no entries for ordinations until after 1559. Booth's death in the same year as Fisher resulted in the appointment of Edward Fox to Hereford. His brief episcopate covered approximately the same period as that of Shaxton at Salisbury. Like Shaxton, he was a Cambridge man and Doctor of Theology. Unlike Shaxton, he was

---

[7] See Bowker, *The Henrician Reformation*, p. 39.

[8] Bowker, *The Henrician Reformation*, p. 77; BL Cotton ms Cleopatra F.ii, fol.130.

frequently involved in diplomatic missions abroad and conducted no ordinations personally.

The conservative reaction which followed the Act of Six Articles was reflected in the reduction in the proportion of ordinations conducted by diocesan bishops. From 1540 to the end of the reign of Henry VIII only six diocesan bishops are recorded as having held their own ordinations in the fourteen sees where such celebrations were conducted. Bonner celebrated one ordination of the twenty conducted in the period between 1540 and 1544 while his fellow Oxford canonist, Arthur Bulkeley, the first Bishop of Bangor to reside in the diocese for over a century, conducted all the ordinations held during his episcopate. Robert King, Bishop of Osney (subsequently Oxford) conducted the three ordinations held in his newly created diocese during 1544. King had been consecrated Bishop of Rheon *in partibus* in 1527, and acted as suffragan to John Longland in Lincoln Diocese where he conducted thirty-five ordination services between September 1529 and March 1542. John Bird, a former religious like King and also like him an Oxford theologian, conducted all ordinations held in his diocese of Chester from its creation to his deprivation in 1554. The other two bishops, John Skip and William Repps, had much in common with Shaxton. All three were Cambridge men, Doctors of Theology who had studied at Gonville Hall; Shaxton and Repps had been almost exact contemporaries, while Skip had taken his BA some eight years after Shaxton. Repps conducted a single ordination at Norwich, the majority being celebrated by his suffragan, the bishop of Thetford. Skip on the other hand conducted around half the ordinations of his episcopate. The bishops who delegated the task of ordaining in the latter years of Henry VIII were in general numbered among the most conservative.

A reduction in the number of candidates for holy orders in the period of the Edwardian Reformation led to a decrease in the number of occasions on which ordinations were celebrated. On average, less than half the number of services is recorded as having taken place compared with the decade before the Reformation Parliament. Even more striking is the significant reduction in the number of candidates on whom orders were conferred on those occasions, revealed by even the most cursory glance at the episcopal registers for the period. The situation in the diocese of Exeter provides a clear example of this trend. During the long episcopate of John Veysey, from 1517 to his retirement in 1551, orders were conferred, on average, on five to six occasions each year in a number of locations in the diocese, including the Lady Chapel of Exeter Cathedral and the Priory Churches of Bodmin and St Germans. After the dissolutions of 1535 and 1538, the overall number of ordinands fell, in common with the situation in other dioceses, though there were still sufficient candidates for at least five ceremonies to be conducted in both

1542 and 1543. Regrettably, the final folio of the Exeter ordinations register for Veysey's episcopate which is still extant is darkened and faded, and the final entry is dated 29 March 1544. It seems very likely that the entries for ordinations for the remainder of the episcopate have been lost. Coverdale's ordination register, covering the period from 20 December 1551 to 22 May 1553, has survived complete.[9] Coverdale conducted all six ordinations of his two-year episcopate, and on no occasion were there more than four candidates. On the first occasion, 20 December 1551, four men were ordained deacon; in the subsequent session, on 26 December, two of those men were ordained priest. On 1 January 1552, Coverdale conferred the orders of deacon and priest on one man, John Crose, 'in uno et eodem die'. At the next session he conducted, [3] July 1552, Coverdale admitted two men to the order of deacon; another was admitted to the same order on 24 July. Coverdale's final celebration as Bishop of Exeter took place on 22 May 1553, when he ordained Henry Reding priest, and Thomas Richard to both diaconate and priesthood also 'in uno et eodem die'.[10] Coverdale also conducted an ordination service in London diocese on 19 March 1553 for Nicholas Ridley. The Exeter ordinations register for the brief period between Veysey's restoration and death shows a return to the frequency of conducting ordinations found earlier, but without a significant increase in the numbers of candidates to match; for much of 1554, only one or two ordinands were presented on each occasion. The explanation may be found in the approach of the two bishops to the use of suffragans to carry out episcopal functions. Almost all ordinations from December 1532 to the point at which records cease in 1544 were conducted by William, Bishop of Hippo *in partibus infidelium*, on behalf of John Veysey; he also carried out all the ordinations during Veysey's restored episcopate. It has already been noted that Coverdale was active

---

[9] The statement of J.A. Vage, that in Exeter 'no-one at all was ordained between 1544 and 1551' ('The Diocese of Exeter, 1519–1641: A Study of Church Government in the Age of the Reformation', Cambridge PhD, 1991, p. 44), while valid on the basis of existing statistical evidence, must be questioned on the basis of the state of the register itself and the unlikelihood that ordinations which had been both frequent and regular with relatively large numbers of candidates should suddenly cease in 1544.

[10] Coverdale's Register, Devon Record Office Chanter Catalogue 16, fols.12r–13r. Christopher Haigh has suggested that, during the period of the Edwardian Church, 1547–53, 'there were no ordinations in the dioceses of Chester, Durham and Exeter' (*English Reformations*, p. 182). In the case of the first two, Dr Haigh is supported by the researches of W.F. Irvine ('The Earliest Ordination Book of the Diocese of Chester, 1542–7 and 1555–8', *Miscellanies Relating to Lancashire and Cheshire* vol. IV, Lancashire and Cheshire Record Society 43 [1902], 25–126). It may be that for Exeter he follows Dr Thompson, who omits Coverdale from his analysis of ordinations carried out by diocesan bishops between 1500 and 1558 ('The Pastoral Work of the English and Welsh Bishops', Table I, p. 179).

in Exeter diocese as a preacher during the later 1540s, and that this was perceived by Hugh Latimer as a failure on Veysey's part to undertake adequately his episcopal duties. It is quite possible that Coverdale was unwilling to employ Veysey's former suffragan. William *Hypponensis* had been papally provided to his see before the break with Rome, and had exercised an episcopal ministry in the West Country for twenty years before Coverdale's appointment; it is very likely that he was not a supporter of the Reformation. There is strong evidence on the other hand that Coverdale took the personal practice of episcopal functions very seriously, in his case resulting largely from the long and intense influence of the Continental Reformation upon him which had begun at Cambridge in the 1520s. Veysey's Marian successor at Exeter, James Turberville, like Coverdale, had taken his doctorate in theology while abroad; also like Coverdale, he exercised a personal practice of conducting ordinations in his diocese throughout his episcopate. Despite a gap of around eighteen months between his provision to the see and his first ordination celebration on 13 March 1557, he is not recorded as having made use of the services of a suffragan to conduct ordinations on his behalf. He conducted five ordination services in each of the two years of his active ministry in this area, celebrated at the times which had been customary in the diocese during the episcopate of John Veysey.

The pattern of ordinations in the other dioceses for which records survive covering the period of the Edwardian Reformation is similar to that of Exeter. In London, the replacement of the conservative Bonner by Nicholas Ridley led to a significant increase in the proportion of ordinations conducted by the diocesan bishop. It is notable that on the three occasions when Ridley did not personally confer orders, he delegated the task to fellow Reform-minded diocesan bishops, Coverdale and Robert Ferrar, Bishop of St Davids. The London ordinations register is more explicit than any other surviving register for the period in stating that the new Ordinal had been used. The entry for 24 June 1550, the first of Ridley's episcopate, clearly states that the ordinations were carried out by the Bishop of London according to the new rites of the English Church.[11] At Oxford and Norwich during Edward's reign the task of conducting ordinations was largely left to suffragans. Robert King, who had been quite diligent in celebrating personally in the latter years of the reign of Henry VIII, delegated more than half of the ordinations in his diocese from the accession of Edward VI to his death in 1557. Thomas Thirlby is recorded as conducting only one

---

[11] 'iuxta ritum modum et formam ecclesie Anglicane nuper saluberrime edite et ordinate'; London Diocese Ordinations Register June 1550 – December 1577, Guildhall Library MS9535/1, fol.1r; see also Ridley's episcopal register, MS9531/ 12 Part 2, fol.319r.

ordination, at Norwich in September 1550, throughout his nineteen years as a bishop. During his years at Norwich, the majority of ordinations were carried out by John Salisburye, bishop of the suffragan see of Thetford.

There seems to have been an increase in the number of occasions on which ordinations were conducted after the accession of Queen Mary. It has also been suggested that large numbers of candidates offered themselves for the priesthood in a misplaced confidence of a Catholic future, resulting in record levels of ordination in many dioceses.[12] Most significantly, this was the first period where more diocesan bishops than suffragans undertook this duty. There may have been a number of factors, unrelated to the bishops' own inclinations or convictions, which contributed to this. It had become more difficult to fill vacant bishoprics with suitable candidates; Exeter, for instance, was returned to the charge of John Veysey who had to be brought out of retirement at the age of ninety. Restoring the process whereby new suffragans could be provided was less important than ensuring the legal reinstatement and confirmation in office of the late Henricians whose episcopal status in relation to Rome was, to say the least, unclear. Moreover, the new bishops tended to be drawn from those whose careers to date had been in theology or the universities and whose experience of matters of state was often limited. The tendency for such men was to incline towards the spiritual and sacramental functions of the episcopal office and away from the sphere of diplomacy and statecraft which had been the ambit of so many of their forebears. Bonner conducted a greater proportion of the ordinations in his diocese after his restoration than he had before his deprivation in 1549. Tunstall conducted all ordinations held in the diocese of Durham from 1556 onwards, save one held by his suffragan, Thomas Sparke, Bishop of Berwick. The gap in ordinations between 1547 and 1555 there and in Chester diocese probably represents an actual cessation rather than the loss of records; two deacons ordained in Chester in 1547 appear in the lists of priests for 1554 and 1555.[13] Similarly, the lack of ordination lists in the St Davids register for the episcopate of Henry Morgan seems to be due to a total lack of candidates, who only began to present themselves after 1561, and then at first only in small numbers.[14] Goldwell, in character with his profession as a Theatine, celebrated personally on five occasions between 19 September 1556 and 17 April 1557 in his cathedral at St Asaph.

[12] A suggestion made by Christopher Haigh in a paper, 'The Restoration of Catholicism in the Reign of Mary Tudor', given to the Tudor and Stuart seminar at the Institute of Historical Research, London, on 5 November 1990.

[13] Irvine, 'The Earliest Ordination Book of the Diocese of Chester', p. 25.

[14] Williams, G., 'The Second Volume of St David's Registers, 1554–64', *The Bulletin of the Board of Celtic Studies*, XIV (1950–52), p. 47.

Thomas Watson, Bishop of Lincoln, appears to have conducted all five ordinations in his diocese held between 17 September 1557 and 24 September 1558. A member of St John's College, Cambridge, and its Master from 1553, Watson provides a direct connection back to John Fisher, whose plans to create a well-educated pastoral clergy found their most concrete expression in the ideals and existence of that institution.

The question of whether the Church could, under extraordinary circumstances, deviate from the norm of episcopal ordination of its ministers was addressed by the 1540 commission on questions of doctrine. The English Church was at the end of a period of uncertainty, particularly with respect to the episcopal office which bound it together, and matters of jurisdiction and authority particularly relating to its relationship with the King had been tidied up by a series of acts of Parliament. A number of doctrinal questions remained unresolved, including some which related to the spiritual significance of the episcopal office. The majority of episcopal members of the commission were of the opinion that the bishop was the sole minister of ordination under all circumstances. Only Cranmer and Barlow considered that under certain conditions lay men were able and permitted to make priests and to authorize the exercise of priestly functions by laymen. While Cranmer's opinion was that both bishop and civil magistrate had authority to make priests by virtue of the divine authority committed to them, Barlow stated that the bishop has no authority to make priests without the authorization of the Christian prince. Tyndale's opinion, stated in *The Obedience of a Christian Man*, is here reflected, to the extent that the only requirement for 'the making of our spiritual officers' is to choose an able person, 'and then to rehearse him his duty, and give him his charge, and so put him in his room'.[15] Several of the other commissioners including Nicholas Heath considered that the permission of the prince was required for the bishop to exercise his authority to ordain, but excluded the possibility that laymen, even in times of necessity, were able to make priests, a doctrine found in the *Defensor pacis* of Marsilius.[16]

In its discussion of the sacrament of order, the Bishops' Book of 1537 had stated that the minor orders were instituted by the apostles' successors, and that the New Testament mentioned only 'deacons or ministers, and . . . priests or bishops'.[17] The act of conferring orders retained its sacramental character, while its essence, prayer and imposition of hands, was derived from the New Testament. The more conservative King's Book of 1543 retained the minor orders alongside

---

[15] Tyndale, *Obedience*, p. 202.
[16] BL Cotton ms Cleopatra E.v. fols.45v, 58v–59r. Chapter 3 discusses this question in greater detail. *Defensor pacis*, p. 92.
[17] Lloyd, *Formularies*, p. 105.

the priests and deacons expressly mentioned in the Scripture.[18] As in the earlier book, it belongs to the episcopal office to pass on the Church's ministry 'by the consecration and imposition of the bishop's hands'.[19] The act of consecration associated with the imposition of hands suggests that the anointing and other ceremonies associated with ordination in the medieval rites were given a level of importance which they did not have in the doctrine as formulated in the Bishops' Book, or indeed in the majority of replies to the relevant question posed in 1540.

An Act of 31 January 1550 (3 and 4 Edward VI, c.12) empowered the King to appoint six prelates, and six other men to complete the liturgical reform begun with the Prayer Book of 1549 by the preparation of a new Ordinal, which appeared at the beginning of March 1550. It seems possible that much work of preparation had already been done, and the new form may even have been used experimentally in an ordination held by Cranmer and Ridley in St Paul's towards the end of 1549.[20] Nicholas Heath, conservative Bishop of Worcester, refused his assent in Council on 8 February, and was committed to the Fleet on 4 March. Finally, he was deprived of his see in October 1551. His successor in the see when it was combined with that of Gloucester in 1552 objected to the book on very different grounds. John Hooper, when offered the bishopric of Gloucester made vacant in 1549 by the death of John Wakeman, declined to undergo consecration in the 'Aaronic habits' required by the new Ordinal, and objected particularly to the 'shameful and impious form of the oath'. The elect was required to swear allegiance to the King's Supremacy '. . . so helpe me GOD, al sainctes and the holy Euangelist'.[21] Imprisoned for some months for his refusal, he eventually explained his reasons to the King, and was summoned before the Council on Ascension Day, 1550, where 'the matter was seriously agitated in the way of interrogatory'. His chief opponent was Nicholas Ridley, who was amongst those who considered vestments to be *adiaphora* and their use therefore permitted. Hooper accused the bishops of being 'children of the world, superstitious and blind papists', to which Ridley retorted with accusations of Anabaptism.[22] This probably reflects

---

[18] *Ibid.*, p. 281,

[19] *Ibid.*, pp. 277–8.

[20] Procter, F., and Frere, W.H., *A New History of the Book of Common Prayer* (London, 1901), pp. 60–1; Strype, *Cranmer*, Book II, Chapter XI, p. 273. If the new rite was used in 1549, the fact is not noted in Ridley's episcopal register; the first ordination of his episcopate recorded therein took place on 24 June 1550 (Guildhall Library MS9531/12 Part 2, fol.121r). Further, according to Strype, Ponet was the first bishop to be consecrated 'after this new form', also in 1549 (*ibid.*, p. 274).

[21] Brightman, *The English Rite*, vol. I, p. 950.

[22] The violence of Ridley's opposition to Hooper probably had its roots in the clash between them on the matter of jurisdiction over the strangers' churches which met in the Austin Friars' church in London. Ridley sought to establish a 'godly unity' in his

a clash of personalities between the two men rather than a fundamental crisis of doctrine. Hooper's scruples were shared by John Bradford, though in his case the parts of the service to which he objected were omitted from his own ordination without serious argument; Bradford was a close personal friend of Ridley.[23] Ultimately, the discussion was concluded to the mutual satisfaction of all parties, and Hooper took upon himself the charge committed to him, the King himself removing the offending clause of the oath.[24] The form of the oath in the 1552 Ordinal retained this inoffensive nature: '. . . so helpe me God through Iesus Christ.'[25] He was discharged from custody, according to the merchant Richard Hilles in a letter to Bullinger,

> after he yielded up his opinion and judgment upon certain matters which are here regarded by us as matters of indifference. And this Lent, habited in the scarlet episcopal gown, after he had been initiated or consecrated after the manner of our bishops, he preached before the king's majesty, many of the [bystanders] either approving or condemning his dress, just as they were guided by their feelings.[26]

The new rite for conferring the Church's ministry on suitable candidates was a considerable simplification of the old forms of ordination. Published and annexed to the Book of Common Prayer, and in English, it also became available to a much wider public. The Ordinal makes no provision for the conferring of minor orders or of the subdiaconate; much of the ceremonial of the medieval rites was excised, as had been anticipated in the 1537 Bishops' Book. Only three orders of service were provided, one for each of the orders of bishop, priest and deacon. In all three rites the central act of ordination was the laying on of hands, accompanied by an imperative formula. The bishop remained the ordinary minister of the ordination of deacons and priests, the archbishop of the province being responsible for conferring the episcopate on his suffragans. In the case of the consecration of an archbishop, it was the other metropolitan who was to preside.

diocese after the deprivation of Bonner, which was threatened by these autonomous congregations which considered themselves exempt from episcopal jurisdiction. John à Lasco, with support from Hooper, was the prime mover in this dispute, and it is notable but perhaps unsurprising to find him Hooper's main supporter in the controversy over the Ordinal. Hopf, C., 'Bishop Hooper's notes to the King's Council', *Journal of Theological Studies*, 44 (1943), pp. 194–9; *Original Letters*, vol. II, p. 573; Brigden, *London*, pp. 464–6.
[23] Trueman, C.R., *Luther's Legacy: Salvation and English Reformers, 1525–1556* (Oxford, 1994), p. 26 note 53.
[24] Hooper to Bullinger, London, 29 June 1550, *Original Letters*, vol. I, p. 87. Procter and Frere, p. 61.
[25] Brightman, p. 950.
[26] Hilles to Bullinger, London, 22 March 1551, *Original Letters*, p. 271.

'The Fourme of Consecrating of an Archebisshoppe or Bisshoppe' found in the Ordinal of 1550 was repeated, with a few significant alterations (chiefly regarding vestments, and the rite of handing over the instruments, or *traditio instrumentorum*) in the book of 1552. While the principal source was the Sarum ordinal, other influences were apparent in a number of passages. It is very likely that the rite for conferring orders given by Martin Bucer in his treatise *De ordinatione legitima* served as a model for the compilers of the 1550 English Ordinal.[27] For example, the interrogation of the bishop-elect by the archbishop, which in both 1550 and 1552 versions of the Ordinal takes place after the Litany, though chiefly derived from the Sarum rite is closer to Bucer in a number of places, giving it a more Reformed tone. The Ordinal, following Bucer, called upon the elect to affirm both the sufficiency of the Scriptures for salvation and his intention to teach the same to his people. Neither *sola scriptura* nor justification by faith were to be found in the Sarum form of the interrogatory. The elect's undertaking to uphold orthodoxy is derived almost verbatim from Bucer:

> [Ordinal] *The Archebishoppe.* Be you ready with al faithful diligence, to banish and driue away al erronious and straunge doctryne, contrary to god's worde, and both priuately and openly to call upon, and encourage other to the same? *Aunswere.* I am ready, the lord beyng my helper.
>
> [Bucer] Estis parati . . . ad arcendam a fidelibus, depellandamque omnem doctrinam alienam, priuatisque admonitionibus, et adhortationibus . . .
> Parati sumus, Domino nos adiuuante.[28]

Bullinger may have had an influence on the simplicity of the Ordinal and on its final shape. In *De episcoporum* he had set out a model for the way in which bishops should be consecrated. Following the example of apostolic simplicity, the elect should stand in the sight of the congregation; after prayer by the people, the '*seniores ecclesiae*' should lay hands on the candidate.[29] There is a certain ambiguity in the passage over the *seniores ecclesiae* who are expected to lay hands on the elect, and it could be taken as an argument for the ordination of a bishop by the college of presbyters, an ambiguity which is to be found also in the writings of the

---

[27] Some Anglican liturgists disagree, considering the Ordinal to be purely within the Catholic tradition and not influenced directly by Reformed thinking; see Firminger, W.K., 'The Ordinal', in *Liturgy and Worship*, ed. Clarke, W.K.L., and Harris, C. (London, 1932), pp. 626–82.

[28] *The First and Second Prayer-Books*, pp. 315, 461; Bradshaw, *The Anglican Ordinal*, p. 20; Brightman, vol. I, p. 1008; Whitaker, *Martin Bucer and the Book of Common Prayer*, pp. 4–6, 175–83.

[29] *De episcoporum*, fol.100v.

early Church.[30] Bullinger had argued that ancient ordination rites knew no ceremony other than a single imposition of hands.[31] The words which accompanied the imposition of hands, the central act of consecration, in the Ordinals of 1550 and 1552 were taken from 1 Timothy 2:6–7, with the addition of the imperative formula 'Accipe Spiritum Sanctum,' which had become current in Latin rite ordinals from the fourteenth century.[32] Other than that of Bucer and Bullinger mentioned above, it seems that the Ordinal contains little or nothing derived directly from Continental Reform thought, and is based almost exclusively on a reworking of traditional sources.[33]

It is instructive to compare two opposing, and yet almost contemporary views of the episcopate found in the writings of John Hooper, Edwardian Bishop of Gloucester and Worcester, and Thomas Watson, Marian Bishop of Lincoln. Watson, in his 1558 collection of sermons for public distribution entitled *Holsome and Catholyke doctryne*, linked the provision of suitable ministers of the Church to the importance of the sacraments.[34] God is the ultimate source of the grace and power of order, the Church acting as the mediator of that grace through the ordaining bishop. Hooper's opinion, expressed seven years earlier, was that the minister holds office with the approval of the Church, and when that

---

[30] Jerome, for instance, had stated that presbyters and bishops were originally one office, and that the primitive bishops were elected from amongst the presbyterate. The ambiguity was often used to support equality of ministers, while in Tyndale's New Testament, the Greek *presbyter* was often translated *senior*.

[31] *De episcoporum*, fol.98v.

[32] As, for instance, in the pontifical of the fifteenth-century Bishop of Exeter, Edmund Lacy: 'The consecrator lays his hands upon the head of the elect, saying to him: Receive the Holy Spirit [*Accipe spiritum sanctum*]. All other bishops present do and say the same . . . .' One of the main arguments against the validity of Anglican orders made by Leo XIII in 1896 was that the words 'Accipe Spiritum Sanctum' are insufficient to designate either the grade of order being conferred, or the powers attached thereto. The Ordinal which accompanied the 1662 Book of Common Prayer sought to correct this defect by qualifying phrases (in the Form of Ordaining or Consecrating of an Archbishop or Bishop, for instance, the formula begins 'Receive the Holy Ghost, for the Office and Work of a Bishop in the Church of God . . .'), though this was understood by the Pope as having come too late to maintain an unbroken succession of validly ordained bishops; it also failed to resolve his reservations about defective intention or the validity of the orders of Matthew Parker's episcopal consecrators. *The First and Second Prayer-Books*, pp. 316–17, 462–3; Brightman, p. 1014; Ott, *Fundamentals*, p. 456.

[33] See, for instance, the discussions of the Ordinal in Cuming, G.J., *A History of Anglican Liturgy* (London, 1969), pp. 92–5, 114, and in Clarke and Harris, *Liturgy and Worship*, noted above, as well as the detailed dissection of sources to be found in Brightman.

[34] Watson, *Holsome and Catholyke doctryne*, fol.cliiii, r. It is interesting to note that the publication of vernacular sermons was a device employed also by Watson's predecessor as Bishop of Lincoln, John Longland.

approval is removed he ceases to be a minister. The act of laying on of hands, a central rite of ordination for both Catholic and Reformed opinion in England, was for Hooper the public expression of the commencement of ministry, of human origin, setting the individual in a relationship with the Church, which continues only as long as the ministry is exercised. There is no question of the transmission of grace in the act of ordination, or of any sense of the idea of indelible character which expresses the Catholic understanding of the permanence of the sacred ministry of the individual;

> albeit that the imposition of hands be tokens of the approbation of the ministers of the church, according to the example of the apostles, yet it may not therefore be called a sacrament.[35]

In this, Hooper followed Zwingli, who denied the doctrine of character as an unscriptural innovation. 'The divine scriptures know nothing of the "indelible character" conferred in recent times on the priesthood.'[36] Hooper's practical response to this doctrine of a ministry defined by its exercise alone seems to have been, in some cases at least, to have conferred that ministry by means other than the formal ceremonies prescribed by the Ordinal. In the Gloucester diocesan records for December 1561, Robert Byocke, curate of Stroud, is recorded as having been accused of unlicensed preaching. He claimed in response that he had been 'made minister' by Hooper in a room of the episcopal palace.

> All the orders that he had given unto him by the said bishop were given him at that one time, but what orders they were he, this deponent, knows not more than that the said bishop willed and charged him to go forward according to the words of the Bible, which he then did hold in his hand, and to preach the same and to minister the sacraments . . . And . . . he has preached and ministered the sacraments ever since unto this present day.[37]

The opinion that ministry in the Church was a function and not a permanent state was taught by Luther as early as 1520, and was stated in very similar terms in Tyndale's *Obedience of a Christian Man* in 1528:

> Subdeacon, deacon, priest, bishop, cardinal, patriarch and pope, be names of offices and service, or should be, and not sacraments. There is no promise coupled therewith.[38]

---

[35] Copy of Bishop Hooper's Visitation Book, *Later Writings*, p. 127.
[36] Sixty-seven theses, 27 January 1523, no.61, in Potter, *Zwingli*, p. 25.
[37] Gloucester Diocesan Records, XVIII, 49–50, in West, *John Hooper and the Origins of Protestantism*, p. 50.
[38] Tyndale, *Obedience*, 'Of Order', p. 196. See also Luther, *De Captivitate Babylonica Ecclesiae*.

The influence of Hooper's connection with Continental Reform thought upon his understanding of the nature and permanence of the Christian ministry is clear. It followed quite naturally from this that he should reject the notion of an apostolic succession of individuals tracing their orders back to Christ, and by which their ministry is legitimated. Tradition and the succession of bishops were false marks of the Church as Hooper understood it.[39] The evidence for valid ministry was to be found in the authentic preaching of the Word of God.[40] For Watson, however, ordination to the ministry was of divine origin, and placed the individual in a permanent relationship with God and the Church. In addition, he allowed to the Church the exclusive right to set men apart for this role, by virtue of the commission given to it by Christ himself when he instituted the sacrament of order,

> wherein grace or spirituall power is geuen to certein Christen men, by the outwarde signe of imposition of the Bishoppes handes vpon them, to exercise effectually the publike ministration of the Churche, whereby what so euer they dooe in the Churche according to the institution of Christe and the Church, is ratified, accepted, and allowed of almighty God.[41]

The sacrament of order was inextricably linked with the right to exercise authority and jurisdiction, for in it 'is geuen to them that be lawfully ordered the ecclesiasticall power of the Churche . . . this power is called in scripture by the name of the keyes of the kingdome of heauen'.[42] He traced the exercise of the Church's ordaining power back to St Paul, supporting his view by reference to the oft-quoted passage from 1 Timothy:

> Dooe not neglecte the grace whiche thou hast in thee, whiche is geuen to thee throughe prophecie, or the inspiration of God by imposition of handes of the order of Priesthoode.[43]

The treatment of the same passage in the King's Book of 1543 is significant in that the thing which is given in the sacrament is not 'grace or power', but 'a gift or grace of ministration'.[44] The balance in the earlier treatment was slightly in favour of an emphasis on service rather than authority.

The permanence of the sacrament of order was often explained by

---

[39] 'A declaration of Christ and his office' (1547), *Early Writings*, p. 82.
[40] 'A godly Confession and protestacion of the christian faith' (1550), *Later Writings*, pp. 90–1.
[41] Watson, *Holsome and Catholyke doctryne*, fols.cliii, v.–clv, r.
[42] *Ibid.*, fol.clvi, r.
[43] *Ibid.*, fols.cliii, v.–clv, r.
[44] Lloyd, *Formularies*, pp. 277–8.

reference to the doctrine of sacramental character. The doctrine had developed by the end of the twelfth century, and was formally defined by Bonaventure, Albert the Great and by Thomas Aquinas; it was professed by Marsilius of Padua in the *Defensor pacis*. It relies on the idea that certain sacraments impart a divine seal or promise and can only be received once. The word *sacramentum* originally meant a sacred and holy thing; it was used to signify the oath of loyalty taken by the Roman soldier, and oaths in general, and in Roman law was a technical term for the pledge which was deposited in the Temple by opposing parties in a suit. Acceptance of the opinion that ordination imparts an indelible sign or character on the soul such that the sacrament cannot therefore be repeated was the essence of the scholastic definition of the permanent nature of order. Denial of the imposition of sacramental character at ordination leads to the conclusion that the ministerial office continues only for as long as its functions are exercised. The 1543 King's Book, unlike its less conservative predecessor taught the doctrine of character imparted in ordination. Baptism and order are both sacraments;

> either of them is given to men by a certain consecration, the one when a man is baptized, and the other when he is ordered: and therefore neither of them may be iterate or repeated in the catholic church of Christ.[45]

The uncertainty of 1537 reflected in the omission of the doctrine from the Bishops' Book posed practical questions for two bishops, Latimer and Shaxton, who in 1539 resigned their sees after the passing of the Act of Six Articles. Latimer was seen at Lambeth a few days after his resignation wearing a priest's gown and sarcenet tippet, and was designated 'clerk' in the *congé d'élire* for his successor, while Shaxton was uncertain whether he should dress like a priest or a bishop.[46] Several years later, in exile in Strassburg, John Ponet signed himself in two letters to Bullinger as '*Anglus*, formerly bishop of Winchester' (letter dated 14 April 1556) and '*Winton*' (the style he would have used as bishop of Winchester, in his final letter to Bullinger of June 1556 before his death in August that year), possibly reflecting an uncertainty on his part of the abiding nature of episcopal office in a bishop deprived of his see or otherwise unable to carry out the functions of the ministry. Those who taught the permanence of the ordained state, once received, had also to reconcile this with the behaviour of many of those who were in that state. Complaints about the state of life of the clergy, and the higher clergy in particular, were all too common in the period. The doctrine of sacramental character meant that even the most ungodly minister still

---

[45] *Ibid.*, p. 281.
[46] Chester, *Latimer*, p. 151. *LP*, XIV part 1, 127, 1354.

possessed the ability to celebrate the sacraments validly. After the restoration of Catholicism in 1553 it was necessary to reaffirm the validity of the sacraments celebrated by the large numbers of ministers who had conformed in the previous reign. Furthermore, the right and duty of priests and bishops to exercise their office, whatever their state of life or perceived evil actions, had to be upheld. The right of those who were most zealous in the persecution of Protestants to call themselves Christian ministers may well have been perceived as in need of clarification. Watson had been quite clear on the matter in his 1558 sermons:

> For that power whiche God hath geuen vnto theym, is onelye to builde, and not to destroye, whiche power is honorable, and to bee estemed and obeyed in all Byshoppes and Priestes, bee they of good lyuinge or noughty liuyng. For the lyfe of an euill Prieste or Bishoppe is no hinderaunce nor preiudice to the effect and vertue of Gods Sacramentes, whiche they truelye minister, no more than the euyll lyfe of a Phisician hindreth the vertue and operation of a good medicine.[47]

He was also quite clear that episcopal ordination was required for the valid exercise of ministry within the Church. This was stated most clearly in a sermon which he preached before the Queen in Lent 1554, where he not only required episcopal ordination for valid ministry, but attacked those who permitted any individual to exercise a form of public ministry, especially in the context of a eucharistic celebration. He also argued against the validity of the orders of those ordained or consecrated according to the rites of the Edwardian Church while allowing the Catholic rite in use during the Henrician schism.[48]

The set of Articles issued by Queen Mary in 1554 seem at first sight to deny the validity of orders conferred under the Reformed Ordinals.[49] Article 15 stated:

> *Item*, touching such persons as were heretofore promoted to any orders after the new sort and fashion of order, considering they were not ordered in very deed, the bishop of the diocese finding otherwise sufficiency and ability in these men, may supply that thing which wanted in them before, and then, according to his discretion, admit them to minister.[50]

---

[47] *Holsome and Catholyke doctryne*, fol.clviii, r.

[48] Watson, *Twoo notable Sermons*, sig.Y.ii,v. The same teaching appeared in his *Holsome and Catholyke Doctryne*, fol.cliiii, v.

[49] The Articles were sent to all the bishops 'by the Queen's Majesty's commandment' on 4 March 1554, the fourth Sunday of Lent. Watson's two published sermons cited above were given before the Queen on the third and fifth Fridays of Lent 1554.

[50] *Articles and Injunctions*, p. 328. W.H. Frere argued in 1896 that the deprivation of clergy ordained under the Edwardian ordinal was for marriage rather than invalidity

The key phrase in the Article was the requirement to 'supply that thing which wanted' in the Reformed ministers.

The essential action for validly conferring the sacrament of order (the 'matter') was, for most scholastic theologians, the handing over of an object or instrument relating to the order being conferred. The chalice with wine and the paten with bread were given to the priestly ordinand, accompanied by a form of words which made specific reference to the offering of the sacrifice of the Mass. Other ministers were handed other appropriate items with an appropriate formula. The technical term for this rite was the *porrectio* or *traditio instrumentorum*. The essential nature of the rite for the valid conferral of holy order was formally defined by the Council of Florence in 1439 in the bull of union of Pope Eugenius IV.[51] The *traditio* itself is not found in any surviving rite for ordination to the orders of deacon or priest, or of consecration to the episcopate, before the tenth century, though it forms the rite for conferring minor orders in the early third-century *Apostolic Tradition* (usually attributed to Hippolytus of Rome). The decrees of Pole's legatine synod of 1555/6 expressed *verbatim* the scholastic view of the *traditio*, as defined by the Council of Florence.[52] The 1550 Ordinal retained a limited version of the *traditio*. Deacons were handed a New Testament, and priests a Bible and a chalice. Bishops were handed a pastoral staff (a Bible was also laid open on their neck, but this rite is not a *traditio* as such). In the 1552 revision, the new priest was to be handed only a copy of the Bible, and the giving of the pastoral staff was replaced in the consecration of bishops by the same act; the ceremony of laying the Bible on the new bishop's neck was removed. However, the accompanying words in the medieval rites all suggested the notion of sacrifice, an idea which the Edwardian liturgical reformers were careful

of orders, indicating an acceptance of the validity of their orders by those in authority. He added to this the suggestion that there is some evidence that 'a certain number' of Edwardian clergy were left in possession of their benefices and not reordained, and found no evidence that proceedings were ever taken on the grounds of invalidity of orders only (*The Marian Reaction*, pp. 109–10, 124, 136). In the case of the reordinations held especially in Exeter and London dioceses in the first year of Mary's reign, he believed this to imply 'an entire disbelief on the part of some one in the validity of the Edwardine Order' which was later supplanted by a view that Edwardian orders were irregular and needed supplementing in some way (*ibid.*, pp. 121, 133). Frere believed that the correct form and intention were necessary for the valid conferral of orders; in this he agreed with Leo XIII, whose bull *Apostolicae curae* was published after *The Marian Reaction* had gone to press (see Frere's p. 157, note 1). However, unlike Frere, Leo XIII considered the Edwardian ordinals to be defective in form and intention, and therefore incapable of conferring the sacrament of order.

[51] Council of Florence, Session VIII (22 November 1439), Bull of Union with the Armenians, *Conciliorum oecumenicorum decreta*, p. 549; Ott, *Fundamentals*, p. 455.
[52] Bray, ed., *The Anglican Canons, 1529–1947*, pp. 88–9.

to omit from the Books of Common Prayer and Ordinals wherever it could be taken to be associated with the eucharist. For more radical Reformers, though, the *traditio* in any form was an unacceptable and illogical innovation. Hooper argued that the font and water should be given as well as the bread, chalice and book, 'for the one is a sacrament as well as the other'.[53]

Confusion over the validity of orders conferred by the Reformed rites was widespread. In May 1551, Daniele Barbaro reported to the Venetian Senate that the new Ordinal contained a form of conferring holy orders which did not differ from the Catholic rite 'save that they take oath to renounce the doctrine and authority of the Pope'.[54] Bonner, writing after the Marian restoration of Catholicism, denied the validity of orders conferred under the Reformed rites because such ordinations failed to confer the authority to offer the sacrifice of the altar:

> the late made minysters in the tyme of the scysme, in theyr newe deuised ordination, hauinge no authorite at al giuen them to offer in the masse the body and bloude of our sauyour Chryst, but both they so ordered (or rather disordered) and theyr scysmaticall orderers also, vtterlye dispising and impugninge, not onely the oblation or sacrifice of the masse, but also the reall presence of the body and bloude of our sauious Chryste in the sacrament of the Aultar, therfore I say, that all suche bothe dampnably and presumptuously dyd offende against almyghty God, and also most pitefullye begyled the people of thys realme, who by thys meanes were defrauded of the most blessed body and bloude of oure sauiour Chryst.[55]

Cardinal Pole, on the other hand, may well have regarded the 1550 *traditio* as sufficient, though it is unlikely that he did so for the 1552 rite. His instructions from Pope Julius III (*Breve de facultatibus*, 8 March 1555) on the procedure to be followed are not clear. Clergy whose orders were clearly valid ('rite et legitime promoti') were to be allowed to continue in their position. Those who had not received orders ('non promoti') were, if suitable, to be retained in their cure and ordained. Otherwise, Pole was given a general authorization to deal with those whose orders were doubtful or irregular, and those conferred by heretical or schismatical bishops. In his instructions to the bishops he took

---

[53] Third Sermon upon Jonas, 5 March 1550, *Early Writings*, p. 479. For a discussion of the use of this action in the English Ordinal and other Reformed rites, see Carleton, 'The *traditio instrumentorum* in the Reform of Ordination Rites'.

[54] *Calendar of State Papers, Venetian*, vol. V, *1534–1554*, ed. Brown, R. (London, 1873), p. 349.

[55] *A Profitable and necessarye doctryne*, sig.Aa.iv,r. The same argument was fundamental to the nineteenth-century condemnation of Anglican orders by Pope Leo XIII.

this to mean that orders received from such bishops were validly conferred so long as the accustomed form and intention of the rite were preserved. The Bull *Praeclara carissimi* (20 June 1555) of Pope Paul IV confirmed Pole's instruction, but with the condition that those ordained by a bishop not 'rite et recto ordinato' were to be reordained. This added the further confusion of the validity of the episcopal consecration of the minister to that surrounding the matter and form prescribed by the Ordinals.[56]

In at least some places, ordination under Edwardian rites was considered wholly invalid, and reordinations are recorded as having taken place. In London diocese in the period just before Christmas 1553, the lists for those receiving first tonsure and minor orders are very long, suggesting that the thing that was lacking, the *porrectio instrumentorum* which constitued the essential form of the conferral of minor orders, was being supplied.[57] This would be fully in accord with Bonner's own opinion on the question. The confusion was subsequently clarified by the papal Brief *Regimini universalis* (30 October 1555). Those bishops were validly consecrated who, even during the schism, were themselves ordained and consecrated 'in forma ecclesiae'. This was taken to mean the use of traditional ordination rites (chiefly the Sarum ordinal), which were used at least to the accession of Edward VI, but excluding the Edwardian ordinals. The episcopal consecrations of Hooper and Ferrar were not recognized on the occasion of their degradations from the clerical state which preceded their executions for heresy in 1555. The rite of 1550 had been used at their consecrations, and as a result they were degraded only from the order of priesthood.[58] Latimer, who had been consecrated in 1535 under the old ordinal, was degraded from the episcopal office before his execution according to Foxe, though Ridley's degradation was from that of priest only, even though he had been consecrated in 1547 before the new ordinal was in use.[59] It has been suggested that, after the procedure carried out for Hooper and Ferrar, Brooks (as the head of the commission charged with the examination of Latimer and Ridley) had assumed that all the Protestant bishops with the exception of Cranmer (whose consecration had taken place before the Henrician schism) were to be treated as priests only.[60] Despite this denial

---

[56] Frere, *The Marian Reaction*, pp. 147, 150, 155–6. *Praeclara carissimi* and *Regimini universalis ecclesiae* are printed in Appendix XVI (pp. 223–32 and 232–5 respectively).

[57] London Diocese Ordinations Register June 1550 – December 1577, Guildhall Library MS9535/1, fol.16 onwards.

[58] Loades, *The Oxford Martyrs*, p. 217.

[59] *Acts and Monuments*, vol. VIII, pp. 518–42; however, D.M. Loades casts doubt on the veracity of this, suggesting that no record of Latimer's degradation survives. Loades, *op. cit.*, p. 217.

of his episcopal state, Ridley wore a bishop's tippet with his furred black gown to the place of his execution.[61]

The English Church had been separated from Rome for around twenty years by the time Queen Mary began the process of healing the breach. In those twenty years a new rite of ordination had been used which was ambiguous at least in the validity of the orders it conferred. In addition, the validity of the episcopal orders of the bishops who carried out those ordinations was questioned. Quite apart from this, a major difficulty faced by Pole was the fact that twenty-three of the twenty-four bishops in full legal possession of their sees on the accession of Mary had been consecrated after the separation of England from papal authority, and had therefore been appointed by royal authority and without papal sanction. Only Cranmer had been consecrated bishop with all due papal authority before the Henrician schism. In addition, several of the bishops who had been deprived under Edward VI, and who would be expected to play a key role in the restoration of Catholicism, had themselves been appointed after the schism. Pole decided at an early stage that, provided that the correct ordinal, that in use before the break with Rome, had been used, the consecrations of the Henrician bishops were valid.[62] This permitted the reinstatement of conservative Henrician bishops, such as Gardiner, Bonner and Heath, as well as the retention of several others who were prepared to comply with the new situation. It is notable that only one bishop inherited or appointed by Mary and still in office at her death was prepared to conform with the Elizabethan settlement.

The difficulties of ensuring that the Church had a constant supply of ministers of Word and Sacrament were surmounted throughout the period of Reformation to the death of Mary by a bench of bishops which, though changing in its constitution often according to the prevailing wind of the times, nonetheless exhibited a considerable degree of continuity. Even where major changes took place, there was always a significant body of bishops who held office across the period of transition and who could ultimately trace their ministry back to the Apostles. Where different understandings of the nature of holy order led to practical difficulties, a solution was found to enable the daily life of the Church to continue at a local level. If a pivotal point in the process of Reformation and the Church's ministry has to be found, it must surely be the almost total replacement of the bench of bishops within a year of the accession of Queen Elizabeth. Such was the level of discontinuity that the deprived and imprisoned Bonner in 1564 was able successfully to avoid the capital charge of twice refusing the Elizabethan Oath of Supremacy. The certificate of refusal was sent to the Court of King's Bench by

---

[60] Loades, *op. cit.*, p. 217.
[61] Chester, *Latimer*, p. 214.

Robert Horne, the Bishop of Winchester (in whose jurisdiction Bonner was being held). Bonner's defence was that the oath was not delivered as stated on the certificate, since Horne was not Bishop of Winchester having been consecrated by Matthew Parker who was himself not consecrated according to English law. The relevant Act (the restored 1533 Appointment of Bishops Act) required consecration by four bishops in legal possession of their sees, and as the one bishop in that state in December 1559 (Kitchin of Llandaff) declined to take part in the consecration, Parker's consecration was unlawful. Rather than let the case come to trial and risk the possibility that the Elizabethan consecrations should be declared unlawful, an Act was passed in 1567 which retrospectively validated the legality of all consecrations performed in the reign.[63]

---

[62] Loades, *op. cit.*, p. 217.
[63] See Carleton, 'English Catholic Bishops in the Early Elizabethan Era', pp. 12–13.

Chapter Nine

CONCLUSION: THE OLD EPISCOPATE IN A NEW ORDER

By the end of November 1559, the episcopate in England and Wales had all but died out. The virtual extinction of the office in the realm was a serious problem for a monarch committed to an episcopal polity. When the first Elizabethan bishop came to be consecrated in December, no bishop in legal possession of an English or Welsh see (as required by the restored 1533 Appointment of Bishops Act) could be found to perform the consecration. Matthew Parker, Elizabeth's first Archbishop of Canterbury, was responsible for the continuation of episcopacy in the English Church through a series of appointments over the course of the next year. While the validity of his consecration has ever since been questioned, it should be noted in its favour that his consecrators had all at one time been accepted as bishops of the English Church by the prevailing administrations. Parker was consecrated using the rite in the 1552 Ordinal. Regardless of the validity of his consecrators' orders, if this rite is not considered to confer the episcopate validly, then the entire succession falls. The argument, therefore, that Coverdale and Scory were unable to consecrate validly having been themselves made bishop by the Edwardian Ordinal is irrelevant, as indeed is the argument that no record of Barlow's consecration survives. The fourth co-consecrator, John Hodgkin, Henrician Bishop of the suffragan see of Bedford, was certainly accepted by Bonner as in valid episcopal orders at the end of the reign of Henry VIII, Hodgkin performing almost all the ordinations held in London diocese between 1540 and 1547.[1] Hodgkin has often been claimed in apologiae for the Anglican succession as the prime link with Augustine of Canterbury and ultimately the Apostles. However, the argument for and against the succession, when the matter came finally to a head in the nineteenth century, rested solely upon the ability of the Ordinal to confer validly the episcopate and presbyterate as understood by the Church.

[1] Guildhall Library, MS9531/12 Part 1, Register of Edmund Bonner, fols.98r–103v (modern foliation).

The consecration of Matthew Parker on 17 December 1559 should have been another stage in the continuous succession of archbishops of Canterbury stretching back to Augustine. Four bishops laid hands on him, upholding the ancient tradition which required at least three of their number so to act. Yet, although three had served as diocesan bishops only a few years earlier, and the fourth had been active as a suffragan bishop in London diocese, none was at the time in legal possession of a see of the English Church. Two had been consecrated using a form of service which in the previous reign had been considered incapable of conferring the office of bishop as understood by the Catholic Church. The same order was used at Parker's consecration, which led to the conclusion that Elizabeth's first Archbishop could be no more in episcopal orders than any other bishop consecrated by the Reformed English rite.

The period which led up to Parker's consecration was characterized by deep division over a number of issues relating to the life and teaching of the Church. The source and nature of authority was questioned in the context both of the royal supremacy and the abrogation of papal jurisdiction in England. Given the dual source of the bishop's power in the late Middle Ages, such issues were of vital import to any discussion of the episcopal office. What is perhaps surprising is the emergence of common features in the understanding of the essence of the office among those otherwise deeply divided.

First and foremost, the English Church learnt (if it did not already know) that the best and most effective bishop was a preacher of the Word of God. The theory was certainly current by 1520, and much early reform had sought to return bishops to the pulpit. As has been demonstrated, few bishops undertook this duty personally, or even provided others to preach on their behalf. The most impressive feature of the study has been the extent to which bishops diametrically opposed in many other ways were of one mind in this matter. The foremost episcopal preacher in 1520, John Fisher, was also the most committed to the conservation of the union of Christendom, even to the point of the shedding of his blood. In 1535, the very year of Fisher's death, Hugh Latimer was raised to episcopal office. Latimer had been a firm advocate of episcopal preaching, and a harsh critic of unpreaching prelates. He was also an individual who had been influenced profoundly by the Reformation, and was to meet his end in the flames for his Protestant beliefs. The most unlikely episcopal partner for Fisher, however, must surely have been John Hooper. His radical Zwinglianism, and notorious disaffection with the outward trappings of episcopacy, were matched with equal vehemence in his requirement that the bishop should be first and foremost an active preacher of God's Word. He, too, was to die for his beliefs. The unlikely combination of such opposing individuals on the bench of bishops, who nonetheless shared a common understanding of the heart of the episcopal office, should be a source of hope for those who can see nothing but division in the period of Reformation in England. Not all bishops were of the same mind, of course; such utter unanimity could hardly be expected. There were often severe disagreements over the content of sermons; Latimer, preaching under Cranmer's licence (granted in 1533 before his episcopal appointment) met opposition from, amongst others, John Hilsey who as bishop was to be a key figure in Cromwell's campaign of preaching in support of the royal supremacy in and around London.[2] Length as well as content was a source of conflict; in a letter of 1547, Gardiner sought to convince Cranmer that ordinary English people 'cannot abide to be longe a teaching', no doubt against the tendency for reformers like Latimer and others to preach for several hours at a stretch.[3] The definition of the episcopal office by the Council of Trent, coming too late for most of the bishops in this study and unwelcome to many others, was paradoxically in accord with the understanding of the English Church, that the bishop should be primarily a preacher.

One of the most surprising results from a study of the theology of episcopal office in the context of the ministry of the Church is the vagueness of the definition of the bishop's office when set aside that of the priest or presbyter. The vagueness permeates all shades of opinion, from the most Catholic to the most Reformed. Scholastic theology was as divided on the matter as any, and even those for whom the bishop was a mere office-holder never clearly defined precisely in what way he differed from the holder of presbyteral office. Official definitions were ambiguous, often referring to two orders found in the New Testament, 'bishops or priests' and 'deacons or ministers'.[4] Even the office of supervisor, a Latin term which some preferred to bishop as the rendering of *episcopus*, was ill-defined in its relationship to the ordinary ministers of the Church. Perhaps this vagueness was what saved the office for the Catholic and Reformed Church of England from the imposition of a presbyteral settlement such as was arrived at in Scotland. Although the rapid return from exile of the more conservative Reformers after the accession of Elizabeth probably had much to do with it, nonetheless the flexibility of the definition saved the existence of the two distinct offices in the ministry of bishop and priest for at least the next ninety years. The role of the bishop in the making of other ministers was for many holders of the office its defining distinctive feature, and as this understanding

[2] Wabuda, 'The Provision of Preaching', p. 100.
[3] *The Letters of Stephen Gardiner*, ed. Muller, J.A. (Cambridge, 1933), pp. 355–6, 311, 314–15; Marshall, 'Attitudes', p. 130.
[4] See, for instance, both the 'Bishops' Book' and the 'King's Book' in Lloyd, *Formularies*.

grew in popularity the personal practice of holding ordinations grew alongside it.

Attitudes to the bishop's role in education and in the preservation of truth against heresy were also very similar after the rhetoric is stripped away. Many educational foundations were laid or enhanced by the bishops of the period, intended both for the provision of a better-educated body of clergy and for the education of the young, in many cases meeting a need resulting from the dissolution of monastic and chantry schools along with the foundations themselves. All the bishops considered themselves to be responsible for the eradication of heresy, in their dioceses and in the nation at large. Various means were employed by bishops of all shades of thought, and it ought to be borne in mind that thoroughly Reform-minded bishops were as prepared to consign heretics to the flames as their Catholic brother bishops. Not all entered into the active prosecution of heresy with the enthusiasm of some of those tarred by the brush of later martyrologists, though it has become clear that the image of the bishop as the shepherd defending his flock from error was a vital one for many holders of the office.

The place of the bishop in the temporal sphere led him to exercise to an exceptional degree the hospitality which canon law required of all pastors with cure of souls. The way in which this was exercised varied according to circumstances and personal conviction. Wolsey's household, approaching the King's in scale and splendour, could not be matched from the revenues of the poorer sees. However, it seems to have been the case throughout the period that many bishops employed their resources in the relief of the poor. Even when the bishop wedded to his see took also a wife, the quality of hospitality seems not to have suffered as a result.

It would be easy to fall into the delusion that a degree of unanimity existed among the bishops from their general agreement on certain important features of their office. It must not be forgotten that the period was one of considerable division throughout Christendom over such fundamental issues as the nature of the eucharist and the exercise of authority in the Church. Many considerations of the episcopal office were made in the context of one or other of these key areas. Further, on those occasions on which bishops of the English Church found themselves in direct conflict, it was often in relation to one or both of these areas of contention. The debate on the doctrine of the eucharist in the House of Lords (14–18 December 1548), for instance, found Ridley and Bonner at opposite ends of a spectrum of divergent views. Quite frequently the individuals concerned were torn between conflicting loyalties, as when Bonner and Thirlby came to degrade Cranmer from the clerical state in January 1556. Foxe records that their attitudes were affected by their former relationships with the Archbishop. While

Bonner's harshness may have been exaggerated by Foxe in order to emphasize an image he wished to put across, Thirlby's reluctant gentleness rings true for one who had been a friend to the Archbishop, and had retained his office through two changes of monarch. It may be the case that the Queen's commission of Thirlby to this task was motivated by her desire to prove his loyalty to her and his commitment to the restoration of Catholicism.[5] On the other hand, certain bishops seemed so fundamentally opposed as to show little likelihood of reconciliation. Early in Edward's reign, Gardiner came into conflict with the promoters of reform over the question of images. From Zürich, Hooper's reply to Gardiner's *A detection of the deuils sophistrie* (1546) accused the Bishop of Winchester of being the chief defender of idolatry; in the same year, 1547, Ridley preached to the King on images, to which Gardiner replied a few days later.[6] Even supporters of the Edwardian reforms came into conflict; despite their common nemesis as episcopal martyrs under Queen Mary, Hooper and Ridley were in a violent dispute over the new Ordinal, the latter going so far as to accuse the former of Anabaptism. Once Gardiner was restored to power, he seems to have shown his great antipathy for Hooper by making his life in prison as miserable as possible.[7] It seems also that Gardiner held opposing views to even his own colleagues among the Catholic bishops; passages used in a Machiavellian treatise believed to be by Gardiner were cited by Pole to demonstrate the diabolical inspiration behind Machiavelli's thought.[8] The legate also considered that Satan had deceived Cranmer's conscience; in his letter exhorting the imprisoned Archbishop to repentance, Pole accused him of leading the flock of God astray, which for him was the worst crime that a bishop as shepherd and pastor could commit. Normally conciliatory, Pole displayed an unusual degree of intensity in the tone of his letter.[9]

Studies of the process of Reformation in England have in the past often treated the realm as if in a vacuum. This study has unearthed some of the great web of interconnected influences in the religious life of the nation throughout the period in question. The process of reform was enriched by the enforced exile of a number of future bishops. Some were

---

[5] *Acts and Monuments*, vol. VIII, pp. 71–80.
[6] Hooper, *An answer vnto my lord of wynchesters booke* (Zürich, 1547), *Early Writings*, p. 202; Aston, M., *England's Iconoclasts. Volume 1: Laws against Images* (Oxford, 1988), pp. 219, 251.
[7] *Acts and Monuments*, vol. VI, pp. 647–8; Newcombe, D.G., 'The Life and Theological Thought of John Hooper, Bishop of Gloucester and Worcester, 1551–1553', Cambridge PhD, 1990, p. 308.
[8] See Donaldson, P., 'Bishop Gardiner, Machiavellian', *Historical Journal*, 23 (1980), pp. 1–16.
[9] Lambeth Palace Library, ms 2007, fol.246v.

driven abroad by the conservatism of Henry VIII, among them Cover-dale and Hooper who returned with personal experience of Continental reform which, in the reign of Edward VI, complemented Cranmer's experience of Lutheranism from the years immediately preceding his preferment to the see of Canterbury. Others, like Pates, Peto and Pole, left because of their opposition to the Aragon divorce and the royal supremacy, returning in Mary's reign to play an active role in the re-establishment of Catholicism. As Catholic exiles returned, so many of those committed to Protestant reformation sought refuge on the Continent, among them a number of bishops. On their return they had an important influence on the shape of the English Church as reformed under Queen Elizabeth. It is also true that many bishops, particularly in the early part of the period, spent time abroad by choice rather than by force of circumstances. The importance of Continental influences on the progress of reform in England, in all its forms, should not be under-estimated. Key individuals like Cranmer and Pole were not alone in their experience; other bishops, like Tunstall, Thirlby and Latimer's old adversary Nicholas West, had personal experience of Continental reform movements both before and after their appointment to episcopal office. Nor was it a one-way process; Fisher's influence upon Borromeo and other bishops of the Catholic Reformation has been well documen-ted, but it is important to note also the part played by later exiles such as Thomas Goldwell in the development of the post-Tridentine Church. While only one bishop of the period was so important for Roman Catholic Christendom that he should be raised to the altar, the modern Church of England has seen fit to commemorate several bishops of the period in its liturgical calendar, among them no less a figure than Cranmer whose influence upon the final form of the Anglican settlement was so great.

The impact of the continuance of the episcopal office in the Reformed English Church may best be demonstrated by looking briefly at the view of that office held by the first and most important early apologist of the Church of England, John Jewel. A student of Merton and Corpus Christi Colleges at Oxford, after his MA in 1545 Jewel was Reader in Humanity and Rhetoric, reflecting his interest in and study of the new learning. This went hand in hand with a commitment to the promotion of the Reformed religion, which received considerable support after the acces-sion of Edward VI, and in 1551 Jewel was ordained to the ministry. He received his Oxford BTh the following year, and the sermon which he preached on that occasion demonstrated the extent of his commitment to the Reformed cause. After the accession of Mary he was deprived of his fellowship, but unlike a number of others (including Jewel's friend and colleague Peter Martyr) chose to remain in Oxford rather than enter self-imposed exile abroad. He was notary at the trials of Cranmer and Ridley in April 1554, and shortly afterwards signed the Catholic articles, an act of inconstancy which later came back to haunt him, and which he was to regret, despite the fact that his own life would have been in danger had he refused. After the death of Mary, Jewel took part in the Westminster Disputation where he opposed the Catholic bishops and divines, lining up with other Reformers many of whom were soon to be raised to the English episcopate. Jewel himself was appointed to the bishopric of Salisbury in the summer of 1559. Two years later he was set to work by the Queen's Secretary William Cecil on a treatise explaining and defending the Elizabethan settlement. The *Apology of the Church of England* which resulted from this soon became one of the fundamental defining documents of the Anglican Church. Not only was the episcopate retained, but its exercise was seen as purer than in the Roman Church, more in line with the practice of the early Church. For Jewel, the prime qualification for a bishop was the ability to instruct the people in Holy Scripture.[10] Despite the teaching of the Council of Trent (the final sessions of which were about to sit when the *Apology* was first mooted), Jewel saw the bishops of the Church of Rome as manifestly failing to carry out the duty of preaching.[11] It is true that the practice of preaching amongst the bishops (in the English Church as much as anywhere) had fallen into some desuetude. Indeed, the nonpreaching of the prelates of the Church was a major complaint amongst many of Jewel's reforming predecessors. However, it must be admitted that there were a number of notable exceptions to this, and whose own lives and actions served in varying degrees as models for the practice of episcopacy in others. Perhaps the most notable of the English bishops who served as such a model was John Fisher of Rochester, whose own personal practice of preaching, particularly in the vernacular, came from his commitment to Christian humanism and the new learning.[12] Jewel, the Oxford man, and Fisher, the Cambridge man, sat in the same tradition of reform and renewal. For Fisher, however, the unity of Christendom and the fundamental place of the papacy in the Church were paramount, and his approach to the reform of the Church came from continuous growth and development. Jewel, the younger by some fifty-three years, and who grew up in a period of religious change, inclined more towards a break from the immediate past as a way to restoring the Church to its original

---

[10] Jewel, J., *An Apology of the Church of England*, ed. Booty, J.E. (Charlottesville, VA, 1963), p. 140.

[11] *Ibid.*, p. 91. The passage goes on to 'common a word or two' against the pope, specifically suggesting that papal primacy, as taught and exercised, was fundamentally contrary to the doctrine of the early Church and Fathers, and thus, by Jewel's touchstone for ecclesial authenticity, neither valid nor licit in the true Church of Christ.

[12] Fisher's preaching is discussed at greater length in Chapter 4.

pristine state. His approach was to look to the early centuries of the Church as the touchstone and essence of authenticity. By this he was able to retain those features of organization and doctrine, essential to the new Elizabethan Church of England, which were not to be found explicitly in the Scriptures alone. Key to the identity of his Church was the model of the bishop as pastor and head of the diocese, a structure which did not come into universal use until the century after the Apostles. The office was quickly seen by many as of the essence of the Church of England, though it always had its opponents. Indeed, the logical conclusion to which this episcopal/royal axis was to lead in the next century cost the King his head and the suspension of the episcopate as an active force in the Anglican Church.

The day 17 December 1559 was a watershed in the history of the English Church. More than any other event, the consecration of Matthew Parker marked the final and definitive split from the Western Catholicism which subsisted in the Church of Rome and drew its unifying principle from communion with the Pope. From Parker onwards, it could truly be said that the Anglican Church possessed a Protestant episcopate. While the label of 'Protestant' (however inappropriately applied) could be and has been applied to earlier English bishops, it was those who derived their orders from Parker and his successors that constituted a new order. There was indeed a visible continuity with the past; in its dioceses, its churches, in many of its clergy, the visible and administrative context of the English Church remained much as it had been for centuries. Word and Sacrament were restored to what was believed to be a more primitive and pristine form, and were celebrated in locations purged of their superstitious associations. Yet for all that, the English Church at that time underwent a sea change in both its self-understanding and in the face it showed to the world. Parker, the scholarly conservative, was soon joined on the episcopal bench by others of more extreme opinions. While it is perhaps as inappropriate to attach the label 'Puritan' to some of these individuals as it would have been to use the 'Protestant' label of their reforming predecessors, it is nonetheless true that many, such as Edmund Grindal, who later succeeded Parker at Canterbury, had been finely honed in the school of Continental reform. Their desire for more rapid and radical reform of the Church of England was not shared by many of their co-religionists, and more particularly not shared by their Queen and Supreme Governor.[13]

The English Church of the sixteenth century was built upon its

---

[13] The trials which Grindal endured, and the difficulties in which his desire for radical reform left him, are thoroughly set out in Collinson, P., *Archbishop Grindal, 1519–1583: The Struggle for a Reformed Church* (London, 1979).

bishops. On several occasions, the whole edifice was dismantled and rebuilt again from its foundations. Whether dependent upon King or Pope, or on the intrinsic authority of his office, the bishop was a defining feature of the Church. Through periods of change the bishops provided at once continuity with the past and a driving force for constant reform. Even the virtual extinction of the office could be seen as a purging and renewal of an essential part of the Church's and the nation's life. In the new dispensation of the Elizabethan settlement, the office of bishop was a fundamental defining feature of a Church which understood itself as at once both Catholic and Reformed.

APPENDIX I:
PROSOPOGRAPHY OF THE BISHOPS IN
OFFICE 1520–1559

The main part of this list includes all those bishops who held episcopal office in England and Wales between 1520 and 1559; it excludes all those appointed after the death of Queen Mary. Only those bishops who had actual legal possession of their sees are included. As a result, bishops-elect appointed in the latter years of Queen Mary, and bishops appointed by the pope *in curia Romana* but without effect, are excluded from the main list. A supplementary section, with brief details of the individuals in this category, is included after the main list.

Key to the main entries

1. a. Dates of birth and death.
   b. Known membership of a religious order at some time in the bishop's career.
   c. Age on first appointment to a diocese as bishop.
2. a. University (universities) of study, followed by college(s) where membership is known.
   b. Degree(s), and dates of award where known. In some cases, where a choice of dates is given (particularly in the period 1 January to 25 March), the later date has been preferred. This is frequently the case with the degree of Bachelor of Arts, which was often conferred in January. The following abbreviations have been used, following the practice of A.B. Emden in his biographical registers of the Universities of Oxford and Cambridge:

BA/MA	Bachelor/Master of Arts
BCL/DCL	Bachelor/Doctor of Civil Law
LicCnL	Licentiate in Canon Law
BCnL/DCnL	Bachelor/Doctor of Canon Law
DCL&CnL	Doctor of Civil and Canon Law
BTh	Bachelor of Theology/Divinity
DTh	Doctor of Theology/Divinity
BM	Bachelor of Medicine

3. a. Diocesan bishoprics held during the period under study.
   b. Other relevant appointments throughout career, including episcopal appointments outside the period.

Where there is doubt over the accuracy or reliability of a date, place or degree, or where the date of birth is conjectural, the fact is noted with a question mark. The following abbreviations are used throughout:

adm.	admitted	appt.	appointed
depr.	deprived	inc.	incorporated
nom.	nominated	res.	resigned
rest.	restored		

1. Main Prosopography: Bishops having legal possession of their sees

ALDRICH, Robert
1. a. (?)–5 May 1556
   b.
   c.
2. a. Cambridge, King's College
   b. BA (1512), MA (1515), BTh (1517), DTh (inc. Oxford 1530)
3. a. Carlisle, 1537–56
   b. Chaplain to John Longland (before 1534)
   Almoner to Queen Jane (Seymour) (1534–37)

ATHEQUA, George
1. a.
   b. Dominican
   c.
2. a.
   b.
3. a. Llandaff, 1517–37 (res.)
   b. Confessor to Queen Catherine of Aragon

ATWATER, William
1. a. ?1440–4 February 1521
   b.
   c. 64
2. a. Oxford, Magdalen College
   b. BA (1473), MA (c.1476), DTh (1493)
3. a. Lincoln, 1514–21
   b. Confessor to Henry VIII before appointment as bishop. 1506–12 Chancellor of Lincoln Cathedral.

AUDLEY, Edmund
1. a. (?)–23 August 1524
   b.
   c.
2. a. Oxford, Lincoln College?
   b. BA (1467), MA (by 1471), DTh (by 1483), DTh (Cambridge, inc. 1483)
3 a. Salisbury, 1502–24

b. Bishop of Rochester, 1480–92; of Hereford 1492–1502.
   Chancellor of the Order of the Garter, 1502–24.

BARLOW (or FINCH), William
1. a. (?)–1568
   b. Augustinian Canon
   c.
2. a. Has been claimed for both Oxford and Cambridge
   b.
3. a. St Asaph, 1536; St Davids, 1536–48; Bath and Wells, 1548–53 (res.)
   b. Minister to an English congregation at Emden during Mary's reign. Bishop of Chichester, 1559–68.

BAYNES (or BAYNE), Ralph
1. a. (?)–18 November 1559
   b.
   c.
2. a. Cambridge, St John's College
   b. BA (1518), MA (1521), DTh (1555)
3. a. Coventry and Lichfield, 1554–59 (depr.)
   b. Professor of Hebrew, University of Paris (after 1550–1553)

BELL, John
1. a. (?)–2 August 1556
   b.
   c.
2. a. Oxford, Balliol College; Cambridge, ?.
   b. BCL (Cambridge, 1504), DCn&CL (abroad, by 1516), DCL (Oxford, inc. 1531)
3. a. Worcester, 1539–43 (res.)
   b. Vicar General and Chancellor of Worcester, appt. 1518. Chaplain to Henry VIII.

BIRD, John
1. a. (?)–25 October 1558
   b. Carmelite
   c.
2. a. Oxford, Carmelite Convent
   b. BTh (1510), DTh (1514)
3. a. Bangor, 1539–41; Chester, 1541–54
      (depr.)
   b. Prior Provincial and Visitor
      General of his Order in England
      1516–19, 1522–37. Bishop of
      Penrith (suffragan to Llandaff)
      1537–39.

BLYTH, Geoffrey
1. a. (?)–1530
   b.
   c.
2. a. Cambridge, King's College
   b. MA (1490), DTh (1498)
3. a. Coventry and Lichfield, 1503–30
   b. Lord President of the Council of
      Wales, 1512–24.

BONNER, Edmund
1. a. 1500?–5 September 1569
   b.
   c. 38
2. a. Oxford
   b. BCL (1519), BCnL (1519), DCL
      (1526)
3. a. Hereford, 1538–39; London, 1539–
      49 (depr.); 1553 (rest.) –59 (depr.)
   b. Chaplain to Cardinal Wolsey by
      1529. Archdeacon of Leicester
      before appointment as bishop.

BOOTH, Charles
1. a. (?)–5 May 1535
   b.
   c.
2. a. Cambridge, Pembroke Hall;
      Bologna
   b. BCL (Cambridge, 1485), DCL

(Bologna, 1493), DCL (Cambridge,
   inc. 1506)
3. a. Hereford, 1516–35
   b. Chancellor and commissary
      general of the Bishop of Lincoln,
      1501–06.

BOURNE, Gilbert
1. a. (?)–10 September 1569
   b.
   c.
2. a. Oxford, All Souls College
   b. BA (1529), MA (1533), BTh (1543)
3. a. Bath and Wells, 1554–59 (depr.)
   b. Chaplain to Edmund Bonner,
      Bishop of London, in the reign of
      Henry VIII.

BROOKS, James
1. a. May 1512–1558/February 1560?
   b.
   c. 42
2. a. Oxford, Corpus Christi College
   b. BA (1531), MA (1535), BTh (1544),
      DTh (1546)
3. a. Gloucester, 1554–58 (died)/59
      (depr.)?[1]
   b. Master of Balliol College, Oxford,
      1546–55. Chaplain and almoner of
      Stephen Gardiner, Bishop of
      Winchester, 1553.

BULKELEY, Arthur
1. a. (?)–14 March 1553
   b.
   c.
2. a. Oxford
   b. BCnL (1525), DCnL (1525)
3. a. Bangor, 1541–53
   b.

BUSH, Paul
1. a. 1490–11 October 1558
   b. Bonhomme
   c. 52

---

[1] The *Handbook of British Chronology* states that Brooks was deprived in 1559 and died in February 1560. However, Cardinal Pole's Archiepiscopal Register records a vacancy from 1558 caused *per obitum bone memoriae domini Jacobi Brokes ultimi episcopi*; see Lambeth Palace Library, register of Archbishop Reginald Pole, fol.63v, and *Fasti Ecclesiae Anglicanae*, where John Bowsher is given as the royal nominee to the vacant see in 1558 (following Pole's register).

2. a. Oxford
   b. BA (1518) (BTh and DTh?)
3. a. Bristol, 1542–54 (res.)
   b. Prior of Bonshommes, Edington, Wilts., at the dissolution in 1539. Provincial of the Bonshommes. Chaplain to Henry VIII.

CAMPEGGIO, Lorenzo
1. a. 1472–1539
   b.
   c.
2. a. Pavia, Bologna
   b. (Studied imperial law according to *DNB*)
3. a. Salisbury, 1524–34 (depr.) / 1524–39 (deprivation not recognized by the pope)
   b. Created Cardinal in 1517. Papal legate *a latere*, with Wolsey, in the matter of the King's divorce. Held several Italian bishoprics concurrently (including Bologna).

CAPON, John – *see* SALCOT

CHAMBERS, John
1. a. (?)–7 February 1556
   b. Benedictine
   c.
2. a. Cambridge; Oxford?
   b. MA (1505), BTh (Cambridge, 1539)
3. a. Peterborough, 1541–56
   b. Abbot of Peterborough, 1528–40. Chaplain to the King by 1539.

CHRISTOPHERSON, John
1. a. (?)–December 1558
   b.
   c.
2. a. Cambridge, Pembroke Hall, St John's College, Trinity College
   b. BA (1541), MA (1543), BTh (1554)
3. a. Chichester, 1557–58
   b. Master of Trinity College, 1553–58. Dean of Norwich 1554. Chaplain and Confessor to Queen Mary.

CLERK, John
1. a. (?)–3 January 1541

2. b.
   c.
2. a. Cambridge; Bologna
   b. BA (Cambridge, 1499), MA (Cambridge, 1502), DCnL (Bologna, 1510)
3. a. Bath and Wells, 1523–41
   b. Chaplain to Cardinal Wolsey.

COTES, George
1. a. (?)–December 1555
   b.
   c.
2. a. Oxford, Balliol College, Magdalen College
   b. BA (1523), MA (1528), BTh (1534), DTh (1536)
3. a. Chester, 1554–55
   b. Oxford, Dean of Divinity, 1535, 1537–38. Master of Balliol College, 1539–45.

COVERDALE, Miles
1. a. 1488?–19 February 1569
   b. Augustinian Friar
   c. 63
2. a. Cambridge, Augustinian House; Tübingen
   b. DTh (inc. Cambridge, 1563, from Tübingen) (BCnL, 1531, according to Cooper, *Athenae Cantabrigienses*)
3. a. Exeter, 1551–53 (depr.)
   b.

CRANMER, Thomas
1. a. 2 July 1489–21 March 1556 (executed for heresy)
   b.
   c. 44
2. a. Cambridge, Jesus College
   b. BA (1512), MA (1515), BTh (1521), DTh (1526)
3. a. Canterbury, 1533–53 (depr.)
   b. Chaplain to Anne Boleyn.

DAY, George
1. a. 1501?–2 August 1556
   b.
   c. 42
2. a. Cambridge, Corpus Christi College?, St John's College

b. BA (1521), MA (1424), BTh
(1533), DTh (1537)
3. a. Chichester, 1543–51 (depr.); 1553
(rest.) –56
b. Chaplain to John Fisher, Bishop of
Rochester, after 1524. Master of St
John's College, Cambridge, adm.
27 July 1537. Vice Chancellor,
University of Cambridge, 1537–38.

DUNSTAN, Anthony – *see* KITCHIN

FERRAR, Robert
1. a. (?)–30 March 1555 (executed for
heresy)
b. Augustinian Canon
c.
2. a. Oxford, St Mary College
b. BTh (1533)
3. a. St Davids, 1548–54 (depr.)
b. Chaplain to Cranmer and to
Edward (Seymour) duke of
Somerset.

FISHER, John
1. a. 1469–22 June 1535 (executed for
treason)
b.
c. 35
2. a. Cambridge, Michaelhouse
b. BA (1487), MA (1491), DTh (1501)
3. a. Rochester, 1504–34 (depr.)
b. Chaplain and confessor to Lady
Margaret and her household. First
Lady Margaret Reader in Divinity,
University of Cambridge, 1502.
Chancellor, University of
Cambridge, 1504–35. Cardinal
Priest of SS. Vitale, Gervasio, and
Protasio, created 31 May 1535.
Canonized (with Thomas More) 19
May 1935.

FITZJAMES, Richard
1. a. (?)–15 January 1522
b.
c.
2. a. Oxford, Merton College
b. MA, DTh (by 1481), DTh
(Cambridge, inc. 1496)
3. a. London, 1506–22
b. Bishop of Rochester, 1497–1503;

of Chichester, 1503–06. Warden of
Merton College, 1483–1507.

FOX, Edward
1. a. c.1494–8 May 1538
b.
c. 41
2. a. Cambridge, King's College
b. BA (1516), MA (1520), DTh (by
1532)
3. a. Hereford, 1535–38
b. King's almoner. Provost of King's
College, 1528–38. Secretary to
Cardinal Wolsey.

FOX, Richard
1. a. c.1448–14 September/5 October
1528
b.
c. 39
2. a. Oxford, Magdalen College?;
Louvain; Paris; Cambridge?
b. BCL (probably foreign, 1477),
matriculated in faculty of Canon
Law, Louvain (1479), DCL (?, by
1486)
3. a. Winchester, 1501–28
b. Bishop of Exeter, 1487–92; of Bath
and Wells, 1492–94; of Durham,
1494–1501. Chancellor of
University of Cambridge, 1498–
1500. Master of Pembroke Hall,
University of Cambridge, 1507–
1518.

FYCHAN, Edward – *see* VAUGHAN

GARDINER, Stephen
1. a. 1483?–12 November 1555
b.
c. 48
2. a. Cambridge, Trinity Hall
b. BCL (1518), DCL (1521), DCnL
(1522), DCnL (Oxford, inc. 1531)
3. a. Winchester, 1531–51 (depr.); 1553
(rest.) –55
b. Master of Trinity Hall, 1525–51,
1553–55. Chancellor, University of
Cambridge, 1540–47, 1553–55.
Confidential secretary to Cardinal
Wolsey. Chaplain to the King and

almoner. Lord Chancellor 1553–55.

de'GHINUCCI, Geronimo
1. a. (?)–1541
   b.
   c.
2. a.
   b.
3. a. Worcester, 1522–35 (depr.) / 1522–41 (deprivation not recognized by the pope)
   b. Henry VIII's agent in the Roman Curia in succession to Giulio de'Medici.

de'GIGLI, Silvestro
1. a. 1463–16(/18?) April 1521
   b.
   c. 35
2. a.
   b.
3. a. Worcester, 1498–1521
   b. Agent for Henry VII and Henry VIII in the Roman Curia.

GLYNN, William
1. a. 1504–21 May 1558
   b.
   c. 51
2. a. Cambridge, Queens' College, Trinity College
   b. BTh (1538), DTh (1544), DTh (Oxford, inc. 1554)
3. a. Bangor, 1555–58
   b. Fellow of Trinity College, Cambridge, from its foundation (December 1546). President of Queens' College. Lady Margaret Professor of Divinity. Ambassador to Rome, 24 May–24 August 1555.

GOLDWELL, Thomas
1. a. 1500–3 April 1585
   b. Theatine
   c. 55
2. a. Oxford, St Mary Hall; Padua; Louvain.
   b. BA (Oxford, 1528), MA (Oxford, 1531), BTh (Oxford, 1534)
3. a. St Asaph, 1555–58; designate of Oxford 1558

b. 'Camerarius' of English Hospice, Rome, 1538; warden there, 1540–43, 1547–48, 1561–64. Theatine novice, Naples 1548–49; professed 28 October 1550. Superior of Naples Convent 1561. Vicar General to Carlo Borromeo, Archbishop of Milan, 1563–65.

GOODRICH, Thomas
1. a. (?)–10 May 1554
   b.
   c.
2. a. Cambridge, Corpus Christi College, Jesus College
   b. MA, DTh
3. a. Ely, 1534–54
   b. Chaplain to Anne Boleyn.

GRIFFITH, Maurice
1. a. (?)–20 November 1558
   b. Dominican
   c.
2. a. Oxford, Dominican Convent
   b. BTh (1532), BCnL (1533)
3. a. Rochester, 1554–58
   b. Appointed Chancellor to John Hilsey, Bishop of Rochester (another former Dominican friar), 1535. Archdeacon of Rochester, 1537–54.

HARLEY, John
1. a. (?)–by June 1558
   b.
   c.
2. a. Oxford, Magdalen College
   b. BA (1536), MA (1540), BTh? (1550?)
3. a. Hereford, 1553–54 (depr.)
   b. Chaplain to the King, 1551.

HEATH, Nicholas
1. a. c.1501–1578
   b.
   c. 39
2. a. Cambridge, Clare Hall, Christ's College
   b. BA (1520), MA (1522), DTh (1535)
3. a. Rochester, 1540–43; Worcester, 1543–51 (depr.); 1553 (rest.) –55; York, 1555–59 (depr.).

b. Chaplain to the King by 1535.
Lord Chancellor 1556–59.

HILSEY, John
1. a. (?)–4 August 1539
   b. Dominican
   c.
2. a. Oxford, Dominican Convent
   b. BTh (1527), DTh (1533)
3. a. Rochester, 1535–39
   b. Prior of Bristol Convent, 1533.
   Prior Provincial of England
   (appointed by Cromwell), April
   1534.

HOLBEACH (or RANDS), Henry
1. a. (?)–2 August 1551
   b. Benedictine
   c.
2. a. Cambridge, Buckingham College
   b. BTh (1527), DTh (1534)
3. a. Rochester, 1544–47; Lincoln,
   1547–51
   b. Prior of Buckingham College.
   Prior of Worcester at dissolution,
   1540; became dean of new
   foundation. Consecrated Bishop of
   (then suffragan) see of Bristol
   24 March 1538.

HOLGATE, Robert
1. a. 1481?–15 November 1556
   b. Gilbertine Canon
   c. 56
2. a. Cambridge, Gilbertine House?
   b. DTh (1537)
3. a. Llandaff, 1537–45; York, 1545–54
   (depr.)
   b. Prior and Master of the
   Gilbertine House at
   Sempringham. Prior of Old
   Malton. Chaplain to Henry VIII.
   Lord President of the Council of
   the North, 1538.

HOLYMAN, John
1. a. 1495–20 December 1558
   b.
   c. 59
2. a. Oxford, New College
   b. BA (1514), MA (1518), BTh
   (1526), DTh (1530)

3. a. Bristol, 1554–58
   b.

HOOPER, John
1. a. c.1495?–9 February 1555 (executed
   for heresy)
   b. Cistercian
   c. 55
2. a. Oxford
   b. BA (1519), DTh (possibly foreign,
   by 1550)
3. a. Gloucester, 1550–52; Gloucester
   and Worcester, 1552–53 (depr.)
   b.

HOPTON, John
1. a. (?)–by September/November(?)
   1558
   b. Dominican
   c.
2. a. Oxford, Dominican Convent;
   Bologna
   b. BTh (Bologna, 1525), DTh
   (Bologna), DTh (Oxford, inc. 1533)
3. a. Norwich, 1554–58
   b. Prior of Oxford Convent, 1528–
   36?. Private chaplain and confessor
   to Princess Mary during the reign
   of Edward VI. Chaplain to Philip
   and Mary 1554.

KING, Robert
1. a. (?)–4 December 1557
   b. Cistercian
   c.
2. a. Oxford
   b. BTh (1507), DTh (1519)
3. a. Osney, 1542–45; Oxford, 1545–57
   b. Bishop of Rheon *in partibus
   infidelium*, papal provision
   7 January 1527. Abbot
   commendatory of Osney (elected
   22 December 1537) to surrender
   (17 November 1539). Suffragan to
   John Longland, Bishop of Lincoln.

KITCHIN (or DUNSTAN), Anthony
1. a. c.1477–31 October 1566
   b. Benedictine
   c. 68
2. a. Oxford, Gloucester College?; (also
   said to have studied at Cambridge)
   b. BTh (1525), DTh (1538)

3. a. Llandaff, 1545–66
   b. Chaplain to the King by 1545.

KITE, John
1. a. (?)–19 June 1537
   b.
   c.
2. a. Cambridge, King's College
   b. BCnL (1495)
3. a. Carlisle, 1521–37
   b. Archbishop of Armagh 1513–21.
   Archbishop of Thebes *in partibus
   infidelium* 1521–37 (*in
   commendam*).

KNIGHT, William
1. a. c.1476–29 September 1547
   b.
   c. 65
2. a. Oxford, New College; Ferrara
   b. BCL (by 1504), DCL (possibly
   abroad, by 1507)
3. a. Bath and Wells, 1541–47
   b. Chaplain to the King by 1513.
   Prothonotary apostolic by 1514.

LATIMER, Hugh
1. a. 1485?–16 October 1555 (executed
   for heresy)
   b.
   c. 50
2. a. Cambridge, Peterhouse?, Clare
   Hall
   b. BA (1511), MA (1514), BTh (1524)
3. a. Worcester, 1535–39 (res.)
   b. Chaplain to Anne Boleyn.

LEE, Edward
1. a. c.1482–13 September/30
   November? 1544
   b.
   c. 49
2. a. Oxford, Magdalen College;
   Cambridge; Louvain; Bologna
   b. BA (Oxford, 1501), MA
   (Cambridge, 1504), BTh (1512),
   DTh (Louvain or Bologna)
3. a. York, 1531–44
   b. Chaplain to the King, 1520.

LEE, Rowland
1. a. (?)–25 January 1543

   b.
   c.
2. a. Cambridge, St Nicholas' Hostel,
   King's Hall?
   b. BCL (1510), DCnL (1520)
3. a. Coventry and Lichfield, 1533–43
   b.

LONGLAND, John
1. a. 1473–7 May 1547
   b.
   c. 48
2. a. Oxford, Magdalen College
   b. MA (1502), BTh (1511), DTh
   (1512)
3. a. Lincoln, 1521–47
   b. Confessor to Henry VIII.
   Chancellor of the University of
   Oxford, 1532–47.

de'MEDICI, Giulio
1. a. 1478–1534
   b.
   c.
2. a.
   b.
3. a. Worcester, 1521–22 (res.)
   b. Held Worcester *in commendam*
   with other bishoprics. Created
   Cardinal 1513. Elected Pope
   (Clement VII) 1523, succeeding
   Adrian VI (as Pope, unable to
   grant the divorce sought by Henry
   VIII).

MORGAN, Henry
1. a. (?)–23 December 1559
   b.
   c.
2. a. Oxford, London College, St
   Edward Hall, Oriel College
   b. BCnL (1522), BCL (1523), DCL
   (1525)
3. a. St Davids, 1554–59 (depr.)
   b. Chaplain to the King by 1537.
   Vicar General to John Veysey,
   Bishop of Exeter, 1544. Admitted
   to Doctors' Commons in 1528
   where for several years he acted as
   moderator of those who performed
   exercises for their degrees in Civil
   Law at Oxford.

NYKKE (or NIX), Richard
1. a. 1447?–29 December 1535/14
   January 1536?
   b.
   c. 54
2. a. Oxford; Cambridge, Trinity Hall;
   Ferrara; Bologna
   b. BCL (Bologna, 1483), BCnL
   (Bologna, 1483)
3. a. Norwich, 1501–1535
   b. Official and Vicar General in
   spirituals to Richard Fox at Bath
   and Wells, 1492, and Durham,
   1495.

OGLETHORPE, Owen
1. a. (?)–31 December 1559
   b.
   c.
2. a. Oxford, Magdalen College
   b. BA (1525), MA (1529), BTh
   (1536), DTh (1536)
3. a. Carlisle, 1556–59 (depr.)
   b. Lecturer in logic, 1529–31, and
   moral philosophy, 1534–35,
   Magdalen College. President of
   Magdalen College, 1536–52,
   1553–55.

PARFEW, Robert – *see* WARTON

PATES, Richard
1. a. (?)–1565 (in Louvain)
   b.
   c.
2. a. Oxford, Corpus Christi College;
   Bruges; Paris
   b. BA (1523), MA (Paris, by 1531),
   BTh (1536)
3. a. Worcester, 1541 (by papal
   provision; temporalties restored
   1555) –59 (depr.)
   b. Ambassador to Imperial court,
   1533–37, reappointed 1540
   (whence fled to Italy).

PENNY, John
1. a. (?)–1520
   b. Augustinian Canon
   c.
2. a. Oxford?, Lincoln College?
   b. DCL? (Cambridge? – not in Grace
   Books)

3. a. Carlisle, 1508–20
   b. Bishop of Bangor, 1505–08. Abbot
   of St Mary de Pré, Leicester, 1496–
   1508 (*in commendam* from 1505).

PETO, William
1. a. (Before 1467?)–April 1558
   b. Franciscan Observant
   c.
2. a. Oxford; Cambridge, Queens'
   College
   b. BA (Oxford, by 1502), MA
   (Cambridge, inc. 1505), MA
   (Oxford, inc. 1510)
3. a. Salisbury, 1543 (provided by Pope
   Paul III, without effect); provided
   again 1557, res. 1558.
   b. Warden of the English Hospice,
   Rome, 1544–53. Appointed
   Cardinal and Legate *a latere* for
   England, 14 June 1557, after the
   revocation of Cardinal Pole's
   legation (9 April 1547), but
   declined the appointment on
   account of his great age. Confessor
   to Princess Mary in her early years.

POLE (or POOLE), David
1. a. (?)–1568
   b.
   c.
2. a. Oxford, All Souls College
   b. BCL (by 1526), BCnL (1526),
   DCnL (1528)
3. a. Peterborough, 1557–59 (depr.)
   b. Vicar General and official principal
   of Rowland Lee (20 April 1534)
   and Richard Sampson (1543),
   Bishops of Coventry and Lichfield.
   Vicar General of Cardinal Pole,
   Archbishop of Canterbury.

POLE, Reginald
1. a. March 1500–17 November 1558
   b.
   c. 55
2. a. Oxford, Magdalen College; Padua
   b. BA (1515)
3. a. Canterbury, 1555–58
   b. Member of the reform commission
   which produced the *Consilium de
   emendanda ecclesia*, July–

November 1536. Created Cardinal Deacon of S. Maria in Cosmedin, 22 December 1536. Papal governor of *Patrimonium Patri* (the largest of the papal states with its seat of government at Viterbo), August 1541. One of three papal legates appointed to open the Council of Trent, 1542 and 1545. Appointed legate *a latere* to England, 6 August 1553. Chancellor of University of Cambridge, 9 March 1556; of Oxford, 26 October 1556. Ordained priest at Lambeth 21 March 1556 (the day of Cranmer's execution) and consecrated to the archbishopric of Canterbury the following day. Legation revoked (without effect) 9 April 1557.

PONET, John
1. a. c.1514–August 1556
   b.
   c. 36
2. a. Cambridge, Queens' College
   b. BA (1533), MA (1535), BTh (1547), DTh? (by 1549?)
3. a. Rochester, 1550–51; Winchester, 1551–53 (depr.)
   b. Chaplain to Cranmer.

RAWLINGS, Richard
1. a. (?)–15/18 February 1536
   b.
   c.
2. a. Oxford, Merton College
   b. MA (1484), BTh (1493), DTh (by 1495)
3. a. St Davids, 1523–36
   b.

REPPS (or RUGGE), William
1. a. (?)–21 September 1550
   b. Benedictine
   c.
2. a. Cambridge, Gonville Hall
   b. BTh (1509), DTh (1513)
3. a. Norwich, 1536–50 (res.)
   b.

RIDLEY, Nicholas
1. a. 1500?–16 October 1555 (executed for heresy)
   b.
   c. 47
2. a. Cambridge, Pembroke Hall; Paris; Louvain (c.1527–30)
   b. BA (1522), MA (1525), BTh (1537), DTh (1541)
3. a. Rochester, 1547–50; London, 1550–53 (depr.)
   b. Chaplain to Cranmer 1537. Chaplain to the King 1541. Elected Bishop of Durham in succession to Tunstall 1553, but election not confirmed. Visitor for Cambridge University in 1548.

RUTHALL, Thomas
1. a. (?)–4 February 1523
   b.
   c.
2. a. Oxford
   b. BCn&CL (by 1488), LicCnL (1490), DCnL (by 1499), DCnL (Cambridge, inc. 1500)
3. a. Durham, 1509–23
   b. Papal prothonotary by 1499. King's secretary 1500–16. Chancellor of University of Cambridge 1503–04. Privy councillor by 1504. Keeper of the Privy Seal 1516–23.

SALCOT (or CAPON), John
1. a. (?)–6 October 1557
   b. Benedictine
   c.
2. a. Cambridge
   b. BTh (1512), DTh (1515)
3. a. Bangor, 1534–39; Salisbury, 1539–57
   b. Abbot of St Benet's Hulme, Norfolk, 1517–39; Abbot of Hyde, Winchester, 1530–39.

SAMPSON, Richard
1. a. (?)–25 September 1554
   b.
   c.
2. a. Cambridge, St Clement's Hostel, Trinity Hall; Perugia; Paris; Siena

b. BCL (Cambridge, 1505), DCL
   (Cambridge, 1513), DCnL (1520)
3. a. Chichester, 1536–43; Coventry and
   Lichfield, 1543–54
   b. Chaplain to Wolsey and to King
   Henry VIII. Dean of Henry VIII's
   Chapel Royal. Occupied chair of
   Civil Law, University of
   Cambridge, 1512–18. Vicar
   General of Wolsey (as Bishop of
   Tournai), 1514. President of the
   Court of Wales, 1543–48.

SCORY, John
1. a. (?)–26 June 1585
   b. Dominican friar
   c.
2. a. Cambridge, Dominican Friary
   b. BTh? (1539?)
3. a. Rochester, 1551–52; Chichester,
   1552–53 (depr.)
   b. Bishop of Hereford, 1559–85.
   Chaplain to Cranmer.

SCOTT, Cuthbert
1. a. (?)–1565
   b.
   c.
2. a. Cambridge, Christ's College
   b. BA (1535), MA (1538), BTh
   (1544), DTh (1547), DTh (Oxford,
   inc. 1554)
3. a. Chester, 1556–59 (depr.)
   b. Chief of commissioners deputed by
   Cardinal Pole to visit the
   University of Cambridge, 1557.

SHAXTON, Nicholas
1. a. 1485?–5 August 1556
   b.
   c. 50
2. a. Cambridge, Gonville Hall
   b. BA (1507), MA (1510), BTh
   (1521), DTh (1531)
3. a. Salisbury, 1535–39 (res.)
   b. Almoner to Queen Anne Boleyn.
   Acted as suffragan to Thirlby,
   Bishop of Ely, and to the Bishop of
   London, during the reign of Mary.

SHERBURNE, Robert
1. a. c.1454–21 August 1536
   b.

c. 51
2. a. Oxford, New College
   b. BA (1477), MA, BM
3. a. Chichester, 1508–36 (res.)
   b. Bishop of St Davids, 1505–08.

SKEVINGTON, Thomas
1. a. (?)–13 August 1533/16–17
   November 1533?
   b. Cistercian
   c.
2. a. Oxford, St Bernard's College
   b.
3. a. Bangor, 1509–33
   b. Abbot of Beaulieu, Hants. by 1508;
   in commendam to death.

SKIP (or SKYPPE), John
1. a. (?)–30 March 1552
   b.
   c.
2. a. Cambridge, Gonville Hall
   b. BA (1515), MA (1518), BTh (1533),
   DTh (1535)
3. a. Hereford, 1539–52
   b. Chaplain and almoner to Anne
   Boleyn

STANDISH, Henry
1. a. (?)–9 July 1535
   b. Franciscan Conventual
   c.
2. a. Oxford, Cambridge?
   b. DTh (Oxford, by 1502)
3. a. St Asaph, 1518–35
   b. Provincial minister of Franciscan
   order in England 1505–(probably)
   1518.

STOKESLEY, John
1. a. c.1475–8 September 1539
   b.
   c. 55
2. a. Oxford, Magdalen College
   b.
3. a. London, 1530–39
   b. Chaplain to the King, 1518. King's
   councillor, 1521; almoner, 1523.

TAYLOR, John
1. a. 1503?–December 1554
   b.
   c. 49

2. a. Cambridge, Queens' College
   b. BA (1424), MA (1527), BTh (1536), DTh (1538)
3. a. Lincoln, 1552–54 (depr.)
   b. Master of St John's College, Cambridge, 1538–46.

THIRLBY, Thomas
1. a. c.1506–28 August 1570
   b.
   c. 34
2. a. Cambridge, Trinity Hall
   b. BCL (1521), DCL (1528), DCnL (1530)
3. a. Westminster, 1540–50; Norwich, 1550–54; Ely 1554–59 (depr.)
   b. Ambassador to emperor in Spain 1542. Embassy to emperor Charles V, c.1543. Present at imperial court 16 January 1547 (when he signed the treaty of peace at Utrecht) to spring 1548. Ambassador to Charles V, March 1552; still resident at the imperial court 25 August 1553. Special ambassador to the pope, February 1556.

TUNSTALL, Cuthbert
1. a. 1474–18 November 1559
   b.
   c. 48
2. a. Oxford, Balliol College; Cambridge, King's Hall; Padua
   b. DCn&CL (Padua)
3. a. London, 1522–30; Durham, 1530–52 (depr.); 1553 (rest.) – 59 (depr.)
   b. Chancellor of William Warham, Archbishop of Canterbury and auditor of causes, c.1508. Commissary of the prerogative of Canterbury, 1511. Keeper of the Privy Seal, 1528–30. President of the King's Council in the north, 1530–38.

TURBERVILLE, James
1. a. (?)–1570
   b.
   c.
2. a. Oxford, New College
   b. BA (1516), MA (1520), DTh

(abroad, by December 1531), DTh (Oxford, inc. 1532)
3. a. Exeter, 1555–59 (depr.)
   b.

VAUGHAN (or FYCHAN), Edward
1. a. (?)–before 27 January 1523
   b.
   c.
2. a. Cambridge
   b. DCL&CnL
3. a. St Davids, 1509–23
   b.

VEYSEY (or HARMAN), John
1. a. c.1462–28 October 1554
   b.
   c. 57
2. a. Oxford, Magdalen College
   b. BA (by 1487), BCL (by 1489), DCL (by 1495)
3. a. Exeter, 1519–51 (res.); reinstated 1553–54
   b. Dean of Exeter, 1509. Dean of the Chapel Royal, 1514.

WAKEMAN (or WICHE), John
1. a. (?)–December 1549
   b. Benedictine
   c.
2. a. Oxford, Gloucester College
   b. BTh (1511)
3. a. Gloucester, 1541–49
   b. Abbot of Tewkesbury, 1534–40.

WARHAM, William
1. a. c.1456–22 August 1532
   b.
   c. 45
2. a. Oxford, New College
   b. BCL (by 1484), DCL (by 1486)
3. a. Canterbury, 1503–32
   b. Bishop of London, 1501–03. Chancellor of England, 1504–15. Chancellor of the University of Oxford, 1506–32.

WARTON (or PARFEW), Robert
1. a. (?)–22 September 1557
   b. Cluniac Benedictine
   c.
2. a. Oxford?, Gloucester College?

b. BTh (Oxford, 1523). BTh
(Cambridge, 1525)
3. a. St Asaph, 1536–54; Hereford,
1554–57.
b. Abbot of Bermondsey prior to
election as Bishop.

WATSON, Thomas
1. a. c.1516–September 1584
b.
c. 40
2. a. Cambridge, St John's College
b. BA (1534), MA (1537), BTh
(1543), DTh (1554)
3. a. Lincoln, 1556–59 (depr.)
b. Master of St John's College, adm.
28 September 1553. Chaplain to
Stephen Gardiner.

WEST, Nicholas
1. a. 1461–28 April 1533
b.
c. 54
2. a. Cambridge, King's College;
Bologna
b. DCL (Bologna, 1496)
3. a. Ely, 1515–33
b. Vicar General to Richard Fox,
Bishop of Winchester, 1501.
Chaplain to King Henry VII and
to Queen Catherine of Aragon.

WHITE, John
1. a. 1510?–12 January 1560
b.
c. 44
2. a. Oxford, New College
b. BA (1531), MA (1534), BTh (by
1554), DTh (inc., 1555)
3. a. Lincoln, 1554–56; Winchester,
1556–59 (depr.)
b.

WOLSEY, Thomas
1. a. c.1475–29 November 1530
b.
c. 39
2. a. Oxford, Magdalen College
b. BA (1490), MA (grace to proceed
to BTh and DTh)
3. a. York, 1514–30; Bath and Wells, *in
commendam*, 1518–23; Durham, *in
commendam*, 1523–29; Winchester,
in commendam, 1529–30.
b. Bishop of Tournai, 1514–18.
Bishop of Lincoln, 1514. Chaplain
to Richard Fox. Cardinal priest of
St Cecilia, 10 September 1515.
Lord Chancellor, December 1515.
Papal legate *a latere*, appointed
May 1518. Perpetual abbot
commendatory, St Albans Abbey,
1522–30.

2. Supplementary Prosopography: Marian bishops-elect; papal provisions made without legal effect in England and Wales

BOWSHER (or BOURGCHIER), John
1. a. (?)–probably c. 1581
b. Augustinian Canon Regular
c.
2. a. Cambridge, St John's College?
b.
3. a. [nom. Gloucester, 1558]
b. Abbot of St Mary-de-Pratis, near
Leicester, 1533–38. Designated
Bishop of the see of Shrewsbury,
planned but not created by Henry
VIII.

CONTARINI, Gasparo
1. a. 1483–24 August 1542
b.
c.

2. a. Padua (1501–09)
b. (Studied philosophy and theology)
3. a. Salisbury, 1539–42, by papal
provision, without effect
b. Bishop of Belluno. Created
Cardinal, 1535. Member of the
commission which produced the
*Consilium . . . de emendanda
ecclesia.*

MALLETT, Francis
1. a. (?)–16 December 1570
b.
c.
2. a. Cambridge, Queens' College

b. BA (1522), MA (1525), BTh (1534), DTh (1535)
3. a. [nom. Salisbury, 1558]
   b. Master of Michaelhouse College, 1536–46. Chaplain to Cromwell, 1538. Chaplain and confessor to Princess Mary during the reign of Edward VI. Dean of Lincoln, 1554, after the deprivation of Matthew Parker for marriage. Retained the deanery of Lincoln after his appointment as bishop was quietly set aside by Queen Elizabeth in favour of John Jewel.

RAYNOLD, Thomas
1. a. (?)–24 November 1559
   b.
   c.
2. a. Oxford, Merton College, Cardinal College
   b. BA (1522), MA (1526), BTh (1536), DTh (1536)

3. a. [nom. Hereford, 1558]
   b. Chaplain to the King in 1537. Chaplain to King and Queen, 1555. Dean of Exeter, 1555–59. Vice-Chancellor of the University of Oxford, 1556.

WOOD, Thomas
1. a. c.1499–after 1579
   b. Franciscan
   c. 59
2. a. Cambridge
   b. BTh (1536)
3. a. [nom. St Asaph, 1558] (The identity of the Wood nominated to St Asaph on the appointment of Goldwell to Oxford is unclear, and the Franciscan friar reported as still living in the Marshalsea aged 80 in 1579 may be a different individual.)
   b.

APPENDIX II: THE DIOCESES

1. The Southern Province

Canterbury
1503–1532	William Warham
1533–1553	Thomas Cranmer
1555–1558	Reginald Pole

Bangor
1509–1533	Thomas Skevington
1534–1539	John Salcot or Capon
1539–1541	John Bird
1541–1553	Arthur Bulkeley
1555–1558	William Glynn

Bath and Wells
1518–1523	Thomas Wolsey
1523–1541	John Clerk
1541–1547	William Knight
1548–1553	William Barlow or Finch
1554–1559	Gilbert Bourne

Bristol
1542–1554	Paul Bush
1554–1558	John Holyman

Chichester
1508–1536	Robert Sherburne
1536–1543	Richard Sampson
1543–1551	George Day
1552–1553	John Scory
1553–1556	George Day
1557–1558	John Christopherson

Coventry and Lichfield
1503–1530	Geoffrey Blyth
1533–1543	Rowland Lee
1543–1554	Richard Sampson
1554–1559	Ralph Baynes or Bayne

Ely
1515–1533	Nicholas West
1534–1554	Thomas Goodrich
1554–1559	Thomas Thirlby

Exeter
1519–1551	John Veysey or Harman
1551–1553	Miles Coverdale
1553–1554	John Veysey or Harman
1555–1559	James Turberville

Gloucester
1541–1549	John Wakeman or Wiche
1550–1553	John Hooper
1554–1558	James Brooks [John Bowsher or Bourgchier, nom.]

Hereford
1516–1535	Charles Booth
1535–1538	Edward Fox
1538–1539	Edmund Bonner
1539–1552	John Skip or Skyppe
1553–1554	John Harley
1554–1557	Robert Warton or Parfew [Thomas Raynold, nom.][1]

Lincoln
1514–1521	William Atwater
1521–1547	John Longland
1547–1551	Henry Holbeach or Rands
1552–1554	John Taylor
1554–1556	John White
1556–1559	Thomas Watson

Llandaff
1517–1537	George Athequa
1537–1545	Robert Holgate
1545–1566	Anthony Kitchin or Dunstan

[1] Prevented from taking office by the accession of Elizabeth I.

London
1506–1522	Richard Fitzjames
1522–1530	Cuthbert Tunstall
1530–1539	John Stokesley
1539–1549	Edmund Bonner
1550–1553	Nicholas Ridley
1553–1559	Edmund Bonner

Norwich
1501–1535	Richard Nykke or Nix
1536–1550	William Repps or Rugge
1550–1554	Thomas Thirlby
1554–1558	John Hopton

Osney
1542–1545	Robert King

Oxford
1545–1557	Robert King
	[Thomas Goldwell, designate][2]

Peterborough
1541–1556	John Chambers
1557–1559	David Pole or Poole

Rochester
1504–1534	John Fisher
1535–1539	John Hilsey
1540–1543	Nicholas Heath
1544–1547	Henry Holbeach or Rands
1547–1550	Nicholas Ridley
1550–1551	John Ponet
1551–1552	John Scory
1554–1558	Maurice Griffith

St Asaph
1518–1535	Henry Standish
1536	William Barlow or Finch
1536–1554	Robert Warton or Parfew
1555–1558	Thomas Goldwell
	[Thomas Wood, nom.]

St Davids
1509–1523	Edward Vaughan or Fychan
1523–1536	Richard Rawlings
1536–1548	William Barlow or Finch
1548–1554	Robert Ferrar
1554–1559	Henry Morgan

Salisbury
	1502–1524	Edmund Audley
(i)	1524–1534	Lorenzo Campeggio
	1535–1539	Nicholas Shaxton
	1539–1557	John Salcot or Capon
(ii)	1524–1539	Lorenzo Campeggio
	1539–1542	Gasparo Contarini
	1542	[William Peto, without effect][3]
	1557–1558	William Peto
	1558	[Francis Mallett, nom.]

Westminster
1540–1550	Thomas Thirlby

Winchester
1501–1528	Richard Fox
1529–1530	Thomas Wolsey
1531–1551	Stephen Gardiner
1551–1553	John Ponet
1553–1555	Stephen Gardiner
1556–1559	John White

[2] Translation not completed owing to the death of Mary. Oxford diocese remained vacant until 1567.

[3] Two lines of succession are shown for Salisbury. The deprivation of Campeggio by the Henrician Church in schism was never recognized by the see of Rome. Campeggio having died in Rome, the Pope exercised his traditional right to appoint a successor, in the person of Contarini. In the same way, after Contarini's death, William Peto was nominated to the see (which was coincidentally vacant in English law by the resignation of Shaxton), though without effect.

Worcester
1498–1521 Silvestro de'Gigli
1521–1522 Giulio de'Medici
(i) 1522–1535 Geronimo
             de'Ghinucci
    1535–1539 Hugh Latimer
    1539–1543 John Bell

1543–1551 Nicholas Heath
1552–1553 John Hooper
1553–1555 Nicholas Heath
1555–1559 Richard Pates
(ii) 1522–1541 Geronimo
              de'Ghinucci
    1541–1559 Richard Pates[4]

2. The Northern Province

York
1514–1530 Thomas Wolsey
1531–1544 Edward Lee
1545–1554 Robert Holgate
1555–1559 Nicholas Heath

Carlisle
1508–1520 John Penny
1521–1537 John Kite
1537–1556 Robert Aldrich
1556–1559 Owen Oglethorpe

Chester
1541–1554 John Bird
1554–1555 George Cotes
1556–1559 Cuthbert Scott

Durham
1509–1523 Thomas Ruthall
1523–1529 Thomas Wolsey
1530–1559 Cuthbert Tunstall

[4] As at Salisbury, the succession according to English law and that of the Church of Rome differed; in the case of Richard Pates, it was as Bishop of Worcester that he attended a number of sessions of the Council of Trent, though he was unable to take formal possession of his see until 1555.

APPENDIX III:
THE EDUCATION OF THE BISHOPS

Table 1: Membership of Oxford and Cambridge Colleges

Oxford

All Souls
  Bourne
  David Pole
Balliol
  Bell
  Cotes
  Tunstall
Cardinal
  Raynold*
Carmelite Convent
  Bird
Corpus Christi
  Brooks
  Pates
Dominican Convent
  Griffith
  Hilsey
  Hopton
Gloucester
  Kitchin?
  Wakeman
  Warton?

Lincoln
  Audley?
  Penny?
London
  Morgan
Magdalen
  Atwater
  Cotes
  Richard Fox?
  Harley
  Edward Lee
  Longland
  Oglethorpe
  Reginald Pole
  Stokesley
  Veysey
  Wolsey
Merton
  Fitzjames
  Raynold*
  Rawlings

New
  Holyman
  Knight
  Sherburne
  Turberville
  Warham
  White
Oriel
  Morgan
St Bernard's
  Skevington
St Edward Hall
  Morgan
St Mary
  Ferrar
St Mary Hall
  Goldwell

Cambridge

Augustinian House
  Coverdale
Buckingham
  Holbeach
Christ's
  Heath
  Scott
Clare Hall
  Heath
  Latimer

Corpus Christi
  Day?
  Goodrich
Dominican Friary
  Scory
Gilbertine House
  Holgate?
Gonville Hall
  Repps
  Shaxton
  Skip

Jesus
  Cranmer
  Goodrich
King's
  Aldrich
  Blyth
  Edward Fox
  Kite
  West

* Nominated bishops but never took possession of their sees.

King's Hall
  Rowland Lee
  Tunstall
Michaelhouse
  Fisher
Pembroke Hall
  Booth
  Christopherson
  Ridley
Peterhouse
  Latimer?

Queens'
  Glynn
  Peto
  Ponet
  Taylor
  Mallett*
St Clement's Hostel
  Sampson
St John's
  Baynes
  Christopherson
  Day

Watson
  Bowsher?*
St Nicholas' Hostel
  Rowland Lee?
Trinity
  Christopherson
  Glynn
Trinity Hall
  Gardiner
  Nykke
  Sampson
  Thirlby

Table 2: English and Welsh bishops at foreign universities
with subject of study [conjectural subject]

Bologna
  Booth, civil law
  Campeggio, Imperial
    law
  Clerk, canon law
  Hopton, theology
  Edward Lee, theology
  Nykke, civil and
    canon law
  West, civil law
Bruges
  Pates, [theology]
Ferrara
  Knight, [civil law]
  Nykke, [civil and
    canon law]
Louvain
  Richard Fox, canon
    law

Goldwell, [theology]
Edward Lee, theology
  (Greek and
  Hebrew)
Ridley, [theology]
Padua
  Goldwell, [theology]
  Reginald Pole,
    [philosophy and
    theology]
  Tunstall, civil and
    canon law
  Contarini*,
    philosophy and
    theology
Paris
  Baynes, Professor of
    Hebrew

Richard Fox, [civil
  and canon law]
Pates, [theology]
Ridley, [theology]
Sampson, [civil and
  canon law]
Pavia
  Campeggio, Imperial
    law
Perugia
  Sampson, [civil and
    canon law]
Siena
  Sampson, [civil and
    canon law]
Tübingen
  Coverdale, theology

* Nominated bishops but never took possession of their sees.

APPENDIX IV:
THE BISHOPS OF SODOR AND MAN

The see of Man was probably united with that of Sodor, or the South Hebrides, about 1098; at the time, both were part of the province of York. In 1154, Sodor and Man was placed under the charge of the Archbishop of Trondhiem. During the Great Schism, the original diocese of The Isles was split into a separate English succession in the Isle of Man (which was politically under English Lordship) and a Scottish line of bishops, which continued to administer the northern part of the diocese.[1] The see was returned to the province of York in 1458 by a bull of Pope Callistus III. The cathedral was on St Patrick's Island off the Manx coast; it was dedicated to St Germanus and had a secular chapter. In 1517 the diocese had only one archdeaconry and seventeen parishes. Under an Act of 1542 (33 Henry VIII c.31) the English diocese of Sodor and Man was formally established alongside the old Scottish diocese of Sodor or The Isles, and placed in the province of York.

The bishops of Sodor and Man, like suffragan bishops, were not members of the House of Lords; all other diocesan bishops were automatically members by virtue of the temporal baronetcies annexed to their sees. Furthermore, few records survive for the diocese, and no episcopal registers exist for the period up to the dissolution of episcopacy. Further, where bishops of Sodor and Man do appear in the records, they tended to act in exactly the same way, and in the same situations, as bishops suffragan proper. As a result of their exclusion from political influence, the ambiguities over both their standing and their succession, and the scanty material available, they have been excluded from the category of diocesan bishops for the purposes of this study.

Prosopography of the bishops of Sodor and Man
Key to the entries may be found in Appendix I (page 188)

HOWDEN, John
1. a. c.1458?–(?)
   b. Dominican
2. a. Oxford Convent
   b. BTh, DTh
3. a. Sodor and Man, 1523–? (See noted as vacant by 1530, though a letter from 'John, Bishop of Sodor' to Cromwell is dated 13 June 1538: *LP* XIII, i, 1180).
   b. Prior, Black Friars in London (?–?)

MAN, Henry
1. a. (?) – 19 October 1556
   b. Carthusian
2. a. Oxford
   b. BTh, DTh
3. a. Sodor and Man, 1546–56
   b. Prior, Sheen Charterhouse, 1535–39 (dissolution).

[1] Powicke, F.M., and Fryde, E.B., eds., *Handbook of British Chronology*, Royal Historical Society (London, 1961), pp. 202–3.

THOMAS, Stanley
1. a. (?)–1570
   b.
2. a.
   b.
3. a. Sodor and Man, 1530?(after
      1538?)–45? (depr.?); 1555 (by papal
      provision)–1570

b. Took the Oath of Supremacy after
   the death of Queen Mary.
   Conducted a service of ordination
   by special licence of Cuthbert Scott
   in Chester diocese 17 December
   1558.

BIBLIOGRAPHY

Primary Sources

Manuscript

(i) Bishops' registers
Bodleian Library, Ms Oxf.Dioc.Papers d.105
Borthwick Institute, Register 27 (Wolsey); Register 28 (Lee); Register 29 (Holgate and Heath)
Devon Record Office, Chanter Catalogue 14; Chanter Catalogue 16; Chanter Catalogue 18
Ely Diocesan Records, University Library, Cambridge, EDR/G/1/7; EDR/G/1/8
Gloucestershire Record Office, GDR.2A; GDR.11; GDR.14; GDR.15
Guildhall Library, MS9531/9; MS9531/10; MS9531/11; MS9531/12 Part 1; MS9531/12 Part 2; MS9535/1
Hampshire Record Office, 21M65 A/1/20; 21M65 A/1/21
Hereford and Worcester Record Office, Hereford, AL19/14; AL19/15
Hereford and Worcester Record Office, Worcester, BA2648/7(ii); BA2648/9(i); BA2648/9(iii)
Kent County Archives Office, DRb/Ar 1/13; DRb/Ar 1/14; DRb/Ar 1/15
Lambeth Palace Library, Registers of William Warham, Thomas Cranmer, Reginald Pole
Lichfield Joint Record Office, B/A/1/14i; B/A/1/14ii; B/A/1/14iii
Lincolnshire Archives Office, Episcopal Register XXV; Episcopal Register XXVI; Episcopal Register XXVIIIA
Norfolk and Norwich Record Office, ORR/1/1
West Sussex Record Office, Ep.I/1/5; Ep.I/1/6; Ep.I/1/7
Wiltshire County Record Office, Registers of Edmund Audley, Lorenzo Campeggio, Nicholas Shaxton, John Salcot

(ii) Other
British Library, Additional ms 29546
British Library, Additional ms 32093
British Library, Cotton ms Cleopatra E.iv.
British Library, Cotton ms Cleopatra E.v.
British Library, Cotton ms Cleopatra E.vi.
British Library, Cotton ms Cleopatra F.ii.
British Library, Cotton ms Vespasian A.xxv.
British Library, Harleian ms 422
British Library, Royal ms 7.B.xi
Lambeth Palace Library, ms 2007

Printed

(i) Bishops' registers

Bannister, A.T., ed., *Registrum Caroli Bothe, Episcopi Herefordensis A.D.MDXVI–MDXXXV*, Canterbury and York Society Series vol. XXVIII (London, 1921)

Chitty, H., ed., *Registrum Johannis Whyte, Episcopi Wintoniensis*, Canterbury and York Society vol. XXVI (London, 1914)

——, *Registrum Stephani Gardiner et Johannis Poynet, Episcoporum Wintoniensium*, Canterbury and York Society Series vol. XXXVII (Oxford, 1930)

——, *Registrum Thome Wolsey, Cardinalis, Ecclesie Wintoniensis Administratoris*, Canterbury and York Society Series vol. XXXII (Oxford, 1926)

Griffiths, G.M., 'A St Asaph "Register" of Episcopal Acts, 1506–1571', *Journal of the Historical Society of the Church in Wales*, 6 (1956), pp. 25–49

——, 'St Asaph Episcopal Acts, 1536–1558', *Journal of the Historical Society of the Church in Wales*, 9 (1959), pp. 32–69

Hinde, G., ed., *The Registers of Cuthbert Tunstall, Bishop of Durham 1530–59, and James Pilkington, Bishop of Durham 1561–76*, Surtees Society Publications vol. CLXI (London, 1952)

Irvine, W.F., ed., 'The Earliest Ordination Book of the Diocese of Chester, 1542–7 and 1555–8', *Miscellanies Relating to Lancashire and Cheshire* vol. IV, Lancashire and Cheshire Record Society 43 (1902), pp. 25–126

Maxwell-Lyte, Sir H., ed., *The Registers of Thomas Wolsey, Bishop of Bath and Wells 1518–1523, John Clerke, Bishop of Bath and Wells 1523–1541, William Knyght, Bishop of Bath and Wells 1541–1547 and Gilbert Bourne, Bishop of Bath and Wells 1554–1559*, Somerset Record Society LV (1940)

Pryce, A.I., *The Diocese of Bangor in the Sixteenth Century* (Bangor, 1923)

Williams, G., 'The Second Volume of St David's Registers, 1554–64', *The Bulletin of the Board of Celtic Studies*, 14 (1950–52), pp. 45–54, 125–38

(ii) Other

Alberigo, J., *et al.*, eds., *Conciliorum oecumenicorum decreta* (Bologna, 1973)

Aquinas, T., *Summa Theologiae* (60 volumes, gen. ed. Gilby, T.), vol. XLVII, ed. Aumann, J. (London, 1973)

(Becon, T.), *The Catechism of Thomas Becon*, ed. Ayre, J., Parker Society (Cambridge, 1844)

Bonner, E., *A Profitable and necessarye doctryne* (London, 1555)

Bray, G., ed., *The Anglican Canons, 1529–1947*, Church of England Record Society vol. VI (Woodbridge, 1998)

Brooks, J., *A sermon very notable, fruictefull, and godlie, made at Paules crosse the xii daie of Nouebre, . . . 1553* (London, 1553)

Bullinger, H., *De episcoporum . . . institutione et functione* (Zürich, 1536)

Calendar of State Papers, Venetian, vol. V, *1534–1554*, ed. Brown, R. (London, 1873)

Calvin, J., *Institutes of the Christian Religion*, Library of Christian Classics vols. XX and XXI, ed. McNeill, J.T. (Philadelphia, 1960)

Coverdale, M., *A confutacion of that treatise which one J Standish made agaynst the protestacion of D. Barnes in M. D. XL.* (Zürich, 1541?)

Cyprian, *De ecclesiae catholicae unitate*, ed. and trans. Bévenot, M. (Oxford, 1971)

Dowling, M., ed., 'William Latymer's Cronickille of Anne Bulleyne', *Camden Miscellany XXX*, Camden Fourth Series vol. XXXIX (London, 1990), pp. 23–65.

Erasmus, D., *The Correspondence of Erasmus*, vol. VI, *1518–19*, ed. and trans. Bietenholz, P.G., Mynors, R.A.B., and Thompson, D.F.S. (Toronto, 1982)

——, *Ecclesiasticae sive De Ratione Concionandi* (Antwerp, 1535)

The First and Second Prayer-Books of King Edward the Sixth, Everyman edition (London, 1910)

Fisher, J., *Assertionis Lutheranae confutatio* (Antwerp, 1523)

——, *Sacri sacerdotij defensio contra Lutherum* (Cologne, 1525)

——, *A sermon had at Paulis . . . concernynge certayne heretickes* (London, 1526)

Forciglioni, A., *Repertorium totius summe*, 3 volumes (Basle, 1502)

[Fox, E.], *De vera differentia regiae potestatis & Ecclesiasticae, & quae sit ipsa ueritas ac uirtus utriusque. Opus Eximium* (London, 1538)

——, *The true dyfferens betwen the regall power and the Ecclesiasticall power. Translated out of latyn by Henry lord Stafforde* (London, [1548])

(Foxe, J.), *The Acts and Monuments of John Foxe*, ed. Cattley, S.R., 8 volumes (London, 1837–39)

Frere, W.H., and Kennedy, W.M., eds., *Visitation Articles and Injunctions of the Period of the Reformation*, vol. I, *Historical Introduction and Index*, vol. II, *1536–1558*, Alcuin Club Collections, XIV/XV (London, 1910)

Gardiner, S., *De vera obedientia*, in Janelle, P., ed., *Obedience in Church and State* (Cambridge, 1930)

——, *The Letters of Stephen Gardiner*, ed. Muller, J.A. (Cambridge, 1933)

Gee, H., and Hardy, W.J., *Documents Illustrative of English Church History* (London, 1921)

Gleason, E.G., *Reform Thought in Sixteenth-Century Italy*, American Academy of Religion Texts and Translations vol. IV (Ann Arbor, MI, 1981)

Gorham, G.C., ed., *Gleanings of a Few Scattered Ears during the Reformation* (London, 1857)

Hooper, J., *Early Writings of John Hooper, D.D.*, ed. Carr, S., Parker Society (Cambridge, 1843)

——, *Later Writings of Bishop Hooper*, ed. Nevinson, C., Parker Society (Cambridge, 1852)

Jewel, J, *An Apology of the Church of England*, ed. Booty, J.E. (Charlottesville, VA, 1963)

Kirk, J., ed., *The Second Book of Discipline* (Edinburgh, 1980)

Latimer, H., *A notable Sermon of the reuerende father Maister Hughe*

Latemer, whiche he preached in the Shrouds at paules church in London, on the .xviii. daye of January, 1548 (London, 1548)

——, *Sermons and Remains*, ed. Corrie, G.E., Parker Society, 2 volumes (Cambridge, 1844–45)

Lloyd, C., ed., *Formularies of Faith Put Forth by Authority during the Reign of Henry VIII* (Oxford, 1866)

Longland, J., *A Sermonde made before the Kynge, his maiestye at grenewich, upon good Frydaye. The yere of our Lorde God M.D.xxxviij* (London, [1538?])

Marsilius of Padua, *The Defender of Peace. Volume II: The Defensor pacis*, trans. Gewirth, A. (New York, 1956)

Melton, W., *Sermo Exhortatorius* (London, c.1510)

Ochino, B., *A tragoedie or Dialoge of the vniuste vsurped primacie of the Bishop of Rome, and of all the iust abolishyng of the same*, trans. Ponet, J. (London, 1549)

Olin, J.C., *The Catholic Reformation: Savonarola to Ignatius Loyola* (Westminster, MD, 1969)

Pole, R., *Epistolae Reginaldi Poli*, ed. Quirini, A.M., 5 volumes (Brescia, 1744–57)

Reformatio Angliae ex decretis Reginaldis Poli (Rome, 1562)

Ridley, N., *The Works of Nicholas Ridley*, ed. Christmas, H., Parker Society (Cambridge, 1843)

Robinson, H., ed., *Original Letters Relative to the English Reformation*, Parker Society, 2 volumes (Cambridge, 1846/7)

——, *Zurich Letters*, Parker Society (Cambridge, 1842)

Schroeder, H.J., trans., *Canons and Decrees of the Council of Trent* (Rockford, IL, 1978)

Starkey, T., *A Dialogue between Pole and Lupset*, ed. Mayer, T.F., Camden Fourth series, vol. XXXVII (London, 1989)

Thompson, A.H., ed., *The Statutes of the Cathedral Church of Durham*, Surtees Society vol. CXLIII (1929)

——, *Visitations in the Diocese of Lincoln, 1517–31*, Lincoln Record Society vols. XXXIII, XXXV, XXXVII (1940–47)

Tunstall, C., and Stokesley, J., *A letter written by Cutbert Tunstall late Byshop of Duresme, and John Stokesley somtime Byshop of London, sente unto Reginalde Pole, Cardinall, then beynge at Rome, and late byshop of Canterbury* (London, 1560)

Tyndale, W., *The Obedience of a Christian Man*, ed. R. Loveitt, Religious Tract Society Christian Classics Series vol. V (London, no date)

Watson, T., *Holsome and Catholyke doctryne concerninge the seuen Sacramentes of Chrystes Church, expedient to be knowen of all men, set forth in maner of shorte Sermons to bee made to the people* (London, 1558)

——, *Twoo notable Sermons . . . concerninge the reall presence of Christes body and bloude in the blessed Sacrament; also the Masse, which is the sacrifice of the newe Testament* (London, 1554)

Weatherley, E.H., ed., *Speculum Sacerdotale*, Early English Text Society vol. CC (London, 1936)

Whitaker, E.C., *Martin Bucer and the Book of Common Prayer*, Alcuin Club Collections no. 55 (Great Wakering, 1974)

Williams, C.H., ed., *English Historical Documents, 1485–1558* (London, 1967)

Secondary Sources

Books

Aston, M., *England's Iconoclasts. Volume 1: Laws against Images* (Oxford, 1988)

Barraclough, G., *The Medieval Papacy* (London, 1968)

Blench, J.W., *Preaching in England in the Late Fifteenth and Sixteenth Centuries* (Oxford, 1964)

Bowker, M., *The Henrician Reformation: The Diocese of Lincoln under John Longland 1521–1547* (Cambridge, 1981)

Bradshaw, B., and Duffy, E., eds., *Humanism, Reform and the Reformation* (Cambridge, 1989)

Bradshaw, P.F., *The Anglican Ordinal*, Alcuin Club Collections, LIII (London, 1971)

Bridgett, T.E., *Life of Blessed John Fisher* (London, 1888)

Brigden, S., *London and the Reformation* (Oxford, 1989)

Brightman, F.E., *The English Rite*, 2 volumes (London, 1921)

Cavendish, G., *Life of Wolsey*, ed. Sylvester, R.S., and Harding, D.P. (New Haven, CT, 1962)

Chester, A.G., *Hugh Latimer: Apostle to the English* (Philadelphia, 1954)

Churchill, I.J., *Canterbury Administration*, 2 volumes (London, 1933)

Clarke, W.K.L., and Harris, C., eds., *Liturgy and Worship* (London, 1932)

Collinson, P., *Archbishop Grindal, 1519–1583: The Struggle for a Reformed Church* (London, 1979)

——, *The Religion of Protestants* (Oxford, 1982)

Cooper, C.H., and Cooper, T., *Athenae Cantabrigienses* (Cambridge, 1858)

Cross, C., *Church and People, 1450–1660* (London, 1976)

Cuming, G.J., *A History of Anglican Liturgy* (London, 1969)

Davies, E.T., *Episcopacy and the Royal Supremacy in the Church of England in the Sixteenth Century* (Oxford, 1950)

Davis, J.F., *Heresy and Reformation in the South-East of England, 1520–1559*, Royal Historical Society Studies in History Series vol. XXXIV (London, 1983)

Dickens, A.G., *The English Reformation*, Second Edition (London, 1989)

——, *The Marian Reaction in the Diocese of York*, Part 1, *The Clergy*; Part 2, *The Laity*, Borthwick Institute, St Anthony's Hall Publications vols. XI and XII (York, 1957)

Dickens, A.G., and Carr, D., *The Reformation in England to the Accession of Elizabeth I*, Documents of Modern History (London, 1967)

Dickens, A.G., and Tonkin, M., *The Reformation in Historical Thought* (Oxford, 1985)

Duffy, E., *The Stripping of the Altars: Traditional Religion in England, c.1400–c.1580* (New Haven, CT, and London, 1992)

Emden, A.B., *A Biographical Register of the University of Cambridge to AD1500* (Cambridge, 1963)

——, *A Biographical Register of the University of Oxford to AD1500*, 3 volumes (Oxford, 1957–59)

——, *A Biographical Register of the University of Oxford, 1501–1540* (Oxford, 1974)

The English Hospice in Rome: The Venerabile Sexcentenary Issue, vol. XXI (May 1962)

Fasti Ecclesiae Anglicanae (London, 1962–64)

Fenlon, D., *Heresy and Obedience in Tridentine Italy* (Cambridge, 1972)

Fincham, K., *Prelate as Pastor: The Episcopate of James I* (Oxford, 1990)

Fox, A., *Thomas More, History and Providence* (Oxford, 1982)

Frere, W.H., *The Marian Reaction* (London, 1896)

Gleason, E.G., *Gasparo Contarini: Venice, Rome, and Reform* (Berkeley and Los Angeles, 1993)

Guy, J., *Tudor England* (Oxford, 1988)

Gwyn, P., *The King's Cardinal: The Rise and Fall of Thomas Wolsey* (London, 1990)

Haigh, C., ed., *The English Reformation Revised* (Cambridge, 1987)

——, *English Reformations: Religion, Politics, and Society under the Tudors* (Oxford, 1993)

Hall, S.G., *Doctrine and Practice in the Early Church* (London, 1991)

Harper-Bill, C., *The Pre-Reformation Church in England, 1400–1530* (Harlow, 1989)

Hay, D., *The Church in Italy in the Fifteenth Century* (Cambridge, 1977)

Headley, J.M., ed., *San Carlo Borromeo* (Washington, 1988)

Heal, F., *Hospitality in Early Modern England* (Oxford, 1990)

——, *Of Prelates and Princes* (Cambridge, 1980)

Heal, F., and O'Day, R., eds., *Church and Society in England: Henry VIII to James I* (London, 1977)

Heath, P., *Church and Realm, 1272–1461* (London, 1988)

——, *The English Parish Clergy on the Eve of the Reformation* (London, 1969)

Helmholz, R.H., *Roman Canon Law in Reformation England* (Cambridge, 1990)

Hembry, P.M., *The Bishops of Bath and Wells, 1530–1640* (London, 1967)

Houlbrooke, R.A., *Church Courts and the People during the English Reformation, 1520–1570* (Oxford, 1979)

Hughes, P., *The Reformation in England*, 3 volumes (London, 1950–54)

——, *Rome and the Counter-Reformation in England* ([London], 1942)

Jedin, H., *A History of the Council of Trent*, trans. Graf, E. (London, 1957–61)

Jones, N.L., *Faith by Statute*, Royal Historical Society Studies in History Series vol. XXXII (London, 1982)

Loades, D.M., *The Oxford Martyrs* (London, 1970)

——, *The Reign of Mary Tudor* (London, 1991)

Lyndwood, W., *Provinciale* (Oxford, 1679)

MacCulloch, D., *Thomas Cranmer: A life* (New Haven, CT, and London, 1996)

McConica, J., *English Humanists and Reformation Politics under Henry VIII and Edward VI* (Oxford, 1965)

——, ed., *The History of the University of Oxford. Volume III: The Collegiate University* (Oxford, 1986)

McNair, P., *Peter Martyr in Italy* (Oxford, 19, 7)

Mittarelli, J.B., and Costadini, A., *Annales Camalduenses*, vol. IX (Venice, 1773)

Oakley, F., *The Western Church in the Later Middle Ages* (New York, 1979)

O'Day, R., *The Debate on the English Reformation* (London, 1986)

——, *The English Clergy: The Emergence and Consolidation of a Profession, 1558–1642* (Leicester, 1979)

O'Day, R., and Heal, F. eds., *Continuity and Change: Personnel and Administration of the Church in England, 1500–1642* (Leicester, 1976)

Ott, L., *Fundamentals of Catholic Dogma*, [1952] trans. Bastible, J. (Cork, no date)

Pettegree, A., ed., *The Early Reformation in Europe* (Cambridge, 1992)

Pollard, A.F., *Wolsey* (London, 1929)

Potter, G.R., *Huldrych Zwingli*, Documents of Modern History (London, 1978)

Powicke, F.M., and Fryde, E.B., eds., *Handbook of British Chronology*, Royal Historical Society (London, 1961)

Procter, F., and Frere, W.H., *A New History of the Book of Common Prayer* (London, 1901)

Prodi, P., *The Papal Prince, One Body and Two Souls: The Papal Monarchy in Early Modern Europe*, trans. Haskins, S. (Cambridge, 1987)

Redworth, G., *In defence of the Church Catholic: The Life of Stephen Gardiner* (Oxford, 1990)

Rex, R., *The Theology of John Fisher* (Cambridge, 1991)

Ridley, J., *Thomas Cranmer* (Oxford, 1962)

Rupp, E.G., *Studies in the Making of the English Protestant Tradition* (Cambridge, 1949)

Scarisbrick, J.J., *Henry VIII* (London, 1968)

——, *The Reformation and the English People* (Oxford, 1984)

Schenk, W., *Reginald Pole, Cardinal of England* (London, 1950)

Sheils, W.J., *The English Reformation, 1530–1570* (Harlow, 1989)

Shirley, T.F., *Thomas Thirlby, Tudor Bishop* (London, 1964)

Smith, D.M., *Guide to Bishops' Registers of England and Wales*, Royal Historical Society Guides and Handbooks vol. XI (London, 1981)

Southern, R.W., *Western Society and the Church in the Middle Ages*, The Pelican History of the Church vol. II (Harmondsworth, 1970)

Strype, J., *Ecclesiastical Memorials* (Oxford, 1822)

——, *Memorials of the Most Reverend Father in God Thomas Cranmer* (Oxford, 1840)

Surtz, E., *The Works and Days of John Fisher* (Cambridge, MA, 1967)
Swanson, R.N., ed., *Continuity and Change in Christian Worship*, Studies in Church History vol. XXXV (Woodbridge, 1999)
Thompson, A.H., *The English Clergy and their Organization in the Later Middle Ages* (Oxford, 1947)
Thrupp, S., ed., *Change in Medieval Society* (London, 1965)
Tierney, B., *Medieval Poor Law* (Berkeley and Los Angeles, 1959)
Trapp, J.B., and Herbrüggen, H.S., *'The King's Good Servant': Sir Thomas More, 1477/8–1535*, National Portrait Gallery (London, 1977)
Trueman, C.R., *Luther's Legacy: Salvation and English Reformers, 1525–1556* (Oxford, 1994)
Venn, J., *Alumni Cantabrigienses* (Cambridge, 1922)
——, *Caius College* (London, 1901)
Wansbrough, H., and Marett-Crosby, A., eds., *Benedictines in Oxford* (London, 1997)
West, W.M.S., *John Hooper and the Origins of Protestantism*, dissertation der theologischen Fakultät der Universität Zürich zur Erlangung der Doktorwürde (Teildruck, private publication, 1955)
Wilkie, W.E., *The Cardinal Protectors of England* (Cambridge, 1974)
Williams, G., *Recovery, Reorientation and Reformation: Wales, c.1415–1642* (Oxford, 1987)
Wright, A.D., *The Counter-Reformation* (London, 1982)

Articles

Alexander, G., 'Bishop Bonner and the Parliament of 1559', *Bulletin of the Institute of Historical Research*, 56 (1983), pp. 164–79
Baskerville, E.J., 'John Ponet in Exile: A Ponet Letter to John Bale', *Journal of Ecclesiastical History*, 37 (1986), pp. 442–7
Bowker, M., 'The Supremacy and the Episcopate: The Struggle for Control, 1534–1540', *Historical Journal*, 18 (1975), pp. 227–43
Carleton, K.W.T., 'English Catholic Bishops in the Early Elizabethan Era', *Recusant History* 23 (1996), pp. 1–15
——, 'The *traditio instrumentorum* in the Reform of Ordination Rites in the Sixteenth Century', in Swanson, R.N., ed., *Continuity and Change in Christian Worship*, Studies in Church History vol. XXXV (Woodbridge, 1999)
Dickens, A.G., 'Robert Parkyn's Narrative of the Reformation', *English Historical Review*, 62 (1947), pp. 58–83
Donaldson, P., 'Bishop Gardiner, Machiavellian', *Historical Journal*, 23 (1980), pp. 1–16
Dowling, M., 'Anne Boleyn and Reform', *Journal of Ecclesiastical History*, 35 (1984), pp. 30–46
——, 'Humanist Support for Katherine of Aragon', *Bulletin of the Institute of Historical Research*, 57 (1984), pp. 46–55
——, 'John Fisher and the Preaching Ministry', *Archiv für Reformationsgeschichte*, 82 (1991), pp. 287–309

Elton, G., 'The Evolution of a Reformation Statute', *English Historical Review*, 64 (1949), pp. 174–97

Grieve, H.E.P., 'The Deprived Married Clergy in Essex, 1553–61', *Transactions of the Royal Historical Society*, 22 (1940), pp. 141–69

Guy, J.A., 'Henry VIII and the *praemunire* Manoeuvres of 1530–1531', *English Historical Review*, 97 (1982), pp. 481–503

Heal, F., 'The Archbishops of Canterbury and the Practice of Hospitality', *Journal of Ecclesiastical History*, 33 (1982), pp. 544–63

Hopf, C., 'Bishop Hooper's Notes to the King's Council', *Journal of Theological Studies*, 44 (1943), pp. 194–9

Huelin, G., 'Martin Luther and his Influence on England', *King's Theological Review*, vol. 9 no. 1 (1986), pp. 9–13

Loach, J., 'The Marian Establishment and the Printing Press', *English Historical Review*, 101 (1986), pp. 135–48

Logan, F.D., 'Doctors' Commons in the Early Sixteenth Century: A Society of Many Talents', *Historical Research*, 61 (1988), pp. 151–65

——, 'The First Royal Visitation of the English Universities, 1535', *English Historical Review*, 106 (1991), pp. 861–88

MacCulloch, D., 'Two Dons in Politics: Thomas Cranmer and Stephen Gardiner, 1503–1533', *The Historical Journal*, 37, 1 (1994), pp. 1–22

Mitchell, R.J., 'English Law Students at Bologna in the Fifteenth Century', *English Historical Review*, 51 (1936), pp. 270–87

O'Day, R., 'Hugh Latimer: Prophet of the Kingdom', *Historical Research*, 65 (1992), pp. 258–76

Parmiter, G., 'Bishop Bonner and the Oath', *Recusant History*, 11 (1972), pp. 215–36

Pogson, R.H., 'Reginald Pole and the Priorities of Government in Mary Tudor's Church', *Historical Journal*, 18 (1975), pp. 3–20

Redworth, G., 'A Study in the Formulation of Policy: The Genesis and Evolution of the Act of Six Articles', *Journal of Ecclesiastical History*, 37 (1986), pp. 42–67

Russell, E., 'Mary Tudor and Mr. Jorkins', *Historical Research*, 63 (1990), pp. 263–76

Strauss, G., 'Success and Failure in the German Reformation', *Past and Present*, 67 (May 1975), pp. 30–63

Swanson, R.N., 'Problems of the Priesthood in Pre-Reformation England', *English Historical Review*, 105 (1990), pp. 845–69

Tucker, M.A., 'Gian Matteo Giberti, Papal Politician and Catholic Reformer', *English Historical Review*, 18 (1903), pp. 24–51, 266–86, 439–69

Wabuda, S., 'Bishops and the Provision of Homilies, 1520 to 1547', *Sixteenth Century Journal*, 25 (1994), pp. 551–66

Walker, G., 'Saint or Schemer? The 1527 Heresy Trial of Thomas Bilney Reconsidered', *Journal of Ecclesiastical History*, 40 (1989), pp. 219–38

Zell, M.L., 'The Personnel of the Clergy in Kent, in the Reformation Period', *English Historical Review*, 89 (1974), pp. 513–33

Unpublished theses

Brown, K.D., 'The Franciscan Observants in England, 1482–1559', Oxford DPhil, 1986

Carleton, K.W.T., 'Episcopal Office in the English Church, 1520–1559', London PhD, 1995

Dunnan, D.S., 'The Preaching of Hugh Latimer: A Reappraisal', Oxford DPhil, 1991

Hamilton, D.L., 'The Household of Queen Katharine Parr', Oxford DPhil, 1992

Heal, F.M., 'The Bishops of Ely and their Diocese during the Reformation Period: ca. 1515–1600', Cambridge PhD, 1972

Höllger, C., 'Reginald Pole and the Legations of 1537 and 1539: Diplomatic and Polemical Responses to the Break with Rome', Oxford DPhil, 1989

Marshall, P., 'Attitudes of the English People to Priests and Priesthood, 1500–1533', Oxford DPhil, 1990

Newcombe, D.G., 'The Life and Theological Thought of John Hooper, Bishop of Gloucester and Worcester, 1551–1553', Cambridge PhD, 1990

Nicholson, G.D., 'The Nature and Function of Historical Argument in the Henrician Reformation', Cambridge PhD, 1979

Pogson, R.H., 'Cardinal Pole – Papal Legate to England in Mary Tudor's Reign', Cambridge PhD, 1972

Potter, D.L., 'Diplomacy in the Mid-16th Century: England and France, 1536–1550', Cambridge PhD, 1973

Scarisbrick, J.J., 'The Conservative Episcopate in England, 1529–1535', Cambridge PhD, 1955

Thompson, S., 'The Pastoral Work of the English and Welsh Bishops, c.1500–1558', Oxford DPhil, 1984

Vage, J.A., 'The Diocese of Exeter, 1519–1641: A Study of Church Government in the Age of the Reformation', Cambridge PhD, 1991

Wabuda, S.R., 'The Provision of Preaching during the Early English Reformation: With Special Reference to Itineration, c.1530 to 1547', Cambridge PhD, 1992

Index of Scriptural References

Exodus 40:1–16 20
Numbers 19 44
Matthew 9:18–26 68
Matthew 22 12
Matthew 26:20 38
Matthew 28 91
Mark 16 91
Mark 16:15 90
Luke 10:1 38
John 10:1 85
John 10:7 84
John 14:6 84
Acts 20:28 33
Romans 10:14 82
Romans 12:13 117
Romans 13 92, 108

Ephesians 2 91
1 Timothy 2:6–7 169
1 Timothy 3 39
1 Timothy 3:1–7 43, 53
1 Timothy 3:2 124, 129
1 Timothy 3:5 117
1 Timothy 4:14 43, 171
1 Timothy 5:17 33
2 Timothy 1:6–7 40–1, 43
2 Timothy 4 91
Titus 1:5 90
Titus 1:5–9 26
Titus 1:7–9 43
Hebrews 4:14 44
Hebrews 7:26 45
Hebrews 13:2 117

General Index

a Lasco, John 49, 167n
ab Ulmis, John 50n
absentee foreign bishops (*see also*
    residence, episcopal) 54, 55, 58, 64
accipe Spiritum sanctum 41, 169
Act of Six Articles 76, 87, 135, 138, 161
Albert the Great, St 172
Aldrich, Robert 91, 189
Aleander, Jerome 58n
Alexander VI, Pope 31
All Souls College, Oxford 16
Ambrose, St 31, 38, 53, 118
Anabaptism, Anabaptists 137, 140,
    142, 143, 166, 183
Anne Boleyn, Queen 61, 63–4, 191,
    193, 195, 198
apostolic succession 171, 177, 179–80
Apostolic Tradition 174
Aquinas, St Thomas 33–4, 41n, 132,
    172
Arthur, Thomas 63
Askew, Anne 153n
Athequa, George 14, 54, 73, 189
Atwater, William 75n, 189
Audley, Edmund 75n, 102, 189
Augustine, St 33, 34, 43, 118, 148

Badia, Tommaso 58n
Bainbridge, Christopher 79
Bale, John 150, 151n
Balliol College, Oxford 102
Barbaro, Daniele 175
Barlow, William 19–21, 23, 38, 73, 77n,
    97, 106–7, 128n, 165, 179, 189
  appointment 63
  exile 68
  marriage and children 129
  proposal for college of preachers at
    Carmarthen 84–5
Barnes, Robert 72, 79, 82, 106
Barozzi, Pietro 30, 55, 56, 60
Basil, St 38
Baynes (or Bayne), Ralph 101, 153, 189
Beaufort, Lady Margaret 120
Becon, Thomas 89

Bede, St (the Venerable) 33
Bell, John 76, 79, 102, 189
Bembo, Pietro 58n
Bertini, Antonio 30
biblical languages 100, 101, 102, 104,
    106
Bilney, Thomas 63, 86n, 134, 135n, 137
Bird, John 28–9, 73, 76, 85, 131, 161,
    190
Bishops' Book (*see also* King's Book)
    16–17, 37, 46, 88–9, 139, 165–6,
    172
Blyth, Geoffrey 70, 82, 190
Blyth, John (brother of Geoffrey) 70
Bocher, Joan 143
Boleyn, Queen Anne 61, 63–4, 191, 193,
    195, 198
Bonaventure, St 172
Bonner, Edmund 23, 29, 38, 91, 131,
    163, 167n, 175, 176, 177, 179, 190
  appointment 76
  approach to heresy 151–2
  degradation of Cranmer 182–3
  deprivation 142
  foreign embassies 79–80
  ordinations 164
  Profitable and Necessary Doctrine 94,
    148
  prohibited books 135
  visitations 28, 94, 126, 143
Booth, Charles 30–1, 43n, 159, 160, 190
Bourne, Gilbert 150, 152, 190
Borromeo, Carlo (St Charles) 53, 59,
    60, 184, 193
Bourgchier, John *see* Bowsher, John
Bourne, Gilbert 150, 152, 190
Bowsher, John 190n, 200
Bradford, John 167
Bradford, Rodolf 87
Briçonnet, Guillaume 31
Brooks, James 68–70, 93, 109, 130,
    148–9, 150, 176, 190
Bucer, Martin 49, 50, 52, 108, 125, 168
Bulkeley, Arthur 67, 77, 107, 160, 190
Bullinger, Heinrich 47, 49n, 50, 52, 89,
    90, 128, 138, 168–9

Bush, Paul 73, 131, 190
Byocke, Robert 170

Cajetan, Cardinal (Thomas de Vio) 31
Calvin, Jean 47n, 48, 52, 92, 125n, 135
Campeggio, Lorenzo 14, 54, 64, 71n, 79, 160, 191, 203n
Campeggio, Marcantonio (brother of Lorenzo) 54
Capon, John see Salcot, John
Carafa, Gian Pietro see Paul IV, Pope
Cardinal College, Ipswich 104–5
Cardinal College, Oxford 104–5
Carnesecchi, Pietro 146
Catherine of Aragon, Queen 189, 200
celibacy see marriage, clerical
Chambers, John 74, 191
character, indelible 170, 171–3
Charles V, Emperor 145, 199
Christ Church College, Oxford see Cardinal College
Christopherson, John 101, 109, 191
Chrysostom, St John 31, 38, 118
Clement VII, Pope, see de'Medici, Giulio
Clerk, John 14, 54, 55, 79, 191
Clerk, Thomas (brother of John) 55
Cole, Henry 150
Colet, John 31, 32, 85, 101
collectanea satis copiosa 10–12, 17, 104
confirmation 1, 32, 50, 133, 156
consecration, episcopal 19–21, 39, 40–41, 156, 166, 167, 180
Contarini, Gasparo 30, 54, 55–7, 58–9, 96, 130, 144, 146, 200, 203n
Coren, Hugh 18n
Corpus Christi College, Oxford 102
Cortese, Gregorio 58n
Cotes, George 191
Council of Florence (1439) 174
Council of the Lateran see Lateran Council
Council of Trent see Trent, Council of
Coverdale, Miles 71, 72, 73, 134, 179, 184, 191
    biblical translation 100–1
    ordinations 162–3
    preaching in Devon 88
    Tübingen 79
Cox, Richard 18n, 122, 129
Cranmer, Thomas 3, 7, 14, 18, 20, 41, 50, 53, 63, 65, 68, 70, 76, 78, 80,

128n, 134, 157, 165, 176, 177, 184, 191, 192, 197, 198
    admonished by Pole 155
    appointment of bishops 22–3
    approach to heresy 137, 140, 143
    Commonplace Book 38
    consecration 62
    degradation 182–3
    excommunication 139
    execution 150
    homilies 83
    hospitality 121–2, 123
    marriage 129
    new bishoprics 107
    provision of preachers 85, 181
    royal supremacy 22–3
    use of new Ordinal 166
    visitation 133, 140
Crayford, John 18n
Cromwell, Thomas 10, 21, 55, 148n, 160, 201
    1537 oration to Convocation 13
    Barlow's plans for Carmarthen 106
    clerical hospitality 123
    consequences of fall 76
    deprivation of absentee foreign bishops 64
    episcopal resignations 138
    heresy commissions 137
    injunctions of 1536 and 1538 123
    new bishoprics 107
    preachers 107, 181
    vicegerent 65
    Wolsey's educational foundations 105
Crose, John 162
Cyprian, St 1, 37, 43, 132, 136, 148, 149

d'Estraing, Francois 31
da Thiene, Gaetano 59
Day, George 18n, 29, 102, 122, 142, 191
de Burgo, Nicholas 104
de Castello, Adrian 157n
de'Ghinucci, Geronimo 14, 64, 71n, 76, 193
de'Gigli, Silvestro 71n, 76, 79, 193
de'Medici, Giulio (Pope Clement VII) 57, 59, 71n, 76, 158, 193, 195
de Melton, William 159
de Vio, Thomas (Cardinal Cajetan) 31

Dudley, John *see* Northumberland, Duke of
Dunstan, Anthony *see* Kitchin, Anthony

Edgeworth, Roger 18n
Edward VI, King 24, 29, 49, 130, 166–7
election of bishops 7, 20, 61–2, 64–5
English Hospice, Rome 59, 79, 148n, 193, 196
episcopal visitation *see* visitation, episcopal
Erasmus, Desiderius 41n, 43, 53, 81, 84, 100, 101, 102, 104, 105, 121, 143
eucharist 41, 95, 124, 142–3, 146, 174–5, 182
  devotion to 35, 46, 47, 56
  1549 Communion Service 120
Eugenius IV, Pope 174
examination of candidates for ordination 57, 58, 159
excommunication 22, 139–40, 141

Fabri, Johann 53
Fawell, Henry (Bishop of Hippo) 162, 163
Ferrar, Robert 68, 73, 78, 127, 150, 163, 176, 192
  marriage 129
Finch, William *see* Barlow, William
Fisher, John 4, 32, 41, 60, 63, 75, 78, 85, 97, 121, 130, 180, 184, 192
  approach to heresy 134, 136–7
  as a model bishop 53
  biblical languages 100, 106
  devotion to eucharist 35, 56
  education of clergy 105–6, 165
  execution 136–7, 150
  hospitality 120
  influence of St Augustine 43
  office of bishop and presbyterate 34–5
  on clerical marriage 127–8
  ordinations 159
  preaching 82–3, 185
  prohibited books 134, 135
Fitzjames, Richard 75n, 101, 192
Flaminio, Marcantonio 144, 146
Florence, Council of (1439) 174
Forciglioni, St Antonino 30, 43n

Foster, Richard 63
Fox, Edward 10–11, 12, 16, 37–8, 63, 79, 104, 144, 160–1, 192
  and Luther 18
Fox, Richard 43n, 102, 104, 157n, 192, 196, 200
Franciscan Observants 148n
Fregoso, Federigo 58n
Fychan, Edward *see* Vaughan, Edward

Gardiner, Stephen 4, 10, 14, 29, 46, 65, 79, 96, 177, 181, 183, 190, 192, 200
  appointment 63
  De vera obedientia 13, 36
  deprivation 142
  prosecution of heretics 153
  White Horse Tavern meetings 134
  Wolsey's educational foundations 105
Garrett, Thomas 86–7
Gervase of Tilbury 11
Ghinucci, Geronimo *see* de'Ghinucci, Geronimo
Giberti, Gian Matteo 30, 57–8, 59, 60, 108, 126, 144
Gigliis, Silvester *see* de'Gigli, Silvestro
Giustiniani, Lorenzo 30
Giustiniani, Tommaso 30
Gloucester College, Oxford 105
Glynn, Geoffrey (brother of William) 103
Glynn, William 150, 193
Goldwell, Thomas 59, 60, 72, 73, 78–9, 93, 96, 164, 184, 193
Gonville Hall, Cambridge 78, 138
Goodrich, Thomas 64, 128n, 193
Great Bible 13n, 101
Gregory Nazianzen, St 31
Gregory the Great, Pope St 31
Griffith, Maurice 74, 103, 193
Grindal, Edmund 186

Harley, John 131, 193
Harman, John *see* Veysey, John
Harpsfield, Nicholas 154
Hawkins, Nicholas 64
Heath, Nicholas 20, 38, 63, 67, 74, 79, 122, 142, 145, 147, 153, 165, 166, 177, 193
Henry VII, King 197, 200
Henry VIII, King 9, 55, 69n, 99, 122, 193, 195, 200, 201

1540 doctrine commission 18
appointment of bishops 7, 61
Bullinger's *De episcoporum* 50
chaplains 189, 191, 192, 194, 197, 198
clerical marriage 128
deprivations 29
injunctions 15
episcopal households 122
Hilles, Richard 167
Hilsey, John 74, 128n, 181, 193, 194
Hodgkin, John 73, 131, 179
Holbeach, Henry 74, 87, 194
Holgate, Robert 25n, 62, 73, 103, 130, 147, 153, 194
holy order *see* ordination
holy sacrifice *see* eucharist
Holyman, John 150, 194
Hooper, John 47–9, 60, 67, 68, 80, 98, 125n, 140–1, 142, 152, 153, 184, 194
  comparison with Fisher 180
  conflict with Gardiner 183
  degradation 176
  education of clergy 107–8
  execution 78, 150
  exile 138
  household 72, 123–4
  marriage 129
  ministry as office held for a time 169–71
  objections to Ordinal 166–7
  preaching 89–92
  royal supremacy 26–7
  vestments 48–9
Hopton, John 152, 155, 194
Horne, Robert 178
Howden, John 207
Hyppolytus of Rome, St 174

Imperium 12
injunctions, royal 15, 95, 100, 104, 123
Inquisition, Roman 146, 147, 153

Jane Seymour, Queen 189
Jerome, St 33, 35, 36, 37, 38, 43, 118, 143, 169n
Jesus College, Cambridge 134
Jewel, John 184–6, 201
Joan of Kent (Joan Bocher) 143
Joseph, Robert 105
Julius III, Pope 175
jurisdiction, episcopal (*see also potestas*

iurisdictionis; *potestas ordinis*) 14, 24, 42, 65, 66, 82, 171

Katharine Parr, Queen 153n
Kempe, John 157n
King Henry VIII College, Oxford *see* Cardinal College
King, Oliver 157n
King, Robert 74, 161, 163, 194
King's Book (*see also* Bishops' Book) 24, 37, 46, 89, 94, 165–6, 171, 172
Kitchin, Anthony 68, 73, 105, 178, 194
Kite, John 195
Knight, William 79, 195
Knox, John 48, 49, 92

Lateran Council III (1179) 104n
Lateran Council IV (1215) 104n
Lateran Council V (1512–17) 30, 32, 79
Latimer, Hugh 63, 64, 68, 97, 118, 128n, 134, 142–3, 153, 163, 172, 176, 195
  education 123
  execution 78, 150
  hospitality 122–3
  preaching 85–8, 180, 181
  resignation 76, 138
  Sermon on the Ploughers 87–8
Latimer (or Latymer), William 63–4, 143
Layton, Edward 18n
Lee, Edward 15, 22, 23, 38, 63, 70, 83, 100, 195
Lee, Rowland 21, 64, 70, 128n, 195, 196
legate *a latere* 62
legate, Papal 54, 147
legatus natus 8, 62, 63, 147
  title renounced by Cranmer 63
Leo X, Pope 30, 53, 158
Leo XIII, Pope 169n, 174n, 175n
Lippomano, Pietro 55
Lollard, Lollardy 85, 86n, 143, 152
Longland, John 50, 70, 74, 82, 102, 160, 161, 169n, 189, 194, 195
  approach to heresy 135–6
  Christ as model bishop 44–6, 47
  hospitality 120
  preaching 83–4, 97
Lupset, Thomas 143

Luther, Martin 17–18, 24, 27, 72, 83, 90, 122, 128, 135, 170
Lutheranism, Lutherans 86n, 127–8, 134, 135, 145–6, 184
Lyndwood, William 119

Machiavellianism 183
Magdalen College, Oxford 143
Mallett, Francis 142, 200
Man, Henry 207
marriage, clerical 28, 117, 126–7, 129–30, 146, 173n
  bishop wedded to see 130, 182
Marshall, William 10
Marsilius of Padua 10, 19, 81, 132, 172
Martyr, Peter (Vermigli) 49, 52, 58n, 96, 125, 129, 144, 146, 184
Mary I, Queen 26–7, 183, 191, 194, 196, 201
  1554 Articles 94, 151, 173
  clerical marriage 130
  death 148
  deprivations 29, 127, 131
  injunctions 95
  likened to Esther, Judith and St Helena 69
  priorities on accession 68
Mass see eucharist
May, William
Medici, Giulio de see de'Medici, Giulio
Melachthon, Philip 27
Melton, William 32
Michaelhouse, Cambridge 75, 106
minor orders 28, 37, 42, 146, 158, 165, 174, 176
mirror of bishops literature 31
More, St Thomas 32, 85, 102, 135, 136, 192
Morgan, Henry 164, 195

Nazianzen, St Gregory 31
Nicholas of Lyra 41n
Northumberland, Duke of (John Dudley) 49, 55
Nykke (or Nix), Richard 63, 79, 103, 137, 138, 153, 196

Ochino, Bernardino 51, 96, 146, 151
Oglethorpe, Owen 18n, 23, 38, 103, 150, 196

Oratory of Divine Love 96, 144
Ordinals
  1550
    25, 37, 38–40, 92, 141, 158, 166, 167–9, 174, 176
  1552
    25, 40, 50, 92, 141, 158, 167–9, 174, 176, 179
  1662
    169n
ordination 14, 19–20, 25–6, 35, 39–40, 54, 181–2
  by abbots 32–3
  by laymen 22–3, 165
Ormaneto, Niccolo 59–60

Pace, Richard 79, 144
pallium 62
Parfew, Robert see Warton, Robert
Parker, Matthew 4, 21n, 73, 94, 134, 169n, 178, 179, 180, 186
Parr, Queen Katharine 153n
Partridge, Nicholas 50n
Pates, Richard 70, 78–9, 184, 196, 203n
Paul III, Pope 30, 58, 130, 145
Paul IV, Pope 54, 56n, 57, 58, 59, 63, 144, 145, 146–7, 154, 176
Pecham, John 9, 119
Penny, John 73, 196
Peter Martyr Vermigli see Martyr, Peter (Vermigli)
Peto, William 72, 147–8, 184, 196, 203n
Pinnock, John 160
Pole (or Poole), David 102, 196
Pole, Reginald 16, 29, 37, 51, 54, 56n, 59, 60, 63, 70, 98, 101, 130, 143–5, 147, 148, 149n, 157, 183, 184, 196, 198
  1536 commission of cardinals 58, 144
  admonition of Cranmer 155
  education 99–100, 108, 109
  English heresy proceedings 153–4, 155
  exile 79
  household 125–6
  on the validity of orders conferred during schism 174, 175–6, 177
  praise of Fisher 53
  preaching 93, 96, 146
  presiding at Council of Trent 95, 96, 145
  study abroad 78

Ponet, John 27, 29, 50, 51, 68, 130, 150–1, 166n, 172, 197
porrectio instrumentorum see traditio instrumentorum
potestas iurisdictionis (*see also* jurisdiction, episcopal; *potestas ordinis*) 11, 22, 32, 34, 139
potestas ordinis (*see also* jurisdiction, episcopal; *potestas iurisdictionis*) 22, 32, 34, 139
presbyterate 32, 35, 36–7, 38, 42, 169n, 181
printing, control of by bishops 59
Priuli, Alvise 144
provision, papal 62, 64, 66

Quinones, Francisco de 54
Quirini, Vincenzo 30

Rands, Henry *see* Holbeach, Henry
Ratisbon Colloquy 145–6
Rawlings, Richard 197
Raynold, Thomas 201
Reding, Henry 162
Redman, John 18n
Repps, William 138, 161, 197
residence, episcopal (*see also* absentee foreign bishops) 31, 54–5, 56, 57, 59, 64
Reuchlin, Johann 53
Richard, Thomas 162
Ridley, Nicholas 52, 67, 98, 134, 162, 176, 177, 182, 183, 184, 197
    against Anabaptist errors 140, 142, 166–7
    execution 68, 78, 150
    ordinations 159–60, 164
    use of new Ordinal 163
    vestments 49
Robertson, Thomas 18n
Rogers, John 150
royal supremacy 25, 29, 63, 138
    1540 doctrine commission establishment 15
    exercise 14
    orthodoxy 24
royal visitation *see* visitation, royal
Rugge, William *see* Repps, William
Ruthall, Thomas 197

sacrament of order *see* ordination

sacramental character *see* character, indelible
Sadoleto, Jacopo 58n, 96, 144
St John's College, Cambridge 82, 103, 106
Salcot, John 64, 72, 197
Salisburye, John 164
Sampson, Richard 77, 196, 197
Savonarola 30
Schmalkalden 79
scholastic theology, scholasticism 34, 35n, 41, 101, 103, 146, 174
Scory, John 67, 68, 73, 74, 131, 179, 198
Scott, Cuthbert 29, 109, 150, 198, 208
seminary 58, 74–5, 99, 108–9
Seymour, Edward, Duke of Somerset 55, 125n, 192
Seymour, Queen Jane 189
Shaxton, Nicholas 64, 128n, 138, 160, 172, 198, 203n
Sherburne, Robert 63, 76, 79, 103, 104, 198
Skevington, Thomas 73, 198
Skip (or Skyppe), John 64, 161, 198
Somerset, Duke of *see* Seymour, Edward
Sparke, Thomas (Bishop of Berwick) 164
spirituali 145, 146
Standish, Henry 14, 72, 73, 74, 75n, 102, 134, 148n, 198
Starkey, Thomas 99, 144
Statute of Provisors 7
Stillington, Robert 157n
Stokesley, John 16, 37, 51, 79, 83, 100, 137, 160, 198
subdiaconate 37, 42, 156, 158
succession, apostolic *see* apostolic succession
suffragan bishops 65–6, 71, 82, 157, 158, 159–60, 164, 207
sumptuary legislation 122, 125–6
superintendent 50–1

Taylor, John 198
Taylor, Rowland 87
Theatines 59, 72
Thirlby, Thomas 18n, 23, 38, 67, 76, 77, 103, 152, 163–4, 182–3, 184, 198, 199
Thomas, Stanley 208

traditio instrumentorum 21, 41, 168, 174–5, 176
Trent, Council of 31, 35n, 42, 55, 93, 95, 96, 98, 135, 145, 146, 151, 181, 185
Tresham, William 18n
Trinity College, Cambridge 101
Trinity Hall, Cambridge 103
Tunstall, Cuthbert 16, 22, 23, 51, 56, 63, 65, 77, 79, 85, 88, 142, 184, 197, 199
  deprivation 29, 67
  equality of bishops 37
  heresy, prohibited books 134–5, 136
  ordinations 159–60, 164
  preaching 93–4
Turberville, James 152, 163, 199
twofold justification 145–6
Tyndale, William 9–10, 99, 100, 165, 169n, 170

Valdés, Juan de 96, 145
validity 28, 173, 175, 176, 177, 179
van Kempen, Jan 96
Vaughan, Edward 199
Vermigli, Peter Martyr *see* Martyr, Peter (Vermigli)
vestments 41, 48–9, 91, 166, 167, 168
  pallium 62
Veysey, John 55, 65, 88, 103, 161–2, 163, 164, 195, 199

visitation, episcopal 14–16, 24–5, 58, 94, 103, 126, 133, 136
visitation, royal 15, 24, 103, 133

Wakeman, John 90, 166, 199
Warham, William 8–9, 21, 83, 102, 135, 136, 157, 199
  hospitality 121
  inhibition by Wolsey 62–3
  support for Colet 101
Warton, Robert 73, 105, 107, 199
Watson, Thomas 41, 46–7, 56n, 95, 101, 109, 150, 154, 165, 169, 171, 173, 200
Warwick, Earl of (John Dudley) *see* Northumberland, Duke of
West, Nicholas 52, 120, 137, 184, 200
White Horse Tavern, Cambridge 134
White, John 150, 200
Whitmay, Andrew 87
Wiche, John *see* Wakeman, John
Wigmore, monastery of 16
Wolsey, Thomas 4, 53, 64, 75n, 85, 121, 128, 129n, 134, 135, 158, 182, 190, 191, 192, 198, 200
  absenteeism 54, 55
  death 144
  educational foundations 104–5
  inhibition of Warham 62–3
Wood, Thomas 201

Zwingli, Huldrich 47, 48n, 170